THE
ROSE GARDENS
OF ENGLAND

THE
ROSE GARDENS
OF ENGLAND

MICHAEL GIBSON

The
Globe
Pequot
Press

Old Chester Road, Chester, Connecticut

First published 1988 by
William Collins Sons & Co Ltd
London · Glasgow · Sydney
Auckland · Toronto · Johannesburg

ISBN 0 87106 749 8

Photoset by Ace Filmsetting Ltd, Frome
Originated in Hong Kong by Bright Arts (HK) Ltd
Printed and bound in Spain by Cronion S.A.

Photographs by Marianne Majerus

*While every care has been taken to ensure that
details of opening times etc. are correct, the Publishers
cannot accept responsibility for any errors contained
in the book and advise you to telephone any garden
before visiting.*

Library of Congress Catalogue
card number: 87-836-19

Contents

CONTENTS

Map of England's Rose Gardens

NORTHUMBERLAND

TYNE AND WEAR

DURHAM

CUMBRIA

CLEVELAND

NORTH YORKSHIRE

Pennyholme
Sleightholme Dale Lodge
Aislaby Hall
Castle Howard
Newby Hall

LANCASHIRE

WEST YORKSHIRE

HUMBERSIDE

MERSEYSIDE
Windle Hall

GREATER MANCHESTER

SOUTH YORKSHIRE

Arley Hall

CHESHIRE

Cholmondley Castle

Chatsworth
Haddon Hall

DERBYSHIRE

Hodsock Priory
Brewery House Cottage

Doddington Hall

LINCOLNSHIRE

NOTTINGHAM SHIRE

Flintham Hall

Dam Farm House

STAFFORDSHIRE

Shugborough

LEICESTERSHIRE

Little Ponton Hall
The Manor House, Bitchfield

Mannington Hall

SHROPSHIRE
David Austin Roses

WEST MIDLANDS

NORFOLK

Elton Hall

Peter Beales Roses

Arthingworth Manor

CAMBRIDGESHIRE

Warwick Castle
WARWICKSHIRE

NORTHAMPTONSHIRE

SUFFOLK
Helmingham Hall

HEREFORD & WORCESTER

Ivy Lodge
Hidcote Manor
Kiftsgate Court

BEDS.

Duxford Mill

Lime Kiln

Winslow Hall

GLOUCESTERSHIRE

BUCKS.

HERTFORDSHIRE

Glazenwood
ESSEX

Alderley Grange

OXFORDSHIRE
Oxford Botanic Gardens
John Mattock Roses
The Manor House, Hambleden

The Manor House, Bledlow
Great Barfield

The Gardens of the Rose

Capel Manor

Hyde Hall Garden

Sheldon Manor
Kellaways

BERKSHIRE

The Old Rectory

Queen Mary's Rose Garden
GREATER LONDON
Kew Gardens
Syon Park
Hampton Court Palace

AVON

WILTSHIRE
Broadleas Gardens

Corsley Mill

West Green House

Wisley Garden

SURREY
Polesden Lacey

Parsonage Farm

KENT
The Old Parsonage

East End Farm

Heale House

Broadhatch House
Jenkyn Place
57 Church Road, Bramshott

Sissinghurst Castle

SOMERSET
The Manor House
Hinton St Mary

Mottisfont Abbey
The Hillier Arboretum
Fairfield House

Nymans

WEST SUSSEX

Ketches
EAST SUSSEX

HAMPSHIRE

Watermeadows
Cranborne Manor Gardens

Berri Court

Charleston Manor

DORSET

Introduction

When does a rose garden simply become a garden with roses? And where should the line be drawn to define a suitable candidate for *The Rose Gardens of England*? In the event I had to take a fairly flexible approach in choosing the gardens for this book as they varied so much in their make-up.

Back in the days of Queen Victoria it would have been an easier decision to make. In the earlier part of her reign, at least, roses were grown rather like vegetables, for cutting for the house, and were confined to a separate rose garden. It was often a walled enclosure some distance from the house, for the roses of those days were not the neat and upright Hybrid Teas and Floribundas that would have fitted admirably into Victorian bedding schemes. They were large, unruly bushes, like the Bourbons, or tall ungainly growers, like the Hybrid Perpetuals, or they were the even earlier Damasks, Albas, Centifolias and so on which would have looked quite out of place.

Roses had in fact been grown on their own from a much earlier date thanks to the ideas of the Empress Josephine, wife of Napoleon I. The documentation of the Château de Malmaison, Josephine's home near Versailles, is remarkably complete. She had a passion for flowers of many kinds and purchased Malmaison, with its several hundred acres of grounds, in 1799. A Scot, Thomas Blaikie, was employed to landscape them and, apart from the plants and flowers she grew, there was quite a collection of rare animals and birds. However, it was the plants and the roses in particular that interested Josephine the most. She gathered together a marvellous team of botanists, gardeners and horticulturalists and used their expertise to great effect. Among them was André Dupont, after whom *Rosa × dupontii* was named, and who was later to found the rose collection at the Luxembourg gardens in Paris.

With single-minded passion, Josephine set about making a collection of every species and variety of rose then known to be in existence, going as far afield as America for some of them. As wife of Napoleon, she could pull strings to get what she wanted. When England and France were locked in combat in the middle of the Napoleonic Wars a certain Mr Kennedy, a partner in the Hammersmith nursery firm of Lee and Kennedy, was granted diplomatic immunity to bring roses from England for her garden. After her divorce from Napoleon in 1809, Josephine moved permanently to Malmaison and devoted all her time to this remarkable garden.

We do not know for certain just how many different roses she collected, but it was probably in the region of 200. In 1912 Jules Gravereaux of the Bagatelle Rose Gardens in Paris published a monograph, *Les Roses de la Malmaison*, which he admitted to be incomplete despite considerable research, and which contained 167 varieties of Gallica alone. However, we do know quite a bit about the Malmaison roses from a contemporary source, as Pierre Joseph Redouté painted 170 of them for his three-volume set of plates, *Les Roses* (which had an accompanying text by the botanist, Thory). The first volume was published in 1817, three years after the Empress's death.

Following Josephine's example, the fashion for rose gardens spread through the aristocratic world so that before long many of the French châteaux had their own. Then, at the end of the Napoleonic Wars, rose gardens appeared further afield on the Continent and, in due course, in England and then America, but they were still confined to the houses of the wealthy. This was a time when labour was cheap and manure was free. It came direct from the stables of the stately homes that grew the roses to their flower beds, dug in by platoons of gardeners.

There were some notable nurserymen in the

years that followed who did their best to widen the market for roses. Lee, whose firm in Hammersmith was mentioned earlier, introduced standard roses from France, which were used extensively for lining rose walks. Thomas Rivers of Sawbridgeworth in Hertfordshire brought out *The Rose Amateurs' Guide* in 1837, the year in which Queen Victoria came to the throne. It included his nursery list, in which one third of the varieties could be bought as standards, quite a change from the present-day catalogues in which they figure as an afterthought. The cheapest roses, incidentally, were one shilling each.

Other great rose nurserymen of the period were Lane of Berkhamsted and Adam Paul of Cheshunt (later of Waltham Cross). It was Paul's son, William, who was responsible for one of the most remarkable rose books ever written, *The Rose Garden*, first published in 1848 when William was only twenty-five. The most comprehensive treatise on every aspect of roses and rose growing yet written, it was clearly a product of the time as his descriptions of varieties are divided into two sections, one for summer, and the other for autumnal roses. Recurrent roses had not been around for very long in the West and Paul, rather misguidedly and presumably from lack of experience of them, advised the disbudding of roses like the Bourbons early in the year to ensure prolific flowering later on. There are a few varieties on which this might have a beneficial effect, but not many, and I have certainly never tried it.

This was still a time when another gardening writer, Shirley Hibberd, could say, 'Fifty roses in a batch may look fine, but ten clumps of five each may have a very paltry appearance unless the rosarium is on so small a scale as to be beyond the reach of criticism.' However, most of the writers of the period produced books which helped to spread knowledge of the rose beyond the confines of the walled gardens of the rich, and clubs and societies for rose growers sprang into being. Perhaps the greatest influence of all was exercised by Canon Hole, (later Dean of Rochester), the Rev. Honywood d'Ombrain and Mr Edward Mawley when in 1876 they founded what was to become The Royal National Rose Society, and began to hold rose shows that brought the rose to the attention of the public. In a remarkably short time Hole and d'Ombrain and the rest of the remarkable band of horticulturalists they gathered round them (including A. Foster-Melliar and the nursery-owning clergyman, Joseph Pemberton) had produced books which sold and sold. Unfortunately the reverend writers were hotly competitive and (with a nod of respect to their cloth) as ready to tan the hide off each other and everyone else in sight with their entries in the rose shows they organized. So their descriptions of how to grow roses do tend to concentrate on producing show blooms. If there is one class of rose that really does need to be grown in isolation so that it can receive the extra bit of attention it needs, it is the exhibition rose. As a result, the myth that roses should not be mixed with other plants in the garden was, to some degree, perpetuated. As William Robinson was to put it later on in his *The English Flower Garden*: 'Shows, too, have had a bad effect on the Rose in the garden, where it is many times as important as a show flower. The whole aim of the man who showed roses was to get a certain number of large blooms grown on the Dog Rose . . . at the least cost.'

It was Robinson of course, together with Gertrude Jekyll and a number of others round about the turn of the century, who brought the rose to the fore in garden planting schemes. Robinson and Jekyll were not, as is often claimed, the first to think like this but they both, through their writings and example, wielded far more influence than any who came before them. Their ideas are still very much alive today and their thinking can be seen in many of the gardens in this book.

There are very few gardens nowadays that grow nothing but roses, though there are still some that have a separate rose garden contained within a larger whole. If I had picked only the latter to describe, a great deal of interest to the rose grower would have been missed. Roses *should* be grown with other things and some of the most wonderful gardens of all have roses blended in with other plants, reaching unbelievable altitudes up trees, ramping over walls, tumbling down banks and generally behaving with almost unseemly abandon.

So I have chosen gardens both large and small that make a real feature of their roses in one way or another, as well as those that have a rose garden proper contained within them.

All the gardens discussed are open to the public, even if only in a limited way, but as many of them are private gardens it is not possible to guarantee that they will remain so for ever.

A great many of the gardens come under the National Gardens Scheme and their *Gardens of England and Wales Open to the Public*, published yearly, will tell you their latest opening times.

Seeing them all has been a labour of love for my wife and myself, the kind of commission that comes only once in a lifetime. We cannot thank the owners enough for making us so welcome and for the time and trouble they took in showing us around and answering our questions. Grateful thanks are due, too, to the Area Organizers of the National Gardens Scheme, to Marianne Majerus for taking such marvellous pictures of the gardens, and to Nigel Raban, Past President of The Royal National Rose Society, for his meticulous checking of the manuscript.

We spent two summers in our car, an elaborate schedule on the back seat to refer to at the beginning of each day to make sure that we arrived at the right place at the right time. Map reading was brought to a fine art, for many of the houses we visited were remote and singularly lacking when we got there in any indication that we had arrived. There is no place on earth so deserted as an English village when there is a need to ask the way. One could be on the moon. Many was the time when we arrived within a quarter of a mile of our destination with twenty minutes to spare, only to circle in a whirlpool of ever-mounting desperation through the lanes and byways before finally homing in on our target, generally in the nick of time. This is not, however, to be taken as a counsel of despair. We visited most gardens by arrangement when they were not open to the public. When they are, the direction signs will be out. Follow these and all will be plain sailing.

I have written about the gardens as we found them. It must not be forgotten, however, that a garden is a living thing. The majority of those in this book have enthusiastic and knowledgeable owners and with such people a garden never stands still. It develops over the years and so changes may come. Visitors may not find everything exactly as I have described it: a flowerbed may have been moved, a view may have been opened up by the removal of a hedge or even a clump of trees, but almost any change made, except possibly a change of ownership, will probably be for the better. One thing, however, will not, and that is a hurricane. All these gardens were visited before the disastrous night in October 1987 which devastated so many gardens in the South of England. Some of those in the book were inevitably affected and may take time to recover, so before planning a visit telephone to make sure that they are open.

Some counties have been covered in depth, as they seem to be teeming with rose gardens. Others, my own county of Surrey among them, have done less well. There are even counties, such as Cornwall, that do not appear in the book at all, but that is no reflection on the owners of gardens in those areas. It is simply that the type of soil, the climate and many other factors must be right if roses are to give of their best and the right combination is not present everywhere.

With some misgivings I have deliberately ignored the new rose classification when mentioning Hybrid Teas and Floribundas. Between eighty and ninety per cent of the roses described in this book are shrub roses of one kind or another and have clusters of flowers. Suddenly to refer to one group of roses only as cluster-flowered (the Floribundas) seems to me to be utterly confusing. Removing confusion was the primary aim of the new class names but it would seem that in this, and in a few other ways, the new classification needs further thought. It is only when you try to use it that certain weaknesses become apparent.

We have come a long way from the time of the Empress Josephine and her Malmaison garden, and since Dean Hole began to spread the word that roses were a good thing for everybody. No-one could have put it better than him when he said: 'He who would have beautiful Roses in his garden must have beautiful roses *in his heart*!' This could certainly be said of the owners of the gardens I have seen.

I sincerely hope that in reading about the gardens in this book and, in due course, when you visit them, you will gain as much pleasure from them as I have.

Michael Gibson

The Rose Families

For the benefit of those to whom the rose families are something of a mystery, here are some brief notes that may be of help. I have taken the families in historical sequence, but it must always be remembered that a new class of rose does not appear overnight. It evolves slowly over a period of many years so in most cases you can only give very approximate dates. In addition, the rose is nothing if not promiscuous so that, as a result of chance interbreeding in the wild and chance crosses in nurseries (long before it was realized that the raising of hybrids could be controlled), many roses do not fit precisely into any category.

The species or wild roses These are the originals from which all later rose varieties came and they occur only in the Northern hemisphere. They have, with one exception, simple, five-petalled flowers, but the term species is also used rather loosely to include close relatives which may have more petals, but which are otherwise similar in habit of growth.

Gallica roses Generally considered to be the first roses cultivated by man, from which all other cultivated roses are descended. A typical Gallica makes a short, twiggy, upright bush with rather rough leaves, with bristles as well as thorns, and with flowers held well above the foliage. Also known as Provins roses.

Damask roses Probably a cross between *R. gallica* and the species *R. phoenicia* produced the first Damask. They originated in the Middle East (not necessarily in Damascus as is often claimed) and, though they were known in Roman times, precise dating is not possible.

Alba roses A Damask crossed with a near relative of the Dog Rose, *R. corymbifera*, resulted in the first Albas, thought to have been brought to the United Kingdom by the Romans. They figure in many of the early Dutch flower paintings and are mostly large, upright shrubs with fine grey-green leaves.

Centifolia roses An Alba crossed with a Damask resulted in the first Centifolia some time in the sixteenth century. They were largely developed in Holland (and were known as Holland roses) until taken up by the French, when they became Provence roses. They are the original Cabbage roses and make large, rather lax, shrubs with sumptuous, many-petalled flowers.

Moss roses The majority of these came from sports of Centifolias, which they otherwise resemble, but there are also some Damask Mosses. The so-called 'moss' is a glandular growth on the flower stalks and buds that is said to resemble moss.

China roses These are roses brought to the West from China early in the eighteenth century, mostly cultivated varieties of great antiquity and all of them recurrent flowering, as opposed to the Western roses that bloomed only once at midsummer. Though not all completely hardy, they were able to pass on their most valuable characteristic to the following:

Bourbon roses A chance cross between a Damask and a China rose early in the nineteenth century resulted in the first fully recurrent Western rose family, the Bourbons. They make vigorous, lusty shrubs with large, double flowers, and no trace of the frailness of many of the Chinas.

Portland roses These are contemporaries of the Bourbons, which may have resulted from a similar cross or from one between a Gallica and a China. The original Portland was sometimes known as The Scarlet Four-Seasons Rose because of its continuous blooming. They comprise a small family whose popularity was rather eclipsed by the Hybrid Perpetuals.

Rosa roxburghii, *the Chestnut Rose.*

Hybrid Perpetuals Bourbons mixed with other Chinas produced these, less overpowering than many of the Bourbons but rather leggy growers. Nevertheless very popular with the Victorians.

Hybrid Teas The product of yet another China rose, the Tea, united with Hybrid Perpetuals and/or Bourbons and recognized as a new class in 1867. The long petals of the Tea rose resulted eventually in the high-centred, classical bloom known and admired nowadays. It is in marked contrast to the cupped or globular blooms of most of the old roses, which had short centre petals.

There are various other rose groups or families, such as the Rugosas from Japan and China, that do not figure much in the mainstream of rose development. Others include the Noisettes, a group of climbers originating in America but largely developed in France; the Polyanthas, which gained their cluster-flowering habit from ramblers and led on to the Floribundas; and the Pernetianas. The latter were the first bright yellow garden roses, introduced in 1900 by the French nurseryman, Pernet-Ducher, as a result of his using a Persian species, *R. foetida persiana*, in his breeding programme.

One of the parents given for the Noisette roses is the Musk Rose, *R. moschata*, and as it is mentioned several times in this book a word about it might be in order. It is certainly an ancient rose and described again and again by writers from the past, but the descriptions given differ quite widely. Even Shakespeare refers to it, though it seems likely that he is, in fact, talking about the Field Rose, *R. arvensis*, which is native to the United Kingdom. This has single white flowers, the only point in common in all the various references to Musk Roses, and a reasonably informed guess is that by Shakespeare's time all such roses were called Musks, regardless of the fact that there was somewhere, lost in the mists of time, a genuine *R. moschata*. This would account for the name Musk Ramblers being used for the Far Eastern tree-climbing roses with their huge sprays of sweetly scented, single, white blooms. It has taken much research over many years by Graham Thomas and others to unearth what would appear to be the real thing and restore it to the specialist nursery lists – a short climber or scrambling rose from Europe and the Middle East with single white flowers from July until well into September. How the Hybrid Musks got their name is described on page 105.

11

SOUTH

Broadhatch House

Bentley

*Off A31 Farnham–Alton road, turn up School Lane in
centre of Bentley. After road swings sharp right, you
pass The Old Rectory. Broadhatch House is beyond it,
on right.*
Tel. 0420 23185
Mr and Mrs P. Powell
Open, garden only, under the National Gardens Scheme.

For over thirty years Mr and Mrs Powell have
been working on their 1.4 hectare (3½ acre)
garden and have achieved some marvellous
colour effects, particularly in the way both foliage and flowers blend together, not just with
the roses but with the many border plants and
shrubs as well.

The roses climbing on the walls of the house
are fairly traditional though none the worse for
that. Among them are 'Paul's Lemon Pillar',
which after seventy years is still about the best

white climber although only flowering once in
the season, 'Etoile de Hollande' and 'Mme Caroline Testout' and, as you move away from the
house on a broad grass walk between two herbaceous borders, there are some more climbers
and ramblers, trained on wires at the back of
them. Two *Wichuraiana* hybrids are included
that are not often seen nowadays; coppery-
orange 'Léontine Gervais' and 'Thelma', with
its fragrant soft-pink flowers.

At the end of this walk there are steps leading down to a circular sunken garden surrounded by a yew hedge. Here you will find beds
of the Hybrid Musks 'Felicia', 'Penelope', 'Wilhelm' and 'Will Scarlet', the last two being comparatively recent additions to the family and
not Pemberton originals. 'Wilhelm' (syn. 'Sky-
rocket') was raised by Kordes in Germany and
'Will Scarlet', a sport from it, was discovered by
Graham Thomas when he was managing the
Sunningdale Nurseries. The central bed in the
garden contains 'Peace' and in beds on top of
the low stone walls just inside the yew circle
are lavenders and other grey-leaved plants.

*Below: Looking towards Broadhatch House from the sunken garden. The roses are 'Felicity', 'Wilhelm',
'Peace', 'Will Scarlet' and 'Penelope'. Opposite: A corner of the main rose garden,
with 'Iceberg' and 'Rosemary Rose' in the foreground.*

Back towards the house, and to one side of it, can be found a pink and white bed containing the indispensable 'Iceberg', the pink Floribunda 'Busy Lizzie' which flowers pretty well continuously, and the Polyantha 'Katharina Zeimat' whose white blooms have a pleasing delicacy and a sweet fragrance. Raised by Peter Lambert in Germany in 1901, it rarely makes a plant more than 60 cm (2 ft) high and so is well worth bearing in mind for patio planting.

From here, you continue to the rose garden proper, passing on the way magnificent displays of paeonies, which do exceptionally well on the heavy soil of the area.

There are few modern roses in the rose garden except for those that blend in well with the old ones, like 'Iceberg' (once again), 'Rosemary Rose' and 'Chinatown', and several of David Austin's English Roses, 'Charles Austin' and 'Graham Thomas' among them, the latter, together with 'Chinatown', bringing good strong yellows into the planting scheme. 'München' is another modern rose, with deep garnet-red flowers.

Of the many old varieties in this good and fairly comprehensive collection, a few stand out. The Rugosa 'Belle Poitevine' is one of the best of the family but is rarely grown for reasons at which it is impossible to guess. It is every bit as good as 'Roserie de L'Hay' which is seen everywhere, and its pink flowers are followed by good hips, a bonus not forthcoming from the other rose. Even more rare is the utterly enchanting blush-pink 'Fimbriata', otherwise known as 'Phoebe's Frilled Pink'. Also a member of the Rugosa family, it has carnation-like blooms on the lines of the Grootendorst varieties but a more delicate colour, and is not a tall grower. Even shorter, though, is its neighbour, the miniature Centifolia 'Burgundy Rose', with flowers of dark purplish-pink with wine-red suffusions. It will not make much over 1 m (3 ft) and forms a dense bush with dark green leaves.

Even though many of the old roses in this garden are familiar varieties, they are worth seeing because they are so well grown. Among those doing particularly well are Portland 'Comte de Chambord', 'Perle d'Or', the Gallica 'President de Sèze', 'Gruss an Aachen', the Moss 'William Lobb', the Damask (or Portland) 'Rose de Rescht', brought to England by Miss Nancy Lindsay (some say from Persia, some say from France), the rampant 'Mrs Anthony Waterer', 'Boule de Neige' (which could often

do with more rampancy and here has it), and the species R. setipoda, which bears fine hips in the autumn.

Beyond the rose garden you arrive eventually at the boundary wall and here you can see R. californica 'Plena', 'Rambling Rector' and 'Maigold' trained against the mellow brickwork and a bush of Viburnum tomentosum 'Rubra', which has the usual tiered branches of tomentosum but pink flowers rather than white. Back past the tennis court you come to the summer house over which grows the very vigorous rambler/climber called 'Countess of Munster', about which little seems to have been written. Something to ponder over as you make your way back to the house, finishing the tour of this very pleasing garden.

Fairfield House

Hambledon, Hants

Leave A3 south of Petersfield and follow signs for Clanfield and then Hambledon. House on right entering village.
Tel. 0705 132431
Mr and Mrs Peter Wake
Open under the National Gardens Scheme.

Stately cedars of Lebanon and spreading beech trees frame the scene as you approach up the drive from the west side, originally the front of the house. It dates from about 1820 and is in what used to be called Regency Colonial style, with wide verandas on the west and south sides. Over these are copper canopies supported by slender iron pillars and wrought-iron screens which, together with the white rendering of the walls, give a lightness and elegance to the whole façade.

Realizing this, the Wakes have chosen only those roses that emphasize this lightness for the walls and to twine round the pillars and screens; dainty 'Climbing Cécile Brunner', 'Françoise Juranville', the deep-pink miniature 'Climbing Pompon de Paris' and white 'Adelaide d'Orleans', near twin of 'Félicité et Perpétue'. In the beds under these on either side of steps that lead down from the veranda to a paved area below are roses mainly in pale pinks and whites. Two of them are 'Little White Pet' and 'The Fairy', the latter growing with almost unparalleled vigour and breaking like pink surf over the edges of the paving. In contrast, on the south face of the house, together with other climbers, is the unfading, deep-crimson 'Souvenir de Claudius Denoyel' with its intense, sweet fragrance.

Moving up a grassy slope round the other side of the house you pass beds on the right in which are numerous shrub roses. Among these are two of David Austin's English Roses (the majority of which are useful in that they are decorative and at the same time not too vigorous for use in a small garden). The two here are 'Yellow Charles Austin' and pink-flowered 'Mary Rose', named after Henry VIII's flagship which was recently raised from the Solent after some 400 years under the water. Size is not, of course, something that the Wakes have to worry about too much, for this is a big garden, and the much larger 'Fritz Nobis' and 'Celestial', together with 'Mutabilis' and 'Ferdinand Pichard', keep the Austin varieties company.

Continuing up the slope you pass the end of the tennis court where roses – 'Félicité et Perpétue' is one – are trained on the side net-

ting while nearby the massed white blooms of 'Kiftsgate' can be seen as it slowly devours a substantial tree.

The old walled kitchen garden lies ahead, some 0.8 hectares (2 acres) of it, now grassed down except along the wall at the top end and down the eastern side. In the grass are planted numerous small trees and shrub roses, the latter, unencumbered by neighbours and only marginally held in check by rustic wooden cradles, free to express themselves in all their glory. But immediately on your left, before the climb up the gentle slope has really begun, is a beautiful planting of willow, sumach, variegated weigela and many other foliage shrubs and trees with *Alchemilla mollis* at the base, and over and through all of which the long shoots of 'Francis E. Lester' weave their way, lighting the whole in summer with huge clusters of star-like blooms.

Roses you pass – and are likely to linger at – as you move on upwards are: 'Cerise Bouquet' (kept in check only by vigorous cutting back), *R. forrestiana*, *R.* × *dupontii*, grey-leaved *R.*

The Regency Colonial style veranda of Fairfield House. 'François Juranville' and 'Adélaide d'Orléans' emphasise the lightness and elegance of the façade.

*Sweetbrier roses beside the steps near the tennis court
at Fairfield House in Hambleden.*

soulieana (from Western China), *R. hugonis*, 'Belle de Crécy', 'Mutabilis', *R. moyesii* 'Geranium' and others. To plant all these and their other roses, the Wakes, who look after the whole garden with very little outside help, had to dig at least 1 m (3 ft) down into the chalk on which Fairfield stands and put in masses of leaf-mould to take its place, but they have been amply rewarded for all their backbreaking work.

Among the roses and trees in the walled garden you come suddenly on a wooden dovecote on a tall pole with fantail pigeons posing decoratively about it, just asking to be photographed. Beyond this is the top wall of the garden against which the Van Fleet climber of 1905, 'Alida Lovett', has recently been planted. The buds of this rose are long and pointed, opening to create slightly fragrant flowers in shell pink with sulphur yellow shadings, a very attractive combination that one finds again in 'Frühlingsmorgen'. Nearby is what promises eventually to be one of the tallest trees in the garden when it reaches maturity, a *Metasequoia gliptostroboides*.

About half-way down the slope, on the eastern side of the garden, the violet-crimson tones of the rambler 'Améthyste' show vividly against the wall. On the right you pass more roses, 'Felicia', 'Maiden's Blush', *R. × alba* 'Maxima', and towards the bottom is 'Jaquenetta' which Mr Wake considers to be one of the best of the Austin roses, with beautiful apricot-pink single flowers. Near the bottom, too, is the singularly beautiful 'Erfurt' and on a short pergola near the end of the oval swimming pool grow 'The Garland', 'François Juranville', 'Rambling Rector', 'Albertine' and a pink jasmine called 'Stephanie'. The tennis court is just below the pool and the netting is put to good use at this side as well for the support of 'Phyllis Bide', a very worthwhile climber that received a Gold Medal from The National Rose Society (before it became Royal) in 1924. It is one of the few climbers that you can describe, hand on heart, as being perpetually in flower throughout the summer, as it produces an endless succession of its yellowish-pink blooms. Used quite a lot in breeding other good roses, notably by Jack Harkness, it was very difficult to get hold of until comparatively recently. Its companion on the netting is the very striking *Clematis florida* 'Bicolor' in purple and cream, and not far away the apple-like scent of the foliage of the Penzance Sweet Brier 'Meg Merrilies' fills the air on a warm evening.

An arch leads through from the pool area to a narrow strip of what is predominantly a vegetable garden on the other side of the wall, but even here there are roses. 'Seagull' has been allowed to climb an old apple tree, 'Adélaide d'Orléans' is on the back of a changing room for the swimming pool, and also there are one of the Moyesii family and 'Sparrieshoop'. This last was raised by Kordes from the earliest of the Floribundas, 'Else Poulsen' (crossed with 'Baby Château'), and the Sweet Brier 'Magnifica', better known as one parent of 'Fritz Nobis'. Coppery, dark-green foliage and single flowers in a warm, rosy, salmon pink distinguish it.

There are more than sixty ramblers and climbers and over one hundred other kinds of rose at Fairfield House, and surprises abound; yet another walled garden is located across a yard below the tennis court, adjoining the house on the eastern side. Roses to be found here include the very vigorous purple-flowered Moss rose 'William Lobb' which climbs into a Mount Etna broom; 'Goldfinch' is on a wall next to the clematis 'Nellie Moser' at a point where some steps lead up to the Vine House; the too-seldom-seen 'Poulsen's Park Rose' (admittedly better in the early summer than in autumn) and 'Buff Beauty' fill one corner; the Gallica 'Charles de Mills' reaches heights its maker never intended in the shade of the south wall and 'Roseraie de l'Hay' mingles with *Buddleia alternifolia*. Yellow roses in this garden include 'Golden Wings', 'Arthur Bell' and 'Graham Thomas'. The latter is next to a small aviary up which the clematis 'Royal Velours' grows, its flowers so dark a purple as to be almost black. 'Mermaid' is behind it, and on the wall of the house 'Parkdirektor Riggers' is a mass of scarlet bloom.

'Poulsen's Park Rose' features again in the small garden attached to a nearby cottage that forms the Wakes' weekend retreat. A very vigorous grower, it can reach 1.5 to 1.8 m (5 to 6 ft), with both large and small clusters of shapely double flowers in a soft silvery pink. Nearby 'Leverkusen' is in fine form on one wall, 'Mme Alfred Carrière' on another, while 'Phyllis Bide' once more and 'Mermaid', 'New Dawn'

and 'Pink Perpetue' are also worth looking at.

The enthusiasm of the Wakes for their garden is evident in the choice of plants, the skill with which they are blended and the exemplary cultivation of everything you see. It is a garden of the dedicated.

57 Church Road

Bramshott

Bramshott road signposted on A3 between Hindhead and Liphook. House on left in village, just before church.
Tel. 0428 722375
Mrs Hazel Le Rougetel
Open, garden only, by appointment.

This must be one of the smallest gardens, if not the smallest, in the country devoted almost exclusively to old roses. Old because Mrs Le Rougetel has no time (and possibly no room) for the moderns with the exception of 'Horstmann's Rosenresli', a very good white Floribunda from Germany which is, in fact, a reasonably respectable thirty years old. This is one of several white roses in the small front garden, which is right on the street, the 1885 Hybrid Perpetual 'Gloire Lyonnaise', 'Yvonne Rabier', the climber 'Mme Alfred Carrière' and *R. wichuraiana* being some of the others.

Through the house to the back garden and the first thing you see is a half-moon-shaped bed of 'Raubritter' cut into the brick patio and recessed slightly below the level of the rest. Most effective. The rest of the garden is basically wide borders round the perimeter containing roses and some other plants, designed specifically to give the maximum of colour all the year round. Some surprisingly large roses have been fitted in without appearing to overwhelm the others, *R.* × *cantabrigiensis* and *R. virginiana* 'Plena' (The St Mark's Rose) for instance, while that rampant climber *R. helenae* is quite happily accommodated in a purple-leaved *Prunus*. In winter the clusters of orange hips take the place of the tiny white flowers for several months.

There are some interesting and unusual roses to be found as well as many that are familiar and these include the creamy-white flowered Dunwich rose, which forms a low, impenetrable thicket, the Portland rose

'Marbrée' (marbled pink and white) of 1858, the Tea rose 'Duchesse d'Albe' with nodding, deep pink blooms, the Gallicas 'Boule de Nanteuil', 'Ohl' and 'Henri Fouquier' and two China roses. One is 'Duke of York' and the other a variety that Mrs Le Rougetel brought back herself from China. It is called 'Tipsy Imperial Concubine' and the flowers are appropriately flesh coloured.

Another rose to make a special note of in this garden is a cross that the owner has made between *R. rugosa* 'Typica' and *R. nitida*, which has small, single, Rugosa-like pink flowers and remarkably fine foliage which, like that of its other parent, turns a rich copper colour in the autumn.

Measuring 18 by 18 m (20 by 20 yds) approximately, this garden is a wonderful example of what can be done with roses in a small space and demolishes completely the belief held by many that shrub roses are all too big for the average modern garden.

The Hillier Arboretum

Between villages of Ampfield and Braishfield, 3 miles north-east of Romsey. Signposted from A31.
Tel. 0794 68787
Hampshire CC are Corporate Trustees.
Open all day Monday to Friday all year round. Open from 1 p.m. to 6 p.m. Saturdays, Sundays and Bank Holidays, from March to second week in November.

To give some idea of the scale on which things are done at the Hillier Arboretum here are a few statistics. The gardens cover something like 64 hectares (160 acres) and in them grow over 10,000 woody plants, which means, of course, shrubs and trees, by far the biggest collection in the United Kingdom. They come from both the southern and the northern hemispheres and from all the continents except Antarctica. To grow well in Hampshire most of them must obviously come from temperate regions with a climate something akin to that of southern England, but rather surprisingly a number of plants from subtropical regions seem to thrive as well.

There are nine National Collections here so that, all in all, it is not a garden for a quick gallop round. Allow plenty of time and your rewards will be rich at any time of year, but come in June and July for the roses as most of them are either species or old garden varieties. While there are some beds of Hybrid Teas and Floribundas, the management feel that these two groups are so often well displayed in other gardens that the Arboretum should concentrate on the wild or species roses and the old garden families. As the garden already has one of the best collections of species in the country this seems a sensible policy to develop.

The Arboretum originated as the garden of Jermyns House, which was bought by Sir Harold Hillier in 1953, the garden being gradually extended and the surrounding land used for the famous Hillier Nurseries. In 1961 these were moved, but the expansion of Sir Harold's collection of trees and shrubs continued. In 1976 a Charitable Trust was created to secure the Arboretum's long-term future, and in 1977 responsibility for the Trust passed to Hampshire County Council, who manage the gardens with the help of a distinguished committee of horticulturalists.

The car park is situated conveniently close to the Plant Centre which has beyond it the Plant Centre Field, now a wide open space but which will be used eventually for the Arboretum's shrub collection, leaving the rest of the garden to the ever-increasing collection of trees. The Plant Centre is a good spot to start from and if you follow the path you will arrive first of all at the western end of the Whitegate Border, a wide grassy avenue some 180 m (200 yds) or so long, planted with shrubs on either side. However, an exploration of this can wait, for ahead and to the left is the main rose garden, a large part of it surrounded by high wire-mesh fencing to keep out marauding deer.

In the winter this fencing is not attractive, but during the summer months it is covered by a wide variety of climbing and rambling roses, both old and new. Among the most interesting of these are 'Cupid', a vigorous climber dating back to 1915 with very large, nearly single, peach-pink flowers, 'Phyllis Bide' (the beauties of which I have extolled elsewhere) and 'Gerbe Rose', which dates from 1904 and has reddish, almost thornless shoots of about the right vigour for a pillar rather than an arch or pergola, and double, quartered blooms in soft lilac-pink and cream.

Also trained on the fence are 'Max Graf', which is, of course, a *Wichuraiana* rambler though we are more used to thinking of it as a ground-cover rose, and 'Complicata', more usually considered as a scrambler through other shrubs than as a climber. The rare white-flowered rambler 'Astra Desmond' is also there, as is the very robust Bourbon 'Blairii No. 2' and *R. soulieana*, which I would previously have categorized as the only non-climbing member of the *Synstylae* group of roses. Normally it makes a great arching mound some 3 by 3 m (10 by 10 ft) covered with attractive grey-green leaves and white, single, star-like flowers, but at the Arboretum it is comparatively restrained and climbs with the best of them up the mesh of the fence. Near it, however, 'Seagull' romps away in its usual exuberant fashion.

The rose garden has, at least for the time being, several irregularly shaped beds of Hybrid Teas and Floribundas, but a much greater number of beds planted with old roses in considerable variety. You can find there 'Crimson Globe' (a Moss rose raised by William Paul), 'Violacea' (a Gallica, also known as 'La Belle Sultane', with almost single deep crimson flowers which fade to violet as they age), the soft, warm pink Damask 'Coralie', and the fairly modern Bourbon 'Adam Messerich', to mention only a few of those not too frequently seen in other gardens. Unusual too, nowadays, is a bed of Polyantha roses and the one here has in it such varieties as the deep orange-scarlet 'Paul Crampel', 'Yvonne Rabier', 'Little Dorrit', 'Ideal' (a dark velvety crimson sport from 'Miss Edith Cavell'), 'Gloria Mundi' and the much more modern 'Yesterday', raised by Jack Harkness in 1974 and which has, incidentally, 'Phyllis Bide' in its parentage.

The Polyanthas were, of course, the forerunners of the Floribundas and came about in the first place after large-flowered roses were crossed with *R. multiflora*. This produced small bushy varieties growing as a rule to about 60 cm (2 ft) and with double flowers in clusters. They were immensely popular for a while but went out of favour for two reasons. They were prone to disease, especially to mildew, and they had a great tendency to sport. While this had the advantage of producing a number of interesting new varieties, in a garden a maverick was likely to pop up in the middle of a carefully thought out bedding scheme, which was not so welcome. In addition to all this, as a result of further crosses of Polyanthas with larger-flowered varieties, the much improved

Floribunda (at first known as a Hybrid Polyantha) was emerging and was really recognized as a new class when the Danish breeder, Svend Poulsen, put his 'Else Poulsen' and 'Kirsten Poulsen' on the market in 1924. Nobody loved the old style Polyanthas any more and with few exceptions they vanished from the nursery lists. 'Yesterday' is a modern type of Polyantha in that it is low growing and has large clusters of flowers, but really it has no right to the name as its parentage is quite different and it more closely resembles a China rose with its delicate, airy growth.

Surrounding the enclosed rose garden at the Arboretum is a large area of rough grass with, like sentinels outside a stockade, a great number of individual species roses (unfortunately many unlabelled) and a collection of deutzias. Among the rarer roses are red-flowered *R. banksiopsis* from Western China and *R. sericea*, as well as the better-known *R. sericea pteracantha* (the one with the enormous flat thorns), both of them having only four petals in their single white flowers and being among the earliest roses to bloom in the spring. Also there are *R. nutkana hispida*, *R. prattii*, *R. giraldii* (the flowers of which are pink with a white centre), *R. wardii* 'Culta' and a vast bush of *R. setigera* (The Prairie Rose) with its deep-pink blooms, soft green leaves and dark red shoots. The Threepenny Bit Rose, which used to be called *R. ferreri persetosa*, is also there, now known as *R. elegantula* 'Persetosa'.

As you may remember, the Whitegate Border begins near the rose garden. Along this is a spectacular planting of mixed shrubs with a few roses intermingled among them. It is worth branching off the grass path that divides this to see the climbing roses along the fence that rings the Plant Centre Field, which is just on your right, and you can return to the border later. *R. setigera* is used here as a semi-climber and then there is 'Blush Noisette', 'Paul's Himalayan Musk Rambler', 'Alida Lovett' (a large-flowered climber even though an offspring of *R. wichuraiana*), 'Bobbie James', 'Rêve d'Or', 'Bleu Magenta', 'Silver Moon' and 'Goldfinch', the white and yellow of which led Vita Sackville-West to describe it as 'scrambled eggs', and many more.

Returning to the Whitegate Border and turning right at the end brings you to the Centenary Border, which again has shrubs planted on either side of a wide grass path. This time, however, there are roses in profusion all along its length. Most of them are species and many are of vast proportions. *R. roxburghii* for instance must be 3.7 to 4.5 m (12 to 15 ft) tall and as much across, and there is another huge specimen of a rose called 'Toby Tristram', of which there are only a very few plants in existence, one of them in my own garden. It is a pink-flowered seedling, I understand, of 'Kiftsgate', which certainly explains its vigour, but it is not in any of the reference books. And it is not the only rose in the Arboretum in this category for there is a climber on the office block called 'Betty Sherriff' (named clearly after the wife of the plant hunter of that name) about which I am sure the Curator would welcome some information I was unable to supply.

Jenkyn Place

Bentley

Take turning signposted Crondall off A31 in centre of Bentley. House 400 m (yds) or so on left.
Tel. 0420 23118
Mr and Mrs G. E. Coke
Open four days a week, garden only.

This is not so much a rose garden as a garden with roses in great profusion and with a wealth, too, of other fascinating plants. A plantsman's garden, in the best sense, its owners have assembled a superb collection of the desirable and the unusual, each plant placed in its right setting and in the right relationship to its neighbours.

If you enter the garden through an oak gate in a stone wall to one side of the forecourt in front of the house, you arrive in the Dutch Garden, walled on two sides, with the old dairy on the third and an open terrace on the fourth. On one of the walls you will find the climber 'Belle Portugaise', raised in Lisbon Botanic Garden in 1903, a Tea rose with large, loosely double flowers in creamy-salmon, and salmon-pink 'Lady Waterlow', also raised in 1903, is there too. 'Crimson Conquest', a climbing Hybrid Tea with quite small double flowers, weaves in and out of the stone balustrade of the terrace.

The modern rose garden, reached by steps facing the Sundial Garden, has four beds of Hybrid Teas, each bed containing three varieties. The rest of the beds and the east and west walls are planted with climbers, species and old

garden roses, *R. pomifera* 'Duplex' (or Wolley-Dod's Rose), the double form of *R. pomifera*, first found in the garden of the Rev. Wolley-Dod, *R. farreri*, various Moyesii varieties, *R. andersonii*, a possible relative of the Dog Rose, *R. × cantabrigiensis*, *R. × dupontii*, and the hybrid Rugosa 'Conrad Ferdinand Meyer' which, the Cokes assure me, perhaps alone among others of this family, appears to be free from rust. From the Modern Rose Garden you pass through the small pink and white garden. Here the clematis-like climbing rose 'Ramona' graces one wall, which gives it necessary protection, and a mixture of pink and white is provided by a large thicket of one of the many unnamed Scotch roses which covers itself with small, globular flowers early in the season. 'Frau Dagmar Hastrup' adds charm with soft pink flowers and creamy-yellow stamens.

Passing 'Bobbie James' scaling an old apple tree, you reach the end of a long grass walk with wide herbaceous borders on both sides, a justly famed feature of this garden. No roses here, but a multitude of interesting plants, among them some outstanding oriental poppies with the raspberry red 'Sultana' and 'Lavender Girl' catching the eye. As you reach the end of this walk you find yourself below the terrace that forms the south side of the Dutch Garden and can now see the south wall of the old dairy. On this the *R. foetida* hybrid, 'Reveil Dijonnais', normally a shrub, with very light green shiny leaves and vivid orange and red flowers, is here used as a climber. A seedling from Pernet-Ducher's 'Rayon d'Or' was probably one of the parents and, appropriately enough, 'Gloire de Dijon' is climbing nearby.

A turn to the right and then another right again brings you to a spectacular double border of lupins with a *Robinia hispida*, the Rose Acacia, on one side of it, trained along wires, espalier fashion, to counteract its habit of shedding its rather brittle branches in windy weather. On the other side of the lupins is the small old rose garden, all of the bushes inside wooden frames which keep the more lax growers reasonably upright. Amongst them is 'Fantin-Latour', along with the Gallica 'Empress Josephine', 'Reine des Violettes', 'Variegata di Bologna', *Centifolia × muscosa*, 'Tuscany Superb' and others, with a hedge of 'Rosa Mundi' at the bottom.

If you now move down the garden towards the tennis court, bearing to the left, you pass a row of various Pemberton Hybrid Musks at the bottom of a slight dip in the grass. In with them,

Stone walls and arches set off the roses 'Mme Grégoire Staechelin' and 'Mme Plantier' at Jenkyn Place in Bentley.

though why seems to be something of a mystery, is *R. × richardii* (otherwise known as *R. sancta* or The Holy Rose of Abyssinia) which almost certainly dates back to pre-Roman times. In fact, it is likely that it was one of the few roses that was grown in ancient Egypt, at least during the last few dynasties, and it is probably a Gallica × *R. phoenicia* cross. Rather a sprawling grower, with dark green matt leaves, its flowers are a soft rose-pink, fading in time almost to white. Across the way is another curved bed with the incredibly spiny *R. × paulii* and 'Max Graf' showing off its lacquered leaves and single pink flowers.

Moving on you come to where there are small trees and shrubs and a number of roses planted in the grass. Shrubs other than roses that catch the eye are *Philadelphus delavayi* with its richly fragrant flowers, and *Styrax hemsleyana*, which has almost circular leaves and long racemes of pure white pendulous flowers that have gained it the name of 'Snowbell' in America. The roses include *R. × alba* 'Semi-plena' (the White Rose of York), 'Cardinal de Richelieu', 'Mme Ernst Calvat' (a light pink sport of 'Mme Isaac Pereire' and just as good), and 'Zigeuner Knabe' (or 'Gipsy Boy') which is very often classed as a Bourbon but according to Graham Thomas is a seedling of the rambler 'Russeliana', which seems much more likely. I have never seen the latter, but *Modern Roses 8* describes the flowers as being fully double, flat, fragrant and magenta-crimson and coming in clusters, which is pretty close to a description of those of 'Gipsy Boy' apart from the fragrance which the latter lacks. They look more like those of a Gallica than those of a Bourbon, but whatever its pedigree, it is certainly tough. Mine, raised from a cutting, never stops growing and I am seriously thinking of changing its name to one or other of the alternatives that *Modern Roses* gives for it: 'Old Spanish Rose', 'Russel's Cottage', 'Scarlet Grevillea', and 'Souvenir de la Bataille de Marengo'. What a romantic galaxy from the past; nowadays we only have 'Just Joey'.

You are still in the area where trees, shrubs and roses mingle and among them are some of

The hedge of Rosa Mundi near the bottom of the old rose garden at Jenkyn Place.

the best of the modern, or comparatively mod-ern, ones like 'Nevada' and 'Golden Wings', together with the species *R. multibracteata*, the sweetly scented pink *R. californica* 'Plena', *R. fedtschenkoana*, not looking too happy as a standard, *R. sericea pteracantha* with its prehis-toric monster thorns, an enormous *R. roxburghii* (Chestnut Rose) and *R. forrestiana*, from West-ern China, whose pink single flowers come in tight clusters in great profusion and are very fragrant. They are followed by flagon-shaped hips, framed like the flowers in very persistent green bracts. It can reach 2.1 m (7 ft), though it has not achieved that yet at Jenkyn Place.

We move on a little to the sunken garden where the honeysuckle *Lonicera mackii podo-carpa* lords over it at the farther side. Its size is quite staggering, even allowing for the fact that it was planted forty years ago. Hillier's *Manual of Trees and Shrubs* gives a size of 3 m (10 ft) whereas this one must be 6 to 9 m (20 to 30 ft)

across and 4.5 m (15 ft) high and only the flowers, varying between white and yellow, betray its family origins as the homely woodbine. In front of it grows a clump of the Moss rose 'William Lobb' and some climbers trained on wires, 'Easlea's Golden Rambler' among them. Until the winter of 1985–6, with its long spells of bitingly cold winds, the bright yellow 'Lawrence Johnston' was here, too, and is about to be replaced.

Pass through an opening in a high yew hedge by the sunken garden and you return towards the house, between more shrub roses on either side. 'Rose à Parfum de l'Hay' has a reputation of being one of the most sweetly scented of the Rugosas and, as there is a Dam-ask rose in its parentage, it has every reason to be so. Its fragrance is no greater though, than 'Roseraie de l'Hay', for example, which is a better grower as a rule, at least in the United Kingdom. But 'Rose à Parfum de l'Hay' certainly looks good at Jenkyn Place, as do a number of other Rugosas nearby such as 'Agnes' and 'Nova Zembla'. However, the widespreading 'Mrs Anthony Waterer' was, when last I saw it, having rather a struggle to escape from under the branches and finely cut leaves of a burgeoning *Sambucus nigra* 'Laciniata', and, as a consequence, its loosely double, bright crimson flowers were notably absent. Much more eye-catching was an *Aesculus* × *mutabilis* 'Induta', a member of the chestnut family with yellow markings on the apricot flowers.

Steps flanked by stone lions lead you nearer to the house, passing the North American species roses, *R. arkansana* and *R. blanda* (the Hudson's Bay Rose), and the low-growing *R. nitida* in the autumn colour garden as its narrow, shiny leaves turn a vivid scarlet at the close of the year.

Apart from the main plantings of roses, there are still individual treasures to be found at Jenkyn Place. William Paul's *R. rubiginosa* hybrid of 1909, 'Refulgence', sports it thorny shoots and scarlet crimson flowers on one wall and the vigorous climber *R. filipes* can be found on another. And finally spare a moment for a suitably unusual rose in this garden of rare and lovely plants, 'Cooper's Burmese Rose' or 'Cooperi', which grows on a sheltered wall in the Sundial Garden. It rather resembles *R. laevigata* (The Cherokee Rose) in its white, single flowers and shiny leaves, but its origin is uncertain. Its beauty is not.

Mottisfont Abbey

Four and a half miles north west of Romsey just off
A3057 Romsey–Stockbridge road.
Tel. 0794 40757
The National Trust
Grounds open April to end September every day except
Friday and Saturday from 2 to 6 p.m. and on
Wednesdays and Sundays from 7 to 9 p.m. during rose
season. House (Whistler Room and cellarium only) open
on Wednesdays and Sundays, from 2 to 6 p.m.

Built in the twelfth century, the Abbey was an Augustinian Priory until the Dissolution of the Monasteries, when it was converted into a house. It was further altered in the eighteenth century so that not much of the original remains, although the monks' cellarium can

still be seen by visitors. The only other part of the house open to the public is a large room painted in *trompe-l'oeil* by Rex Whistler, but for rose lovers it is the grounds, and the Rose Garden, that must be seen. The setting is magnificent, with wide lawns under fine old trees leading down to the River Test. One of the largest plane trees in England is to be seen here. It has a double trunk and the circumference, 1.5 m (5 ft) above the ground, had reached 10.8 m (36 ft) some years ago.

The Rose Garden, right next door to the old car park, is some distance from the house. It was established in 1972 primarily to conserve the old French roses of the last century, though some other historic varieties were included in the planning by Graham Thomas, at that time the Trust's Gardens' Adviser. The walled kitchen garden was chosen as being ideal for them and in keeping with the Victorian theme. The planting of the earliest roses was sponsored by the Trust's Winchester Centre, which organized a worldwide appeal and, with the help of The Royal National Rose Society (which already had plantings of those roses gathered together from all over the world by Mr Thomas over many years) the Mottisfont collection was rapidly assembled.

In describing a garden it is all too easy to list plant after plant, which rapidly becomes boring and does not convey the feel of the place, which is of equal importance. Also many of the same varieties would be bound to crop up time after time. With a garden such as Mottisfont it becomes more difficult than usual to avoid the list approach as the layout is so simple. Basically it has been (until quite recently) an almost square, walled garden, divided by gravel paths into four roughly equal plots with a circular space and a pool with a fountain in the middle. There are no hidden corners or secret bowers so all that can be said is that here is a collection of old roses, second to none in the country. But I will pick out for mention anything special in the way of varieties or how they are grown.

The old car park, where you first catch a glimpse of some of the roses, has in it, primarily on the walls, the climbers *R. anemonoides*, with lovely pink flowers but with rather few leaves (in general and not just at Mottisfont), its deeper-pink sport 'Ramona', two Banksian roses (yellow *lutea* and single white *normalis*), a vast 'Ayrshire Splendens' (the Myrrh-scented Rose) in the corner nearest the sales kiosk, *R.*

Above: *The pool, the focal point of the Mottisfont rose garden, and 'Raubritter'.* Opposite: *Old roses and other plants mixed successfully in a border, with 'President de Sèze' in the foreground.*

brunonii of the grey, drooping leaves, *R. fortuneana*, a cultivated variety of climber brought by Robert Fortune from China in the mid-1840s but not too free with its flowers in the United Kingdom, the rambler 'May Queen' and 'Wolley-Dod's Rose' (*R. pomifera* 'Duplex').

Once inside the garden, if you move clockwise round the outside path, one of the few species roses in the collection can be seen, the Sacramento Rose, *R. stellata mirifica* from Mexico, with rose-coloured flowers and ivory thorns. Not far from it is a huge bush of *R. canina* 'Abbotswood', which came to the attention of Graham Thomas in a Cotswold garden in 1954. It is generally a more manageable garden plant than the original species.

Opposite, constrained to some extent by a frame, as are many of the other roses, is a mystery called 'Violacea'. Often classed as a Gallica, as it has many of that family's characteristics, it will on the other hand go up to 1.8 to 2.1 m (6 to 7 ft) and is more akin to a Damask in its laxness of growth. The flowers are deep crimson with violet-purple flushes. 'Mme d'Arblay' climbs into an old apple tree just beyond, as does 'Complicata' and 'Blairii No. 2', all along the same side of the garden. Many of the roses in the beds are pegged down in true Victorian fashion, even the immense thorny canes of the Rugosa hybrid 'Ferdinand Conrad Meyer', which makes it produce so many flowers that it is worth its place despite persistent rose rust every year. The big Albas at Mottisfont are affected in this way, too, but no old rose collection would be complete without them.

In one corner, the Bourbon 'Variegata di Bologna' has been given its head and is actually climbing a tree, while nearby on a wall is the peach-yellow climbing Tea rose 'Mme Jules Gravereaux', which has large double flowers. Less certain of its welcome from the English climate, that favourite conservatory rose of the past, 'Maréchal Niel', just about keeps going from year to year and actually flowers in the open, even if it hangs its head rather pathetically. Further down the same wall is another climbing Tea, 'Sombreuil' (sometimes known incorrectly as 'Colonial White') and beyond it 'Climbing Souvenir de la Malmaison' has reached something like 4.5 m (15 ft) across and shows no signs of stopping. The lovely 'Lady Waterlow', its soft-pink flowers edged with a

deeper shade, is another climber there, as well as 'Mme Sancy de Parabère'. This is a rose from the small Boursault group, named after the original raiser, a French botanist called Henri Boursault, and has loosely formed, double flowers of soft pink that can be as much as 12 cm (5 in) across. The new wood is thornless and the original Boursault was known at one time as *R.* × *lheritierana*, a name which originated in Thory's text for the Redouté plates. This name was adopted, presumably, to honour another botanist, M. l'Heritier de Brutelle, who had done so much for the young artist, but it was a bit hard on Boursault.

Rather strangely, in front of these climbers and clearly there because they were important roses in the historical sense are *R. foetida* and its two offspring (sports or what have you) *bicolor* and *persiana*. Both their habit and colourings assort rather oddly with the pinks, purples and maroons of the roses about them.

Still on the same path and around the next corner there is a fairly comprehensive collection of Rugosa hybrids, including 'Delicatata', with large semi-double lilac-pink flowers, pink 'Souvenir de Christophe Cochet' and white 'Souvenir de Philémon Cochet' with a pink flush in the centre of the double blooms. 'William Lobb' adopts the Mottisfont habit and climbs a tree opposite.

Box hedges line the paths so far followed and you now move from the perimeter of the garden between the banks of herbaceous plants that provide colour after the majority of the roses have finished flowering. Many more roses are planted in the beds here, too, and there are arches across the paths in places. On these grow, amongst other varieties, 'Princesse Marie', a *R. sempervirens* hybrid with pink flowers, 'Blush Boursault', of the same family as 'Mme Sancy de Parabère', of palest blush-pink with a deeper pink in the centre of the double blooms, and the almost evergreen 'Adélaide d'Orléans', named after one of the daughters of the Duc d'Orléans by its raiser, the Duke's gardener, M. Jacques, in 1826.

In 1987 a triangular walled garden immediately adjoining the first was opened up. Access to it is through the wall of the old garden farthest from the entrance, but at the time of writing it has not been fully planted and most of the roses are not fully grown.

A preliminary tour and an inspection of many of the young plants that are there left me feeling baffled as so many of the names were strange. It was not until I talked to the head gardener, David Stone, that I discovered the reason. A large number of them come from the vast collection (probably the biggest in the world) of old roses at Sangerhausen in East Germany and there they still have, or have collected in more recent years, many of the old roses that have long since vanished from cultivation in the West. The Sangerhausen list contains over 600 varieties and nearly 600 species and their variants. Eventually Mottisfont, once the new roses are really established, will be even more of a place of pilgrimage for lovers of old roses than it is today. 'Enshrined in it', as Graham Thomas has written, 'there will be memories of those who treasured the old roses when their cause seemed forlorn'.

West Green House

Hartley Wintney

Turn north off A30 in Hartley Wintney village and follow country lane for one mile. House on left.
The National Trust
Open Wednesdays, Thursdays and Sundays, from April to end September.

To anyone who thinks he or she knows about old roses, West Green House is both humbling and enormously exciting. It is my idea of a secret garden, a garden of the past, gloriously neglected except in some areas near the house, and with roses in profusion everywhere you go. They scramble up walls and through other shrubs, they struggle in competition with overgrown herbaceous plants, and there is hardly a tree that is not enhanced with the massed white blooms of one or other of the Musk ramblers and climbers. At times you walk beneath a complete canopy of creamy blossom with roses on either side of the path competing for every bit of sunlight that filters through the leaves above. It is an experience not to be forgotten, but you need to have your wits about you if you want to identify the plants, for not a single rose is labelled.

There would appear to be no record of who planted the roses, which mostly date from before the turn of the century, though you can find a few, like the glorious 'Constance Spry', which only goes back to 1961 and which is trained on pillars on the main lawn. Presumably someone must remember who planted these and there are signs of development work to be seen, particularly in parts of the garden where the public are not at present allowed. The house itself, which dates from the early eighteenth century, has been extensively repaired and redecorated in recent years and gives the feeling that it is just stirring back to life. I hope the National Trust does not move too swiftly or too far, for the existing garden possesses a rare and special charm that could be lost all too easily.

You approach the house through woodland. Beside the entrance gate is a cottage with the rambler 'Félicité et Perpétue' climbing over the small porch and the Moss rose 'William Lobb' in close attendance. 'Roseraie de l'Hay' is in the cottage garden behind a picket fence that Tom Sawyer would recognize, and so far identification of the roses has not been difficult, with the proviso that 'Félicité et Perpétue' is *very* like 'Adélaide d'Orléans'.

The entrance to the main garden is, to say the least of it, informal. At the gate you are likely to find a collecting box for your entrance fee (if you are not a Trust member) but not a soul in sight. To find the roses, make your way round the house, passing under a brick arch and taking the path along the back. On the red brick walls are climbers, 'Mme Caroline Testout', 'Albertine' and that charming Tea rose 'Sombreuil', which has creamy-white flowers crammed with petals that open flat and often quartered. A knot garden can be glimpsed through railings to the left and then you are in amongst the roses, greeted at once by the vivid crimson-purple of the rambler 'Violette' scrambling up an old plum tree.

You are now in a big walled garden divided by paths into six sections. Four of these are of equal size, made up of lawns with flower beds round them, while the other two sections comprise a vegetable garden, though this rather prosaic name ill prepares you for the exotic things it contains. And the exotica is not only botanical for there are two immense Victorian-style octagonal fruit cages with curving roof timbers, actually designed by Oliver Ford in 1975. Along the sides of the paths that lead to these lie, jumbled together, old-time pottery

The old waterway, flanked by Rugosa roses, leading from the nymphaeum at West Green House.

'beehives' for forcing rhubarb and other crops and cloches with leaded lights, shaped like candle lanterns.

A walk round the perimeter path is probably the best way to start seeing the roses. The path is edged with box in the traditional way and on the lawn side are fairly narrow beds of herbaceous plants and roses and then the grass, with an occasional rose on a frame or up a tree in the middle.

On the other side of the path are much wider beds, again with a mixture of roses and other plants, but as the former have been allowed their head for many years and been allowed to run more or less wild, even some of the most familiar roses may not be easy to recognize. They may, for instance, be twice their normal size if they have had to struggle for light through surrounding shrubs, or their flowers may differ in size and colour or both. Just the same, walking round the first half of the perimeter it is possible to spot 'Reine des Violettes', 'Commandant Beaurepaire', R. multiflora, 'Blush Damask', R. rugosa 'Alba', 'Félicité et Perpétue', 'Hippolyte', 'President de Sèze', 'Celestial', 'Wedding Day' (on a frame, as is 'Mme Plantier'), 'Ville de Bruxelles', 'Dr Van Fleet' and a great many more that are more difficult to name.

At the half-way point on the path, there is an opening in the wall through which a tree-shaded pond can be seen and a diversion here is well worth while. Turn to the left through the opening along the outside of the wall and more treasures are to be found by the path that leads through the long grass. 'Kiftsgate' is overhead at one spot and nearby is the Damask Moss rose 'Blanche Moreau', very distinctive with its white flowers and coarse brown moss on the flower stalks. The father (or mother) of all the Damask Mosses is here too, 'Quatre Saisons Blanc Mousseux', the white (and mossed) sport of the 'Autumn Damask', while others are R. sericea pteracantha and that other sericea derivative 'Heather Muir' with its large, fragrant, pure white, single flowers. Then there is a crimson China that is probably 'Fellemberg', the Damask 'Trigintipetala', several different Moyesii varieties and R. elegantula 'Persetosa' (late R. farreri persetosa) and many more.

Retrace your steps at the end of this path – it is impossible to do anything else – and going back under the arch continue the walk round the perimeter path. Roses to the left once more include 'Leda', the Painted Damask, so called because the flowers are tipped with crimson, dark red 'Tuscany' and the comparatively modern climber 'Alchymist' on a pillar, showing off its old-style double buff-yellow blooms, flushed with orange in the centre and not unlike those of 'Gloire de Dijon'.

By this time you are at the vegetable garden and on your left is giant rhubarb, together with currants, gooseberries and other fruits, all grown as standards. Ahead is a bank of trees with at least one of the small-flowered white ramblers up each one, intermingling in the top-most branches. Most of them are so high up that positive identification is difficult, but 'Silver Moon' is pretty distinctive with its comparatively large flowers, and I would say that R. gentiliana, R. longicuspis, 'Kiftsgate' and 'Bobbie James' are also present. I wish I could name the enchanting pink rambler up one of the trees. 'Ethel'? 'Princesse Marie'? but too vigorous, probably, for either.

Leave the ramblers for a moment and divert once more through another opening in the wall. Outside it the ground rises and you make your way up a grassy slope past plantings of 'Little White Pet' and a Rugosa that looks from a distance (you cannot get very near for brambles) like 'Mrs Anthony Waterer', to an open space with a formal pool with water lilies on either side and informal cut grass in between. On all sides roses are running rampant with 'Complicata' leading the revels. Ahead are the remains of an old watercourse which used to link up with the pools and you can make out the ghost of steps on either side of this. What appears to be a building of some sort can be seen at the far end of the watercourse but to reach it you have to work your way round to the left from the grass area between the pools, past yet more roses (many of them recently planted) and come at it from the side. You will then find that it is not a building at all but something described as a nymphaeum. It looks like a kind of monument without any particular dedication but with life-sized figures in niches at either side and with troughs of water at the base which at some time must have been linked up with the artificial watercourse. On a plaque at the top, Pope's famous couplet is carved in the stone:

A little learning is a dang'rous thing;
Drink deep or taste not the Pierian spring:

An appropriate sentiment if you have come to the garden convinced that you can recognize every rose ever grown.

A glimpse of the Kentish countryside from The Old Parsonage, framed by the rose 'Cerise Bouquet'.

The Old Parsonage

Sutton Valence

Turn off A20(M) on to B2163 at Great Danes Hotel roundabout; follow signs for Sutton Valence. Turn east into village at King's Head Inn and take upper road through village. Up Tumblers Hill and house is at top on right.
Tel. 0622 842286
Dr and Mrs Richard Perks
Open, garden only, under the National Gardens Scheme.

Not many people can say, as Dr and Mrs Perks can, that their garden contains a twelfth-century castle and one of the finest views in the south of England. When you add to this their wonderful collection of trees, shrubs, shrub roses and other plants you have something rather special.

Roses greet you as you turn in at the gate, for there is a planting of a dozen or so of the pink Hybrid Musk 'Vanity' all down the right-hand side of the drive. From there on there are roses everywhere you go and two 'Allen Chandler'

climbers are the first things you see on the walls of the house as you drive into the forecourt.

From this forecourt a brick path leads along the south side of the house where there is a long lavender border immediately on your right, with a wide stretch of lawn beyond. At the far side of this the land drops away dramatically down the side of a hill offering a magnificent view of the Low Weald of Kent. Behind you, on the wall of the house, are 'New Dawn' and 'Albéric Barbier' and at the far end is 'Lawrence Johnston'. There is a group of shrub roses there, too: *R. hugonis*, the lovely, dark, velvety-crimson Hybrid Perpetual 'Souvenir d'Alphonse Lavallée', 'Rosa Mundi' and the exuberant 'Gipsy Boy' kept under some sort of restraint on a wooden frame. Beyond these you pass through a small clump of trees to emerge on another lawn with more trees round it.

Most of the trees in the garden have been planted over some thirty years by the Perks themselves and one that stands out especially is *Betula ermanii*, with its remarkable satiny white bark.

There are roses planted in the grass all round this lawn, *R. moyesii* in several different forms, 'Sarah Van Fleet', 'Nevada' and, in one corner, 'Scarlet Fire', restrained like 'Gipsy Boy' in a horticultural straitjacket of rustic poles. Also to be found is the rose sometimes known as 'Sissinghurst Castle' but which is really the Gallica 'Rose des Maures' (as explained on page 44), 'Constance Spry', *R. rugosa* 'Rubra', 'Frühlingsgold', *R. ecae* (an unpronounceable name formed from the initials of the wife – Mrs E. C. Aitchison – of the man who found it in the wild in Afghanistan) and many more. There are a number of buddleias planted with the roses, much to the enjoyment of the Red Admiral and Peacock butterflies, and they go well together. If you look back across the lawn in the direction of the house, you can see, looming over some trees at the back of a summerhouse, an enormous *R. filipes*. In front of, and near the summerhouse itself, are a number of bushes of 'Penelope' and the pink Damask 'Ville de Bruxelles'.

However, your path now takes you in the opposite direction through a gap in a rather tangled hedge to where the Kentish countryside comes once more into view. Commanding the prospect stands the ruin of Sutton Castle which dates from 1132 and is associated with the name of Simon de Montfort, Earl of Leicester, soldier and statesman. Though owned by the Perks, the castle is now managed by The Department of the Environment and a wire fence with a gate in it separates it from the rest of the garden.

Down the slope on the far side of the castle is a grove of Kentish Cobs over a hundred years old and Dr and Mrs Perks have carried on with the planting of nut trees all along the steep grassy slope within the garden itself, which lies to your left. This is traversed by shallow steps and narrow paths and as you walk down there are more roses on either side, Scotch roses first of all and then 'Meg Merrilies', *R.* × *paullii*, *R.* 'Macrantha', *R. soulieana*, various Rugosas, *R. fedtschenkoana*, *R. pomifera*, *R. nutkana*, *R. roxburghii*, 'Autumn Fire' and 'Aloha', the latter looking a little out of place among so many species. One other rose, however, is in place, though it is rarely seen and something of a mystery. This is 'Morlettii', also known as *R. inermis morlettii* and sometimes as *R. pendulina* 'Plena'. If you try to track down its origin, you are constantly referred onwards whenever you seem

The Hybrid Musk 'Moonlight' was one of the first raised by Joseph Pemberton.

near an answer. But whatever its parentage, it is an attractive rose with arching, plum-coloured shoots that are almost thornless, clusters of medium-sized magenta-purple blooms and foliage that turns a coppery red in the autumn giving it another few weeks of beauty. It will reach about 1.5 m (5 ft) in height and spread out by about the same. *R. wilsonii* is another one to be found at The Old Parsonage and I can get nowhere in tracking it down. I did not even see it in flower.

A road runs along the bottom of the garden and you follow the line of it inside the wall, gradually climbing up once more through a grove of trees towards the house. Even in this comparatively shady part more roses are planted, not always getting as much light as they would perhaps like but doing remarkably well just the same. I remember near the bottom 'Moonlight', 'Iceberg' and the Bourbon 'Commandant Beaurepaire', but as you climb further you come across the Albas, 'Königin von Danemarck' and 'Great Maiden's Blush', and the Gallica 'Charles de Mills', on frames, the rambler 'May Queen' on a fence, a huge *R. californica* 'Plena' (everybody's favourite) on its own and 'Wolley-Dod's Rose'. A brief diversion along a terrace path directly below the lawn in front of the house and you discover still more roses: 'Wedding Day' and 'Mermaid' on the terrace wall and, on the other side of the path, the soft-yellow blooms of 'Golden Wings', the pink ones of 'Fritz Nobis', *R. davidii* and the particularly graceful and lovely *R. webbiana*. A garden to remember.

Parsonage Farm

Boxley

Leave M20 at junction 7, turn for Maidstone. Turn first right, then right again into Boxley Road. Boxley village green on right with church at one end (small, and easy to miss as you drive through Boxley). House on south side, no nameplate.
Tel. 0622 54510
The Hon. Sir John and Lady Whitford
Open, garden only, under the National Gardens Scheme.

Parsonage Farm lies in a lovely setting just off the village green. It is reached through a wide gateway, beyond which the drive dips down a little towards the house, one wing of which is

an old chapel. To the right, a wide lawn is bounded on the far side by a high stone wall, but immediately beside the drive is a hedge of roses, modern varieties which the Whitfords say they always intend to move but never do. To me it is an attractive feature, but not to those who discount any rose raised after the turn of the century. 'Scarlet Queen Elizabeth', 'Anna Wheatcroft' and a few others are dazzlers and ensure that this bed really catches the eye.

Further on 'Kiftsgate' climbs an apple tree and 'Lawrence Johnston' an enormous pear tree of the variety 'Black Worcester', which dates back to about 1600. 'Mme Alfred Carrière' is on the wall of the house and nearby are 'Cerise Bouquet', not yet as big as it can be, 'Mme Lauriol de Barny', 'Complicata' and a few others. 'Complicata' and 'Cerise Bouquet', rivalling one another in size and number of flowers, make quite a contest, and nearby the rumbustious grower 'Gipsy Boy' ('Zigeuner Knabe') enters the lists as well.

Just by some steps that lead up from the front door of the house to the lawn is the single Hybrid Tea 'Ellen Willmott', the edges of its petals pale pink, shading to ivory, with lemon yellow at the base. A nicely scented rose, it was raised in 1936 at the nurseries of W. E. B. Archer and Daughter of Sellinge, near Ashford in Kent, not all that far from Boxley. Archer was the raiser, too, of that other single Hybrid Tea, 'Dainty Bess', which was one of the parents of this one, together with the Tea rose 'Lady Hillingdon'. 'Ellen Willmott' is a great rarity now, but at least it seems to have outlasted the Archers' other introduction of the same year, the glowing crimson-scarlet Hybrid Polyantha 'Folkestone'.

If, instead of going right down the drive, you turn left just inside the gate, you will see fruit cages and the vegetable garden across the lawn straight ahead, which is slightly higher here than it is nearer the house. Where the two levels meet, there is a planting of low-growing shrubs, amongst them *R. sancta*, the Holy Rose of Abyssinia, and 'Martin Frobisher', a Rugosa hybrid bred by the Canadian Department of Agriculture in 1968 as part of a programme designed to produce roses that would stand up to the harsh Canadian winters. It has fragrant light pink flowers with a darker centre and typically fresh green Rugosa foliage.

At the far end of this bed, steps lead down to the lower lawn and if you turn left and back towards the drive you will find a curved row of

Hybrid Musks planted in the grass, including 'Erfurt', 'Daybreak', 'Cornelia' and 'Francis E. Lester', which will in time make a pretty big shrub as it is normally a vigorous climber. Alternatively, turn right at the foot of the steps and you will soon be moving along the perimeter wall with roses like 'Cupid' trained on it and many more planted in the grass of the lawn in front of it, the larger ones supported on wooden cradles. There you can find another climber used as a shrub, 'The Alchymist', 'Mme Isaac Pereire' of the huge, scented, double blooms, 'Moonlight' in fine form, 'Maiden's Blush', 'Blanche Moreau' (a Damask Moss), the Portland rose 'Comte de Chambord', 'Du Maître d'Ecole, R. californica 'Plena', 'Céleste', R. virginiana and 'Kazanlik', much taller as a rule than other Damasks. This latter, discussed briefly on p. 87, is said by some not to produce enough flowers to make it a good garden shrub, but I have found that if left completely alone it puts on a good display. Prune it and it sulks.

There are also some modern varieties at this end of the lawn which mingle very happily with the older ones. Among them are 'Aloha', 'Rosemary Rose', 'Fritz Nobis' and 'Fred Loads' which, though a very modern vermilion in colouring, has a softness of tone that blends well with its neighbours, soft-pink 'Souvenir de la Malmaison' and the slightly deeper pink 'Baroness Rothschild'. It is interesting that the modern roses among these, together with 'Chinatown' and 'Arthur Bell' elsewhere, do well in the chalky soil of this garden. Near them is a venerable 'Canary Bird' standard, the yellow blooms of which in late May, for all of those who grow it, herald the summer.

Through an arch in the wall and round the corner at the end of the chapel wing of the house you see many climbing roses and other wall shrubs. The strongly scented apricot-pink blooms of 'Compassion' look particularly well against the mellow stonework and 'Mme Grégoire Staechelin' mingles there with Sophora and Campsis radicans of the orange trumpet-like flowers. In the beds in front of them, among herbaceous plants, the tall shoots of R. moyesii are visible as is the thicket-forming growth of R. elegantula 'Persetosa' with its minute pink flowers.

Turn away from this border and another vista opens up, for the grass slopes gently down to a large pond surrounded by trees and shrubs: Salix fargesii with its magnolia-like leaves, R. glauca, R. × paullii (which Lady Whit-

ford would like to move if its spines were not quite so lethal) and a number of others. This is a quiet and shady spot of great beauty with ornamental ducks gliding over the smooth surface of the pool and in the background the gentle chuckle of a small waterfall that leads down to a narrow stream. Along this, immensely tall poplars and other trees tower above a bog garden with many varieties of primula, astilbe and other moisture-loving plants. Arching above the stream is the trunk of a willow that blew down in a gale some years ago and now forms a natural, highly decorative if rather perilous bridge across the water.

There are not many roses in the area of the water garden, but by retracing your steps a little and moving round the north side of the house you can discover more. 'Phyllis Bide' and 'Gloire de Dijon' are on the walls of the house itself and the dusky scarlet 'Soldier Boy' is on a fence opposite. Other shrubs include 'Nevada', the Rugosa hybrid 'Conrad Ferdinand Meyer', Hydrangea sargentiana, which has large velvety leaves (very unlike others of its kind) and curiously bristly stems, and a number of other Rugosas.

And so, through a gateway in a wall on the left, you come back to the front of the house once more, having completed a tour of a garden that has enormous charm and a great sense of harmony with the past.

Sissinghurst Castle

Sissinghurst

One mile east of Sissinghurst village on A262;
2½ miles north-east of Cranbrook. Signposted.
Tel. 0580 712850
The National Trust
Open from April to mid-October, Tuesday to Friday
from 1 to 6.30 p.m.; Saturday and Sunday from 10 a.m.
to 6.30 p.m.

Sissinghurst was never a castle. A country mansion dating from Tudor times, it was one of the more domestic buildings that replaced the fortified manors of the Middle Ages. It became a 'castle' only in the eighteenth century when it was used to house French prisoners of war.

After that the buildings were allowed to decay until they became the ruin that Vita Sackville-West and her husband, Harold Nicolson, first saw in 1930. They bought it and in the ensuing years created what has become one of the most famous gardens in England. Much of the story was told by Miss Sackville-West herself in her weekly gardening articles in *The Observer*, that have now become classics of their kind.

While finding much to admire at Sissinghurst, I cannot worship wholeheartedly at the shrine of the Nicolsons. The division of their garden into a number of small compartments or 'rooms', each with its own theme, I find rather claustrophobic. It has been better done at Hidcote, where each of the compartments is larger and the hedges and walls not so dominant.

The garden is famous for its roses and while there are perhaps more important collections elsewhere, you will not find them used better than they are here. The Nicolsons' particular skill was to be able to visualize just what the effect of one plant would be in association with others, even if it meant waiting years before it was achieved for some plants grow slowly. Not all gardeners have the gift and it needs an uncommon degree of patience to carry it through.

On entering the Castle you pass through an archway in the red brick façade and at once are in a walled garden. Here the scarlet semi-double flowers of the climbing rose 'Allen Chandler' frame the arch and 'Gloire de Dijon', pink, scented 'Blossomtime' and the huge, flat, apricot-pink flowers of 'Meg' cover the walls on either side. The climbing Hybrid Musk 'Francis E. Lester' is on the wall opposite and shrub roses, predominantly *R. moyesii* 'Geranium', are to be found in the surrounding beds.

Through another arch under the great tower you arrive in a second walled garden and can glimpse the famous White Garden through yet another arch to your left. The walls on the approach are adorned with more climbers, 'Cupid', 'Easlea's Golden Rambler' and one very unfamiliar one that turns out to be the climbing version of 'Irish Elegance'. This is one of a series of Hybrid Teas with single flowers produced by the Irish firms of Dickson and McGredy early this century. 'Irish Elegance' is a bronzy orange, and the others are 'Irish Fireflame' (rosy-pink, splashed crimson, and also with a climbing sport), and 'Isobel' in light rose-pink. 'White Wings' is another single-flowered Hybrid Tea that can be found in the Sissinghurst Rose Garden, but this came much

later (in 1947), though it was an offspring of another one, 'Dainty Bess', that goes back to 1925. Pink 'Dainty Bess' has bluish-purple stamens; those of 'White Wings' are chocolate brown.

In the White Garden 'Mme Alfred Carrière' covers one wall of the Priest's House and other roses of appropriate colour are 'Nevada', the 'Double White' Scotch rose and *R. longicuspis*, which covers an enormous iron framework in the centre. Just outside the White Garden the old Sempervirens rambler 'Flora' climbs a tree, its lilac-pink, very double flowers with their deep-rose coloured centres peeping from the foliage.

Moving in the other direction back across the Tower Lawn you reach the Rose Garden itself. The high walls all around are used to good advantage to display such climbers as deep-red 'Etoile de Hollande', 'Paul's Lemon Pillar', 'Gloire de Dijon' and *R. × anemonoides*. In the beds beneath the walls and in the centre beds, too, is a very fine selection of the old garden roses from virtually every family, interplanted with lilies, irises, paeonies (including the very striking almost single white-flowered one, 'Janice') and shrubs like the dainty *Deutzia × elegantissima* 'Rosealind'. The modern roses, (not very many of them, as Miss Sackville-West had little time for them), include mainly those that look like old roses, such as 'Lavender Lassie' and 'Golden Wings'.

Of the older roses to catch the eye as you enter the garden there is, immediately on your left, a fine group of *R. rugosa* 'Alba' with beyond it the purplish-red 'Magnifica', a seedling of the Penzance Brier 'Lucy Ashton' and much used in hybridizing, and the Hybrid Perpetual 'Ulrich Brunner' pegged down in the best Victorian tradition. This was something done by Victorian and Edwardian gardeners as a way of dealing with the often ungainly Hybrid Perpetuals, which had a habit of sending up very long shoots that waved about in the breeze, their flowers clinging on for dear life at the very tips and with nothing but leaves lower down.

To increase the number of blooms the tips of the shoots were tied down in autumn to pegs driven into the ground at suitable spots. In spring, the flowering side-shoots (which would otherwise have remained dormant) would burst into life and produce the much-needed flowers. They were, in effect, given the same treatment that one gives to a climber when training the shoots out sideways along wires in order to produce colour low down.

Other older roses include *R. villosa* with its soft grey-green leaves and pink flowers (also known in other gardens under the name *R. pomifera*), 'Ellen Willmott' which is another single Hybrid Tea from the raiser of 'Dainty Bess', the Bourbons 'Great Western' and 'Coupe d'Hébé' and the rather procumbent Gallica 'Ombrée Parfaite', the petals of which vary from light pink to deep purple in the same flower. Also there is the crimson-magenta 'William III' of the Pimpinellifolia family. 'Coupe d'Hébé', like 'Ulrich Brunner', is pegged down to increase the production of its deep-pink, very double flowers.

On the way to the Cottage Garden you pass a hedge of Sweet Brier (*R. eglanteria*), one of our native wild roses, referred to in Shakespeare's plays as Eglantine. Its pink flowers are rather fleeting, but in a hedge like this it can be very striking while it is blooming and there is a fine display of hips in late summer and autumn. More often, however, you find one of its hybrids – the Penzance Briers – used in gardens instead.

In the Cottage Garden, in fact growing against the South Cottage itself, is the brilliant yellow climber 'Lawrence Johnston', which will light up a wall early in the year but there will be no repeat. Another wall supports 'Mme Alfred Carrière' and in a bed below there is perhaps the most startling yellow of all, that of *R. foetida*, helping to carry out the predominantly yellow, orange and red colour scheme of this garden.

Beyond the Cottage Garden is the Orchard and here a few more roses have been left to fend for themselves in the long grass, the labels either obscured or lost long ago. However, the grey, peeling bark and many-segmented leaves and pink flowers of a huge *R. roxburghii* are unmistakable, as are the flame-pink blooms and red canes and deep-green pointed leaves of the China rose 'Cramoisi Superieur'. The climber 'Wickwar' (see page 66) is, however, labelled.

There is a great deal else to see at Sissinghurst that I have not described, but I have tried to give a fair impression of the kind of roses the visitor will find. It is so famous a rose garden that perhaps visitors may go there expecting too much, and this is why my opening paragraphs were somewhat qualified in their enthusiasm. However, there is only one way to find out if you agree. Go and see for yourself.

Polesden Lacey

Signposted off A246 Leatherhead to Guildford road near Great Bookham.
Tel. 0372 58203
The National Trust
Open daily.

There was a house on the site of Polesden Lacey in the sixteenth century and it was the home for a time of the playwright Richard Brinsley Sheridan. It was he who was responsible for lengthening the famous Long Walk in the grounds, making it much as we see it today. This is a vast grass terrace with a walled drop on one side that looks over the wooded valley that gives such fine views to the south of the house. The terrace is backed by trees, on the farther side of which is the grass amphitheatre of the Polesden Lacey open-air theatre. At certain times during the summer you can combine a visit to the gardens with one to a performance at the theatre in the evening and it is difficult to think of a more pleasant way of spending the day. The house and grounds are now administered by The National Trust.

The house that Sheridan knew no longer exists, the present one having been built in 1824. It is a comparatively small country mansion and could be said to have reached its heyday as a residence between the two wars, when it was owned by Mrs Ronald Greville. She entertained there with truly Edwardian magnificence, and it was at Polesden Lacey that the Duke of York (later King George VI) and his bride spent part of their honeymoon. Fourteen gardeners were employed to tend the grounds and the old nineteenth-century walled kitchen garden was turned into the present rose garden by Mrs Greville herself.

To reach it you walk down the drive or across a grassy slope from the car park and cross the paved terrace in front of the house. On your left is the view across the valley and the house walls on your right are covered with the particularly fine deep-green leaves of the species *Clematis armandii*, though the rather ghost-like creamy-white flowers of early spring will have long since vanished by the time the roses are out.

Ahead of you and slightly to the right you can see the high brick wall that surrounds the rose garden and if you follow the path towards

The colours of the roses at Polesden Lacey are those of varieties from the Edwardian era.

it you can glimpse to your right a rather special dogs' cemetery, half-hidden in a small enclave of yews. This is by no means the rather pathetic and weed-grown collection of half-buried little memorial stones that one usually sees as a long-forgotten relic of the past. It is almost like a military cemetery, some dozen or so gravestones standing up like guardsmen in ordered rows, beautifully cared for despite the fact that five gardeners now do the work once carried out by fourteen. Just beyond this is the tomb of Mrs Greville herself, surrounded by yew hedges on two sides and, as you will be aware from the scent that already reaches you, very near to one of the parts of the garden closest to her heart. For the rose garden was created to her inspiration in the true Edwardian manner.

As with so many Surrey gardens, the soil at Polesden Lacey is far from suitable for roses. It is shallow and chalky and Mrs Greville had all the beds dug out to a depth of 45 cm (18 in) and filled with high-quality loam. For those beds cut in the four great lawns into which the rose garden is divided, roses have been chosen that match those of the Edwardian era in their colourings: that means varieties in red tones, various shades of pink and cream and white, but no bright yellows, which did not arrive in our gardens until a little later in the twentieth century. They are also roses that are more able than most to stand far-from-ideal conditions for, despite Mrs Greville's efforts and despite what has been done since, the chalk still lurks and every so often the roses, tough as they are, have to be replaced and the soil in the beds sterilized before new plantings are made.

There are something like 2400 roses in the four beds and varieties that seem to do well are 'Gail Borden', 'Pascali', 'Peace', 'Red Planet', 'Home Sweet Home', 'Pink Favourite', 'Eden Rose' and 'John Waterer', among the Hybrid Tea varieties, and 'Iceberg', 'Frensham' (mildew not too noticeable), 'Queen Elizabeth', and 'Chanelle' among the Floribunda roses. Also to be found there are one or two Hybrid Perpetuals such as 'Hugh Dickson' and 'Mrs John Laing' and the Hybrid Musks 'Penelope', 'Felicia' and 'Buff Beauty'.

The lawns are bordered by low box and lavender hedges and divided by paths, over which are pergolas running the whole length and width of the garden. The pivot where the paths cross in the centre is formed by a Venetian well head.

The roses on the pergolas are typical of the Edwardian period and all are hybrids of the rambler *R. wichuraiana* or its close relative *R. luciae*. They include 'Dorothy Perkins', 'Excelsa', 'Sanders' White', 'American Pillar', 'Albéric Barbier' and 'Albertine', and also the rather more modern 'Crimson Shower' and 'New Dawn' which, despite their comparative youthfulness, are very much in the same style. On the walls themselves are more ramblers such as the lilac-pink fragrant 'May Queen' whose bright, fresh, green leaves come very early in the season, some climbers like 'Mme Alfred Carrière' and one from the small group of Boursalt roses called 'Mme Sancy de Parabère'.

In the wide beds beneath the walls is a quite impressive collection from most of the old rose families, the Gallicas, Albas, Portlands, Rugosas, Hybrid Perpetuals, Bourbons and a China or two, but not as far as I can see any Damasks, Centifolias or Moss roses. There are, however, a number of species and modern shrub roses, all of them underplanted with no less than eight different species or varieties of geranium, *Alchemilla mollis*, anaphalis and the following hardy fuchsias 'Graf Witte', 'Lady Thumb', 'Happy', 'Chillerton Beauty', 'Rufus', 'Emile Zola', 'Thornley's Hardy', 'Paula Baylis', 'Eva Boerg', 'Blue Bonnet', 'Pee Wee Rose', and 'Sealand Prince'. The species roses include the not-too-often-seen Scotch rose 'Double White' and another one of the same Pimpinellifolia family, 'Andrewsii', three of which planted close together form an absolutely impenetrable thicket of thorny twigs.

In the beds along the south wall and on the shorter west wall a number of the roses have been trained over strong but flexible saplings which have been bent into suitable curves so that they form a frame roughly in the shape of an igloo about 1.2 m (4 ft) high. The roses are tied in to this and produce flowering shoots all along their lengths, making large mounds of blossom. Varieties treated in this way are mostly fairly modern ones and include 'Frühlingsgold', 'Fritz Nobis', 'Cerise Bouquet' and the rather older Hybrid Perpetual 'Georg Arends'. This is an interesting rose as its pink blooms show very clearly the beginnings of a new shape in rose flowers. All the early varieties had short centre petals which resulted in blooms that were either cupped or globular in shape. It was not until the Tea Rose from China, with its much longer petals, was interbred with other roses that things began to change. Gradually a new shape emerged which culminated in roses with the high, pointed centre that is so much admired today. 'Georg Arends', introduced in 1910, shows an early manifestation of this new shape very clearly. I would not, myself, have picked an upright, arching grower like 'Frühlingsgold' for tying over a frame, but just beyond the roses I have mentioned the more conventional pegging down of the climber 'Maigold' works very well.

All told, despite a few varieties that have arrived on the scene since her day, Mrs Greville would probably still be very much at home in her rose garden if she were alive today, though she would miss the great glasshouses that used to stand against the north wall. You can still see traces of them on the brickwork and the beds underneath are not yet fully developed.

Should you come to the garden for a first visit before the roses are out, in April perhaps, do not miss the superb specimen of *Corylopsis willmottiae*, which bears its pale yellow cowslip-like flowers in incredible profusion in a corner of this north wall. It is one of a number of old-established shrubs that grow there and, no doubt, roses will be added in due course.

Wisley Garden

Well-signposted off the A3 and the M25 near Ripley in Surrey.
Tel. 0483 224234
The Royal Horticultural Society
Open every day except Christmas Day. Members only on Sundays.

Wisley Garden is a more than worthy showplace in almost every way for the most highly respected (not to say largest) horticultural society in the world, although the site presents problems. Its 96 hectares (240 acres) are on the edge of typical Surrey heathland, undulating country of Scots pine, birch, oak, heather and gorse. The soil is very sandy, acid and quick-draining, hardly the ideal habitat for growing good roses.

Wisley has a big display garden for modern Hybrid Tea, Floribunda and climbing varieties just at the foot of both Battleston and Weather Hills, the main axes of which are at right angles to each other. Here the roses are grown for five years before being replaced by newer kinds and there is also a raised bed for miniatures at one end.

Those roses that make the grade are planted after their five-year trial period, together with a number of firmly established favourites, in two very long and very wide borders that run up the gentle slope of Weather Hill. The two borders can in a good season be spectacular, but more often than not it is with its cultivation of these and their unwelcoming soil that Wisley falls short of the excellence to be found everywhere else in the garden. In fact, if it were for its bedding roses alone, Wisley might not find itself included as one of the rose gardens of England.

However, the problems that seem to affect most of the modern rose varieties are clearly shrugged off by the shrub roses, and there are many treasures among these to be found elsewhere in the garden. In fact on Weather Hill itself there are very worthwhile climbers such as 'Mme Grégoire Staechelin' growing along the ropes of two catenaries that flank the main rose borders, and to the right as you stroll upwards are two fairly new roughly oval beds that feature a number of modern shrub roses such as 'Robusta' from Kordes of Germany and the lovely creamy-white 'Sally Holmes' and 'Butterfly Wings', both raised by amateurs in the United Kingdom. Mixed with these are many of the latest so-called ground-cover roses such as 'Fairy Damsel', 'Pearl Drift', 'Rosy Cushion', 'Pink Bells', 'Red Bells' and 'White Bells' and others. I say 'so-called' because to my mind a true ground-cover rose has to be a real weed annihilator, and of them all only the 'Bells' series gets anywhere near. Other interesting but rarely seen roses in these beds are 'La Sevillana', 'Anna Zinkeisen', 'Rachel Bowes Lyon', 'Proud Titania', 'Olive' and 'Leander'.

Carrying on up the hill and passing to the left of the Bowes Lyon Pavilion, tucked in behind the Model Fruit Gardens is a long shrub-rose border with a backing of tall trees. See it in the morning if you wish to take photographs as it gets full sun only then. Nevertheless the roses thrive and here you will find such species as

R. virginiana, *R. moyesii*, *R. primula*, *R. glauca* (*R. rubrifolia*) and *R.* × *cantabrigiensis*, some particularly fine specimens of 'Nevada' and in general a mixed bag of old and new. 'Trier' is one variety there of especial interest to rose historians. It has clusters of small white flowers and was raised by the German nurseryman Peter Lambert in 1904. It was the rose much used by the Essex clergyman-cum-nurseryman Joseph Pemberton in breeding his family of Hybrid Musk roses (see also page 116), good examples of which are to be seen in the Wisley Summer Garden, to be found by retracing your steps down Weather Hill and turning left. Two of them, 'Penelope' and 'Felicia', can be rather wayward growers in the sense that they send out long shoots at unpredictable angles, but here they are beautifully restrained on horizontal wires strung between metal uprights. The same treatment also keeps in check the normally almost uncontrollable Penzance Briers, 'Lord Penzance', 'Lady Penzance', 'Amy Robsart' and the less common dark-crimson 'Anne of Geierstein', all raised around the turn of the century by Lord Penzance (see page 76) and many of them named after characters in Sir Walter Scott's novels. There are no fewer than forty-six other different varieties of shrub rose in the Summer Garden, ranging from species like *R. pomifera* to moderns like 'Kassel' and including both lemon and white versions of 'Cécile Brunner'. They are blended in very happily with a number of other plants that flower at high summer.

Just down a gravelled path from the Summer Garden a truly enormous rambler/climber soars up 12 m (40 ft) or more into a tree. So far nobody has been able to make a positive identification, but from its clusters of small white flowers it is clearly of the group rather loosely termed Musk ramblers.

Retrace your steps just a little way and you will see near the Curator's cottage a bed of old roses containing two of particular note, the crimson Centifolia, 'Ombrée Parfaite', and the pink Damask, 'Oeillet Parfait' with petals striped with a deeper pink. Both were raised early in the nineteenth century.

Now move down the grassy slope towards the long, rectangular formal pool. On the left, ahead of you, will be the tall brick walls of the Formal and Walled Gardens. There are interesting roses on the insides and outsides of these walls, including the light pink, fragrant climbing sport of the very first Hybrid Tea, 'La

France', and the climbing Tea rose 'Lady Hillingdon'. There is also the climbing miniature, 'Pompon de Paris', which can be seen again on the front of the laboratory building (which is not as old as it looks) at the other end of the Formal Pool. Other roses on the laboratory walls are the climbing Hybrid Musk 'Francis E. Lester' which was raised in the USA and *R. gigantea*. A climber from China, this does not always survive the climate of the United Kingdom or produce its large, single white flowers with the same freedom that it does in the East, but it is an important ancestor of modern varieties. At one end is the enchanting 'Helen Knight', a hybrid actually raised at Wisley (one gathers with a certain amount of luck) by the one-time Director Frank Knight, a cross (as far as is known) between *R. pimpinellifolia* and *R. ecae*. Imagine a climbing 'Canary Bird' with smaller, even brighter flowers and you have 'Helen Knight'.

Along one side of the pool a number of plants of the miniature climber 'Nozomi' sprawl down a bank and long beds on the other side contain many roses mixed with other plants and shrubs. Many of David Austin's English Roses are among them, including 'The Squire', 'The Reeve' and 'The Knight'.

Heading away from the pool through a gap between the beds you pass between *R.* 'Macrantha' on one side and 'Marguerite Hilling' on the other. The restaurant will now be ahead of you, but do not be tempted in yet because on your left is the last major rose border you will encounter. There are twelve different Gallicas there, two Centifolias and 'Shailer's White Moss', so you complete the tour with quite a flourish of old roses. Elsewhere in the garden you will come across other roses planted individually, such as the huge, tree-climbing 'Paul's Himalayan Musk Rambler' at the far end of the area called 'Seven Acres', which includes a lake and a magnificent heather garden. And in spring the bright yellow of *R. × harisonii* ('Harison's Yellow') lights up several corners. Everywhere in Wisley there is beauty to be found in any month of the year, but June and July are, of course, the best months for roses.

'Complicata' growing successfully in partial shade among the trees at Berri Court.

Berri Court

Yapton

*South-west of Arundel. A27 Arundel–Chichester road,
then B2132 to Yapton. House in centre of village
between Post Office and Black Dog Inn.*
Tel. 0243 551663
Mr and Mrs J. C. Turner
Open, garden only, under the National Gardens Scheme.

You approach Berri Court along a busy village street that carries a good deal of the traffic between Littlehampton and Bognor Regis but suddenly, as you swing in through the gate, all is peace. Mellow brick walls help to shut out the bustle of the world and give support to all manner of roses including, of course, a fine selection of climbers and ramblers.

However, the first thing to catch the eye as you approach the house up the gravel drive is something much less familiar. It is a very handsome shrub – almost a small tree – against one of the house walls. A specimen of *Drimys winteri*, it is native to both Australasia and South America, though this one comes from the latter. The large leaves rather resemble an evergreen magnolia and the creamy-white flowers open in May, a little earlier than those of an enormous 'Climbing Cécile Brunner' which is invading the roof just to its left and has the kind of trunk you sometimes see on ancient wisterias. There are some bedding roses by the drive, including the excellent orange-red Floribunda 'Sarabande'.

The garden is entirely the creation of Mr and Mrs Turner and is divided by its walls into a number of separate gardens, each one with a character of its own. In case anyone is tempted to sigh 'Not another Sissinghurst' the answer is, 'Not a bit of it!' Berri Court is completely original.

To the east the windows of the house look out onto a walled garden that is roughly square and which has broad beds round the edges where shrub roses are mixed with other plants: 'Nevada', 'Canary Bird', 'Stanwell Perpetual', *R. glauca* (*R. rubrifolia*), 'Buff Beauty', 'Frühlings-gold', to name just a few of them. 'Climbing Cécile Brunner' appears once again, threatening to engulf the house from this side also, and other climbers on the walls include an exceptionally fine 'New Dawn', 'Mme Alfred Carrière', the lovely apricot-pink 'Meg', and the

white Hybrid Musk 'Moonlight' which has here been encouraged to go upwards rather than sideways.

If you go through a gate at the far end of this garden, you come out into another with walls on one side only. There is a small pool to the right and above it a double, yellow Banksian rose covers the wall. To the left of the gate are other climbers, while immediately ahead is an area planted entirely with shrub roses, including quite a selection of Pemberton's Hybrid Musks. All down one side is a really spectacular hedge of the most popular one of all, the creamy-apricot 'Penelope' – a demonstration of just how much room a hedge of these roses needs if they are not rigorously cut back (which they should not be if you want them at their best) or disciplined by training on wires. The Polyantha 'Yvonne Rabier' appears among this group but grows to such a height that I quite failed to recognize it.

If you move down a slight slope to the right, the mood changes. You are in the cool shade of the spinney, but there is enough light there nevertheless for many more of the old roses to thrive. There you will find 'Celestial', *R. × centifolia* 'Variegata', 'Ispahan', more Hybrid Musks including 'Cornelia' and quite a clump of the rose-pink 'Vanity' (which really needs close grouping like this because of its ungainly habit), 'Crimson Moss', 'Souvenir du Docteur Jamain' and the seldom seen 'Aurora'.

There is a high wall on one side of the spinney and a low one on the other. On the high one 'Rambling Rector' lives up to its name and on the low one the long shoots, the large, very tapered, grey-green leaves and corymbs of white flowers of another rose said to me *R. brunonii*, probably the form, 'La Mortola'. However, the label (and most roses in this garden are labelled) was *R. moschata nepalensis*, which some authorities say is the same as *R. brunonii* while some disagree. There is so much confusion and argument over these Far Eastern so-called Musk Ramblers that, being something of a novice in this area, I tend to back off when the bickering starts.

As you leave the trees and walk towards the drive you pass Penzance Briers with their scented foliage and, looking a little lost and out on its own, a single 'Old Blush'. Nearby is a wonderful specimen of *Cornus controversa*, the wide-spreading branches of which carry broad clusters of cream-coloured flowers in May and early June. This is only one of the interesting shrubs, trees and other plants that you see everywhere you look, all blending beautifully with one another.

Across the drive, you enter a woodland walk with rhododendrons, exotic acers and other plants that like shade or semi-shade. However, enough light still comes down through the branches and into occasional clearings for some roses to do surprisingly well. There is for instance R. × paulii (the Turners keep ordering the pink form but are sent the original white) and a great shiny-leaved mound of 'Max Graf', over 1.2 m (4 ft) high. Nearby 'Mermaid' coils itself tightly like a python round the trunk of a tree, a considerable feat of training when you remember the stiff and rather brittle 'Mermaid' shoots with their formidable thorns, and 'François Juranville' goes hand-over-fist up another. White-flowered 'Mme Plantier' (a rose of doubtful ancestry, though it almost certainly has some Alba blood in it) is used very successfully as a climber here, too.

There is much more of the garden, but the areas I have covered are those where most roses grow. It is a place created by people with a great knowledge and love of all plants, not just of roses; it is also a place where you can be distracted from a winning shot at tennis by the exquisite soft-pink blooms of the rose 'Fritz Nobis' just beyond the side netting; where the glossy leaves and massive, fragrant, pink double flowers of 'Aloha', that climber without peer, light up a shady courtyard wall away from the other roses. It is without doubt a garden to visit at all seasons.

Charleston Manor

Westdean

On A27 between Lewes and Polegate, turn south at Wilmington on Litlington road. House three-quarters of a mile from turning.
Tel. 0323 870267
Mr and Mrs R. Headlam
Open, garden only, under the National Gardens Scheme and during Charleston Manor Festival in June/July each year.

Described by Sir Nikolaus Pevsner as 'the perfect house in the perfect setting', Charleston Manor has a Norman wing dating back to 1080 that is mentioned in the Domesday Book. On

the south and east sides it is Tudor, while the front of the house is Queen Anne. There are many outbuildings and cottages on the estate and a vast fifteenth-century Tithe Barn, now used as a theatre for the Festival. Flint walls are everywhere, dividing the garden into a number of different compartments. On every one of them climbing and rambling roses are trained, while other roses clamber into trees or cover arches or metal-framed pillars copied in design, I believe, from those in the Parc de Bagatelle in Paris.

I suppose that it might be possible to count how many ramblers and climbers there are, but let us say only that their number is staggering. It is a pity, though, that so few are named, as many of them are no longer in cultivation and are therefore difficult to identify. Such labels as still exist are of the old lead variety on which the shadow of a name written by a gardener of long ago is barely visible. A planting plan of the original rose collection does exist, of the shrub roses as well as the climbers, and the intention is, I understand, that a number of those that are showing their age should be replaced by new bushes of the same variety. I hope this does happen, sooner rather than later, as historically this is one of England's most important rose gardens. It would be tragic if it were not restored to its former glory.

Not that it is not glorious now, and many of the roses can, of course, be named quite easily. As always there are doubts about many of the look-alike multi-flowered white ramblers, and one of the large-flowered climbers on one of the walls that surround the gravel sweep up to the front door of the house baffled me until I poked about and found a lead label that was still readable. It turned out to be the lovely creamy pink 'Gruss an Aachen' in its climbing form. As a low-growing bush it dates back to 1909 and some people hold that it was the first of the Floribundas, without much justification, as its parents were a Hybrid Perpetual and a Hybrid Tea. As a climber it was apparently discovered at the Sangerhausen Rosarium in East Germany and introduced by the nurseryman Wilhelm Kordes in 1937, so it is modern compared to most of the roses in the garden, which perhaps accounts for the legible label. A fine climber, and recurrent to boot, it is a pity that it is not better known.

On first arriving at the house, a small courtyard off the drive to the right leads through into a walled garden. There are herbaceous borders

'Penelope' is among the best of the Hybrid Musks raised by Joseph Pemberton early in this century.

here and a lily pond and a medlar tree in one corner, but not too many roses. Honeysuckle covers the walls and the pale pink 'New Dawn' is there too, a rose that features again and again in the rose gardens of England. Its soft, delicate pink colouring makes it easy to live with, and it is, of course, recurrent, though a sport of a once-flowering rose 'Dr W. Van Fleet'.

At the far end of this first walled garden you pass through a wrought-iron gate into what could fairly be described as a magic world. A brick path stretches into the distance ahead and, over it, on arch after arch, are ramblers and climbers in varieties obviously chosen for their light, airy beauty. 'Bobbie James' is the one to greet you first and is followed by 'Climbing Iceberg', 'New Dawn', 'Félicité et Perpétue', 'Paul's Himalayan Musk Rambler', 'Francis E. Lester' plus many others that I am not too sure about. One is, I think, 'Dr Benschop', which can be seen in the gardens of The Royal National

Rose Society but nowhere else that I know of, and is ex-directory as far as the reference books are concerned. Near the bottom of the path 'Kiftsgate', not surprisingly, rather overwhelms its arch and it can be seen a number of other times throughout the garden, though more often with its blooms nodding down at you from a tall tree.

On either side of this central path with its multiple arches is a wide stretch of rough grass and then a flint wall. In the grass are many free-standing shrub roses, but others are trained on pillars, 'Crimson Rambler' and 'May Queen' coming first to mind. Among the shrubs is a wide selection from all the old rose families and some quite modern ones – 'Trigintipetala', 'Penelope', 'Belle Poitevine', 'Scabrosa', *R. glauca, R. nitida*, 'Charles de Mills' are some of the names picked at random, and one that I tentatively identified as the rainbow coloured 'Radway Sunrise'. Needless to say, on the surrounding walls rambling and climbing roses grow in profusion.

At the far end of this enclosure – it hardly gives the feeling of being a walled garden in the traditional sense as the walls are no more than head height and less than that on the south side – is another wrought-iron gate. Once through this and to the right, you can glimpse another large walled area but there are few roses of much note there except 'Dorothy Perkins' and 'New Dawn', which you can see anywhere. A turn to the left is another matter. There is a long, grassy slope ahead and the ground rises quite steeply to a wood at the top, for Charleston Manor is in a valley. Along the bottom of the slope, heading back in the direction of the house and along the outside of the south wall of the rose garden already discussed, more roses are planted in the grass, 'Trigintipetala' again, 'William Lobb' and 'Kiftsgate' on pillars, a good selection of Rugosas, the Alba 'Félicité Parmentier' and many more. 'Parade' and other climbers cover the outside of the rose garden wall.

As you draw near to the house, you can see on the slope ahead an enormous round flint dovecote and just below it some formal round beds containing roses such as 'Raubritter', 'Felicia' and 'Buff Beauty'. To one side sprawls, in all its vast magnificence, one of the largest bushes of 'Cerise Bouquet' I have ever seen, probably all of 4.5 m (15 ft) across and smothered in thousands of bright cerise-pink blooms.

As you reach the dovecote the house is below you on the left and once again no wall is left unadorned by roses. Ahead, a short yew walk temporarily hides the house, but you emerge at the top of a series of long terraces that lead down to it once more and to a large lawn on the farther side of which, and, in fact, stretching from one end to the other, is the huge Tithe Barn. On the terrace below is a further shrub rose planting and immediately ahead on the terrace on which you are standing are more of the metal-framed pillars like those in the rose garden. On them are 'American Pillar', 'Goldfinch', 'Violette', 'Albéric Barbier' and 'Vielchenblau', while across the way 'Aloha' and 'Albéric Barbier' mingle with sweet peas on the barn walls.

The terraces are edged with low, clipped box hedges and as one progresses down steps towards the lawn, on either side are colourful plantings of begonias with blue powder-puffs of ageratum among them.

After passing through an iron gate at the end of the lawn farthest from the house you are in an orchard-cum-woodland where ramblers of the more adventurous kind like 'Silver Moon' and, need I say it, 'Kiftsgate' disport themselves in the trees. You can wander amongst them for a while and then return towards the house along the side of the barn. Again there are roses, 'Maigold' on one wall, 'Mme Alfred Carrière' on another, and varieties like 'Yvonne Rabier', 'Fru Dagmar Hastrup', R. virginiana 'Plena', 'Iceberg', 'Felicia', 'Scabrosa', 'Belle de Crécy', 'Moonlight' and many more in the beds beneath them. A door in the wall ahead leads back to the front of the house and so back to the drive.

Ketches

Newick

From A272 through Newick take Barcombe Road south. House on right opposite turning to Newick church. Tel. 082 572 2679 Mr David Manwaring Robertson Open, garden only, under the National Gardens Scheme.

Tall shrubberies surround the forecourt at Ketches so the magnificent vista that opens up as you move round the house comes as a great surprise. The view over woods and rolling countryside makes a superb setting for a wonderful garden. Parts of the house go back to 1580, with additions over the years up to Victorian times, and it has a most pleasing façade overlooking the main lawn, with 'Climbing Shot Silk' and 'Etoile de Hollande' obviously revelling on the sunny, south-facing walls. There are roses everywhere you go at Ketches but fortunately it is fairly easy to take a path round the garden and, without doubling back too much, see everything there is to see.

As good a place to start as any is the great curved bed to the east of the main lawn where there is a massed planting of the soft-pink Rugosa 'Fru Dagmar Hastrup', with 'Blanc Double de Coubert' behind it and 'Little White Pet' in the foreground, together making one of the loveliest combinations of roses I have seen. Beyond it a red-leaved *Photinia glabra* 'Rubens' marks the entrance to a shady path between tall shrubs, rhododendrons and others, with roses, 'Albéric Barbier', R. × 'Macrantha' and the white Hybrid Musk 'Pax', scrambling through them, despite the shade.

You come out into the sunlight again at the bottom of the lawn. Here there is a big bed of that wild man of the rose garden 'Cerise Bouquet' and, while it takes courage (and space) for most people to plant just one of such a rampant grower, here there are five or six! When I saw them they were quite small, but when they take off they will be a formidable sight. A group of 'Marguerite Hilling' flourishes nearby and you see this mass planting of a single variety of shrub rose again and again as you go around the garden. It is something that you do not see too often but Mr Robertson, who has created the garden from scratch over some thirty years, has obviously realized how effective it can be.

Across the bottom of the lawn you pass a magnificent oak tree (estimated as being between 250 and 300 years old) and a Spanish chestnut which, with its huge gnarled and twisted trunk, looks infinitely older although it is probably about the same age. Beyond them you move into the shade once more, though only briefly, where mauve-flowered 'Vielchenblau' and white 'Rambling Rector' scramble up on either side through the branches of a grove of shrubs and small trees.

Out into the open once more by the swimming pool and a little above you on the right, for the garden slopes gently, are the massed white blooms of the rambler 'Seagull' on the side wall of the pool. Ahead and to the left is another planting of Rugosas, this time of three varieties: 'Fru Dagmar Hastrup' again, deep-pink 'Scabrosa' and wine-red 'Roseraie de l'Hay', the first two of which are the biggest and best hip-bearers among the Rugosas in late summer and autumn.

Moving on and up past the vegetable garden you pass by 'Frühlingsgold', the Bourbon 'Mme Isaac Pereire' set against a variegated dogwood to great effect, the David Austin-raised and sweetly scented 'Chianti' (the flowers of which form Gallica-like rosettes of deep crimson, turning purple with age) and the White Rose of York (R. × alba 'Semi-plena'). At the top of the slope is an extensive area in which roses have been planted among small trees and some other shrubs. Most of the trees are apples but in among them is a fine specimen of *Acer negundo*, the 'Box Elder' of the USA and noted as a family for its very attractive variegated foliage. One tree has no fewer than three roses growing over it, which seems rather unfair when one of

them is 'Kiftsgate', but there must be worse fates than having it, 'Parade' and the veteran 'Gloire de Dijon' exploring your topmost branches.

Nearby several plants of the Alba rose 'Celestial' form the backing to a garden seat and there are other beds of 'Golden Wings', 'Kathleen Harrop' (a paler pink and rather less vigorous sport of 'Zéphirine Drouhin'), R. webbiana and the rarely seen 'Goldbusch' (or 'Goldbush'). The latter is a Kordes-raised *Rubiginosa* hybrid with yellow flowers that have a hint of peach in them, and despite the fact that Mr Robertson is not enthusiastic about its rather straggling habit, its flowers and their rich fragrance have continued to make it irresistible and have saved it from the bonfire so far.

At the far end of this area of the garden you arrive back at the house again, at the opposite side from where you started. Early-flowering 'Maigold' almost completely covers one wall of a cottage opposite the house and there are a few more shrub roses in beds round about, 'Kassel' and 'Penelope' being the first to catch the eye, together with a quite enormous bush of the American Floribunda rose, 'Apricot Nectar', which is generally considered not to do too well in the United Kingdom.

Ketches is a garden of tremendous charm. Although not a great number of rose rarities can be seen there are many lessons to be learned about how roses of all kinds can be used to the maximum effect, both on their own and in association with other plants.

Nymans

Handcross

On B2114 at Handcross, 4½ miles south of Crawley, just off A23.
The National Trust, under the guiding hand of Anne, Countess of Rosse.
Open from end March to end October, every day except Monday and Friday.

In this garden it is all to easy to think you have spotted 'Paul's Himalayan Musk Rambler' only to find that you are wrong. The first time this happened to me was when I had a distant view of a rambler at the entrance to the rose garden, which turned out to be 'Princesse Marie' instead, a possible Sempervirens hybrid raised in France by Jacques in 1829. The second time, it happened in the rose garden itself where I mistook the Walsh rambler 'Debutante' growing on an arch for it. As all three have large clusters of small blooms in much the same warm pink tone I suppose there was some excuse. But the flowers of the Musk Rambler are much smaller than either of the other two and the leaves are not the same. When I saw the genuine 'Paul's Himalayan Musk' a little later I wondered how I had ever made the mistake. The whole of a vast tree in a dell beyond the front of the house was a foaming waterfall of pink blossom, cascading down from something like 12 m (40 ft). Of all the pink ramblers (not just the three I have referred to), only 'Paul's Himalayan Musk' could achieve such beauty on a similar scale.

The main part of the house at Nymans, the home of the Messel family for many years, was destroyed by fire in 1947 and only one wing is now lived in. The rest forms an extremely romantic-looking ruin that dominates the centre of the garden and in no way detracts from its appeal.

The original rose garden contained many of the roses from the famous collection of Ellen Willmott but over the years there have been many changes and Lady Rosse has taken a particular interest in the old varieties, adding many more. The metal arches and pillars for the climbers and ramblers were erected in the late 1970s.

To reach the garden from the car park you go down a long path at the side of which are some shrub roses and rambling climbers such as 'Kiftsgate', *R. polyantha* 'Grandiflora' (sometimes incorrectly known as *R. gentiliana* and probably, in truth, a hybrid of *R. multiflora* and a garden variety) while others scale trees round about with all the agility of a Moorish Corsair racing up the rigging. The garden is well signposted so you are unlikely to lose your way.

The rose garden is oblong, not particularly big in terms of the scale of the garden as a whole. It has a main central path with others leading off it on either side and a well in the middle. 'Princesse Marie' welcomes you and almost immediately after that, by the side of the path, is a planting of the 'Macrantha' hybrid 'Raubritter' (clearly a favourite at Nymans). This is a low-growing, spreading shrub, here intended presumably for ground cover on a level site. It is also ideal for sprawling down a steep bank in which spring bulbs are planted and which needs cover for the rest of the season. The very profuse flowers are of the same very globular form as the Bourbon 'Mme Pierre Oger' and they hold their shape with very little reflexing of the petals. A most attractive rose, it seems to do well at Nymans despite a rather bad reputation for mildew.

Most of the other roses are those you would expect to find in a Victorian rose garden: Gallicas, Damasks, Centifolias, Albas and the rest, the bigger ones on metal frames, arches and pillars. Some roses have a special interest because they are rarely seen: the American Van Fleet climber 'Breeze Hill', for instance, with its creamy apricot flowers fading to creamy buff, and 'Lady Curzon', another of the 'Macrantha' clan, but this time a hybrid with a Rugosa. Then there is 'Sissinghurst Castle', a Gallica that was discovered in the garden whose name it bears, or perhaps I should say that it was rediscovered there since it appears to be identical to the much older 'Rose des Maures'. In its new incarnation it was introduced in 1947. It is semi-double with deep maroon-purple petals that have paler edges and reverse. Another rose that one rarely sees is 'René André', which is on one of the arches that frame the central well of the rose garden. It is one of the many Wichuraiana ramblers introduced by the French firm of Barbier around the turn of the century. The blooms are a soft yellow, flushed with apricot and pink, and they have a sweet scent reminiscent of apples.

To the left of the main path and some way from it are some of the larger shrubs, an enormous 'Cerise Bouquet', *R. × dupontii*, 'Honorine de Brabant', *R. rugosa* 'Rubra' and the modern German shrub rose 'Bonn', which here grows 2.1 m (7 ft) tall and rather leggy, so that once again 'Raubritter' comes into its own for ground cover under it.

Elsewhere in the garden, one of the finest in Sussex, you can find other roses, but not in profusion. There are a few bedding varieties in the lawn near the house, the tree climbers I have already mentioned, and here and there among extensive plantings of rhododendrons and other lovers of acid soil such as pieris and camellias, are *R. virginiana*, whose pink flowers arrive late in the summer and whose leaves turn to sunset hues in the autumn, the Chestnut Rose (*R. roxburghii* 'Normalis'), the White Rose of York (*R. × alba* 'Semi-plena') and that other fine Alba, 'Maiden's Blush'.

Hampton Court Palace

Right beside Hampton Court Bridge on river Thames at junction of A308 and A309. Well signposted.
Tel. 01 977 1328
The Department of the Environment
Open daily.

The gardens of Hampton Court Palace, on the banks of the river Thames just outside London, are some of the most spectacular in the whole of the British Isles. In spring, when the massed plantings of daffodils are out under the cherry and magnolia trees, they are a magic world of yellow, white and palest pink. At other times they have a more formal look, but they are never less than impressive and are some of the best-looked-after gardens I know.

The palace is always associated with the Tudor period of English history and was built for Cardinal Wolsey, although King Henry VIII took it away from him, but little if any of the original Tudor garden remains. Even the knot garden, so typical of Tudor times, is comparatively modern and what you see today is largely the creation of William and Mary, the work being carried out under the supervision of Sir Christopher Wren. Later, under George III, 'Capability' Brown took, for him, a fairly restrained hand in it, and it was he who planted one of the wonders of Hampton Court, the Great Vine.

Hampton Court has an abundance of mellow brick walls, mostly something like 3 m (10 ft) high, that give enormous scope for climbing plants. The rose garden, conveniently next door to the car park, which itself has climbing roses on the walls, has walls on three sides and a 1.5 m (5 ft) box hedge on the fourth, the south-eastern side. The perimeter beds have plantings of hundreds of Hybrid Tea and Flori-

Looking across the rose garden at Hampton Court with the palace buildings in the background.

bunda varieties, some old stagers, but a lot of very modern kinds, too. In the bed under the south-western wall these are closely interplanted with standard or tree roses on a scale I have not seen elsewhere and this way of using standards can be most effective, even if the numbers usually have to be more modest.

The garden is roughly square, probably 63 to 72 m (70 to 80 yds) each way. The centre lawn, into which ten large beds have been cut, sets off very well the mixed plantings of roses to be found there. Once again there are huge numbers of modern bush roses, but along the centres of each of the ten beds are shrub roses including 'Nevada', *R. primula* (a spring-flowering species with scented leaves), 'Fred Loads', 'Constance Spry', the Hybrid Musk 'Vanity', *R. moyesii* of the bottle-shaped hips, 'Frühlingsgold', 'Canary Bird', 'Marguerite Hilling' the pink sport of 'Nevada' and, perhaps least likely of all, several plants of 'Austrian Copper' (*R. foetida bicolor*), no doubt spreading its black spot far and wide. It is really a fine old mish-mash of old and new, but is very effective just the same, particularly when seen against the background of the walls and several well-established magnolia trees in the beds at one end.

The cultivation, as everywhere in the garden, is immaculate. If you wish to learn how climbing roses should be trained, look on the walls of Hampton Court. There are many climbers outside the rose garden itself, but in it one can find such varieties as 'Albéric Barbier', 'Crimson Glory', 'Dreaming Spires' and a rather surprisingly restrained 'Kiftsgate'. There are several of the less common roses, including the brilliant-yellow 'Lawrence Johnston', named after Major Lawrence Johnston, who created the famous garden at Hidcote in Gloucestershire and who rescued the rose when it was about to be discarded by its raiser, Pernet-Ducher, in 1923. On another wall is a rose labelled 'Belle Sebright', a name that I cannot find listed in any of the record books, though I have discovered a 'Belle Siebrecht' (also known as 'Mrs W. J. Grant'), a climbing sport of which appeared in 1899, so perhaps there has been some confusion in the labelling.

Another rose that you do not find in every garden is the rambler 'Mme d'Arblay', which has the same parents as 'The Garland' though with the seed and pollen parents reversed. It is fragrant with small, blush-pink flowers.

To add interest for those who are not rose fanatics, there are other climbing plants as well, an interesting range which includes *Garrya elliptica*, ceanothus in variety, clematis, abutilon, *Myrtus communis* (the Common Myrtle), *Actinida kolomiktia*, *Callistemon linearis* and *Piptanthus laburnifolius*. And finally, do not leave Hampton Court without seeing the truly magical specimen of *Betula ermanii* just outside the rose garden at the north-western corner. The smooth trunk and branches, white at first glance, contain a subtle blending of many soft colours and the whole thing looks as if it comes straight out of a fairytale illustration.

Kew Gardens

The Royal Botanical Gardens, Kew

Immediately over Kew Bridge, on Richmond Road, Kew Green is on right with main garden entrance at far end. The easiest parking is by the Brentford Ferry gate: turn off Kew Green towards the river down a narrow lane beside the Herbarium building, then left along the river bank to the car park.
Tel. 01 940 1171
Open every day.

Many maps still show a rose garden near to Kew's famous Pagoda, but the roses are no longer there. This is mentioned as a warning so that you do not have a long walk in vain if you enter by the Brentford Ferry gate to the gardens. True, it will be a pleasant walk and you will also see Decimus Burton's dazzling white Temperate House. This, together with his Palm House from the 1840s, must be one of the most impressive examples of horticultural architecture in the world. It is the Palm House you should make for as you come into the garden if you want to see the roses first, as a map on a display board will show you.

The modern rose garden runs along the north-east side of the Palm House, a gigantic half-circle of grass enclosed by a holly hedge on its curved side. The beds are cut into the grass and there is a mixture of both varieties and kinds, not all of them bedding roses in the

Opposite: *Modern roses like 'Iceberg', 'Rose Gaujard' and yellow 'Chinatown' are successfully blended with the old at Hampton Court.*

accepted sense. Two of the beds contain the Hybrid Musks 'Buff Beauty' and 'Penelope' and there are also two large circular beds with 'Nevada' and its pink sport 'Marguerite Hilling' planted in them, one each side of a wide central path. However, for the most part the roses are either Hybrid Teas or Floribundas. 'Cheshire Life', 'Anne Harkness', pink 'Scented Air', 'Molly McGredy', 'Living Fire', 'Korp', 'Golden Shot', 'Softly, Softly', 'Blessings', 'Arthur Bell', 'Southampton', 'Precious Platinum' (one of the best red modern Hybrid Teas) and, of course, 'Peace' are among the varieties on show.

At the north-eastern end of the Palm House, between it and the Lily House, are more roses, bedding varieties together with 'Ballerina', 'The Fairy' and two veteran Hybrid Teas, yellow 'Mrs Pierre S. du Pont', which came from the raiser, Charles Mallerin, in 1929, and 'Sarah Arnot', which is not quite so old but still goes back thirty years. In addition, the scarlet climber 'Parkdirektor Riggers' does not really take too kindly to being used for bedding and is next door to another unlikely candidate, 'Kew Rambler'. This one was actually raised at Kew in 1912 and is a cross between the grey-leaved *R. soulieana* and the American Walsh rambler, 'Hiawatha'. The pointed buds open to light rose-pink single flowers with a white centre round the yellow stamens. They are sweetly scented and come quite late in the season. The leaves are a reminder of the first mentioned parent.

If you now walk down the side of the Palm House farthest from the Rose Garden you will pass a small lake (known as The Pond) on your left, with the Temple of Aeolus across the water and a rich carpet of bedding plants at your feet. Carry on and you will come to more roses round the corner at the far end of the house, but mostly of a very different kind from those seen so far. For here is a series of beds, planted in 1985, showing the history of the rose with examples from most of the main families. The earliest beds are nearest the lake and contain Gallicas, one of the oldest of the Damask roses, 'Trigintipetala', and *R. moschata* growing on a frame. A bed of China roses (including *R. chinensis*) and Centifolias has *R. gigantea* and a rose I feel to be mislabelled, *R. × odorata*, on frames. For my money *R. × odorata* is the first Tea rose and not a climber either, but whatever it may be I would not give too much for the survival of these two Far Eastern beauties out in the open, although I wish them luck.

Other beds have Albas, Hybrid Chinas, Portlands and Bourbons ('Louise Odier', 'Rose du Roi', 'Comtesse du Cayla', 'Mutabilis', 'The Portland Rose' and 'Souvenir de la Malmaison') and Hybrid Perpetuals and Noisettes, while the bed for the Pernetianas and Dwarf Polyanthas has, in addition to all three of the *R. foetida* family, their immediate offspring 'Soleil d'Or' in quite exceptionally fine form, and 'Cécile Brunner' and 'Perle d'Or', here correctly representing the Polyanthas rather than the Chinas with which they are so often classed. Ramblers and climbers are rather scantily represented by *R. wichuraiana* creeping over the ground and 'Paul's Scarlet' on a frame, and apart from these there is a bed of Hybrid Musks and Hybrid Polyanthas, two of the former being Pemberton varieties and the others 'Wilhelm' from Germany and its sport 'Will Scarlet', discovered by Graham Thomas in England. 'Frensham' and 'Dusky Maiden' are the Hybrid Polyanthas (which, of course, became Floribundas in due course) and the Hybrid Teas shown in the final bed are 'Mme Butterfly', 'Ophelia', 'La France' 'Frau Karl Druschki' and 'Mme Victor Verdier', the latter two more usually considered Hybrid Perpetuals. Lastly there is white 'Mme Bravy' (which has no less than seven other names as a testament to its popularity in the middle of the nineteenth century) and which is a Tea rose. There are display boards with some historical information about the various roses at the back of each bed.

The high holly hedge around the modern rose garden also runs down one side of the historical beds, separating them from a much larger area of grass to the south-west where there are beds of species roses planted among fine specimen trees: tulip trees, acers and others.

These roses were situated near the Japanese Gateway at one time but it was felt better that all the roses should be in one area so that the whole of the genus could be seen easily and the species related more closely to the historical section. The move was made in 1985 to coincide with the laying out of the latter and at the time of writing the planting is not completed. Young plants are being grown on in the garden's own nursery and some of the rarer species are difficult to come by as the policy at Kew is to raise from seed from a known provenance. Eventually it is intended to have representatives from all the main botanical sections, *Caninae, Synstylae* and so on.

The pink Floribunda 'Kerryman' is planted along the avenue beside the lake in Queen Mary's Rose Garden.

Queen Mary's Rose Garden

Regent's Park

*Baker Street underground station or, by car, from
Clarence Gate on Outer Circle ring road.*
Tel. 01 486 7905
Open every day.

If you enter the main park by Clarence Gate on the Outer Circle ring road, cross over a footbridge which can be seen straight ahead and, turning to the left with the broad expanse of a lake on your left, skirt round the gardens of Bedford College. This brings you out at the Inner Circle ring road and the entrance to the rose gardens will be right opposite you across the roadway. If you come early enough in the year you will be greeted even before you get inside by a magnificent planting of the yellow species rose 'Canary Bird' behind the railings.

Cross the road and at once you will find climbers such as 'Pink Perpetue' and 'Etude' on the low fence that borders the restaurant area on your left. On the other side of the path the deep-red single blooms of 'Frank Naylor' peep from its deep-green foliage rather than flaunt themselves above it as the flowers of many roses do. Its neighbours are 'Golden Chersonese', 'Scintillation' and specimens of the yellow Rugosa 'Agnes' which have made me stop dismissing it as the poor, straggly grower with wishy-washy flowers I have so often seen elsewhere. Clearly it is thriving in Regent's Park and its double yellow flowers are superb, their scent sensational.

At the end of this first short path turn right along a broad avenue with large beds of Floribundas on each side. The varieties include 'Mr E.E. Greenwell', 'Disco Dancer', 'Iced Ginger', 'Princess Michael of Kent', and many more, while across a wide stretch of grass to the right, along the fence that borders the road, is a further planting, this time of shrub roses. Here you can discover some of the better known ones, such as 'Marguerite Hilling' at her spectacular best, the Rugosa hybrids 'Conrad Ferdinand Meyer' and 'Sarah Van Fleet', several of the Moyesii family, many of the early-flowering yellow species, and also the less frequently seen 'Autumn Fire' and creamy-white 'Frühlingsschnee'. *R. fedtschenkoana* is there too, but so overshadowed by surrounding shrubs as to be, in the gloom beneath them, the Gollum of the rose world.

Continuing along the avenue, trees and a small lake come into view to the left, but the plantings of Floribundas continue to line the path opposite and there are a number of pillar roses as well. Ornamental ducks are only one of the attractions of this beautifully landscaped stretch of water, which leads you eventually right to the focal point of the rose garden. The land rises slightly here and at the higher level there is a round central bed of roses with others radiating out from it in concentric circles. All these are planted with modern Hybrid Teas, and surrounding the whole is a massive catenary of seventy-two tall pillars with ropes

looped between them along which climbing and rambling roses are supposed to drape themselves. In fact only rampant varieties like 'Bobbie James', *R. longicuspis*, 'The Garland' and *R. multiflora* are entirely successful in doing this, but 'Dreamgirl', 'Allen Chandler', 'Francois Juranville', 'Adélaide d'Orléans', 'Cupid', 'Maigold' and 'Rose Marie Viaud' clothe the pillars magnificently even if they are reluctant to venture along the ropes.

Outside the circle of the catenary and backed by trees and taller shrubs (among them the striking plum-purple foliage of *R. glauca* (*R. rubrifolia*) there are large plantings of shrub roses, a fine jumble of old and new. The number is prodigious and the closeness of the planting and the juxtaposition of certain varieties may lead to space problems at a future date, but it is a fascinating collection ranging from the narrow-leaved *R. nitida*, the Centifolia 'Fantin-Latour' and the 'York and Lancaster' rose to moderns like 'Cardinal Hume', 'Charles Austin', 'Sally Holmes' and the yellow rose named after Graham Thomas. All these are very clearly and meticulously labelled and it is

The dazzling scarlet of 'La Sevillana', one of the many modern roses at Syon Park in Brentford.

to be hoped that the public will allow them to remain so.

A path on the far side of the circle leads to the other (and certainly grander looking) gate to the rose gardens. Walk towards it, but before you reach it take the side path that doubles back to your left. On the corner formed by these two paths is a large planting of most of the modern varieties of miniature rose available in the United Kingdom. The bed is slightly raised and the miniatures are backed by some of the taller 'in-between' varieties like 'Anna Ford', too large to be a true miniature but too small to be a typical Floribunda. The whole thing makes a tremendous splash of colour and is a lesson in how these small roses should be used.

Continuing down the side path means leaving the main rose garden, though we have not quite finished with it yet. A large planting of shrub roses soon comes into view on the left with the same indiscriminatingly sociable mixture as before. The low-growing magenta-crimson Burnet rose 'William III' rubs shoulders with the Bourbon 'Coupe d'Hébé', 'Gloire de Mousseux', and 'Mme Plantier', while the moderns 'Lavender Lassie' and 'Marjorie Fair' seem equally at home. Opposite, across the path, are some 'Lawrence Johnston' climbers which have over the years lost their wooden supports and as a result are looking rather as if they do not know which way to go. But this is most untypical of a garden that nowadays has a freshly groomed air. Not too long ago it went through the doldrums after the great days under the care of Millar Gault, but now he, long retired, could certainly be proud of his creation once more.

You now really have left the main rose garden behind, but if you bear to the right on to a winding path between herbaceous borders there are still roses to be seen planted along the way: R. moyesii in variety, some absolutely huge bushes of R. californica 'Plena', which are a mass of pink rosettes early in the year, fully 2.1 by 2.1 m (7 by 7 ft), 'Complicata', R. primula and R. pisocarpa, an American species with lilac-pink single flowers. At the end of this path you emerge near an ornamental fountain and a broad walk takes you back, past the entrance to the Open Air Theatre, towards the restaurant. This walk has been flanked for as long as I can remember with enormous beds of 'Chicago Peace', 'Red Dandy' and 'Iceberg', and they look just as good now as they did on the day they were planted.

Queen Mary's Rose Garden puts on a more than worthy display for a capital city and is unusual in providing such a well-grown and comprehensive collection of roses so near to the city's centre and so accessible to all.

Syon Park

Brentford

Just across river from Kew Gardens. From Kew Bridge go west along Brentford High Street, left at Twickenham Road (traffic lights) and fork left after 100 m (yds). Signposted.
Tel. 01 560 0881
The Duke of Northumberland
Open every day.

Why is Flora, the Roman goddess of flowers, wearing a hairpin? To keep her hair tidy? Well, yes, but not entirely. Syon Park provides the answer, but wait, the rose gardens come first.

These are completely separate from the rest of the gardens and are to the right of the long approach drive. You will have to go past them to reach the car park and then walk back. Signs will direct you to them but the gates in the high wall that separate them from the drive should be indication enough. Of wrought iron, they have two enormous Tudor roses worked into the design at the top.

Inside the gates a gravel path curves away to the left through a grove of trees towards the modern rose garden, but before you reach it there is a planting on either side of equally modern varieties such as 'Summer Holiday', 'Rose Gaujard', 'Apricot Nectar' and the soft-pink David Austin rose 'Chaucer'. This grows taller and more strongly here than in other places I have seen it.

Before you are through the trees you can catch a glimpse of the south face of Syon House, the upper windows of which overlook the rose garden. On its other three sides, the garden is open, with views across the parkland, where cattle graze peacefully, to the river Thames beyond.

The modern rose garden is a large, square area with wide paved paths separating the beds in which many of the best of the modern Hybrid Teas and Floribundas are planted. In fact, nearly all the worthwhile modern varieties can be found there, together with many of the established favourites from earlier years, well-grown and clearly labelled. It is an excellent place to come to if you wish to make a choice of roses to buy for your own garden. There are standards in many of the beds as well.

The outer beds all round are raised about 45 cm (18 in) above the rest, behind low retaining stone walls, and are backed on the north and south sides by hedges of that lovely lavender-pink Floribunda 'Escapade' which, like 'Chaucer', is much taller here than usual. To the east is a hedge with a gap in the centre formed from the Hybrid Musks 'Buff Beauty' and 'Penelope'. It is trimmed to a rather more formal outline than is usually considered advisable if they are to put on their full display of flowers throughout the summer. Their good dark foliage forms a fine background for the other shorter roses even when they are not in flower but when they are, the combination of the two is spectacular.

To leave the modern rose garden you walk back towards the trees and then turn left along the fence that borders the parkland. Against this, there is a long curved rose bed with a few miniature roses just on the corner and then larger ones such as 'Beautiful Britain', 'Trumpeter', creamy-white 'Fleur Cowles', 'Pink Parfait', 'Amber Queen', deep-pink 'Marion Foster' and 'Pink Perpetue', the latter grown more as a spreading shrub than as a climber.

Ahead and to the right are wide stretches of grass with a fine selection of ornamental trees, catalpa, holly, Spanish chestnut, oaks – including the Portuguese oak (*Quercus infectoria*) – various conifers and at least one specimen of the Big Shell Bark Hickory (*Carya lacinosa*). Amongst these, wherever it is light enough, and occasionally where it is not, are plantings of shrubs, including many shrub roses. I learned with surprise that , judging by its enormous size, *R. × paulii* seems to thrive, fungus-like, in semi-darkness, though I would not put my money on it producing many flowers. To be fair, however, there is plenty of light for most of the roses and they really do look splendid in the semi-woodland setting.

Half-way along this stretch of the garden, facing east over the open parkland, is a semi-circular pergola with round concrete posts (sheathed in Netlon) supporting wooden cross-beams. Over this grow climbing and rambling roses, two to a pillar, with clematis as well to give added, and late, colour when the once-flowering ramblers are over. Among the rose

varieties are 'Climbing Cécile Brunner', 'Mermaid', 'Cupid', 'The Garland' and 'Excelsa'.

There are not many roses beyond this point, but moving across the garden to the far side of the tree belt behind the pergola you do pass a few – 'Canary Bird', 'Rose à Parfum de l'Hay', the York and Lancaster Rose (*R. × damascena versicolor*), 'Fellemberg', 'Louise Odier' and the bush form of 'Cécile Brunner'. Beyond these a high brick wall, if you follow it to the right, will lead you back to the gates. Along it are planted many shrub roses, among them 'Kazanlik', *R. pimpinellifolia altaica* and 'Double Pink', various Hybrid Musks, *R. soulieana*, *R. × dupontii*, an assortment of Rugosas, 'Stanwell Perpetual', *R. californica* 'Plena' and a short-growing Gallica 'Du Maître d'Ecole'. Behind them on the wall itself is a good range of climbers, sparkling pink 'Rosy Mantle', *R. helenae* (allotted three times as much space as the others with the possible exception of 'La Mortola'), 'Climbing La France', 'Climbing Lady Sylvia', 'Meg', 'Climbing Allgold', 'Climbing Mme Caroline Testout' and 'Climbing Mme Edouard Herriot' – quite a selection from the best of the older climbing sports.

That more or less completes the rose gardens, but while visiting them it would be a pity to miss seeing the rest of the gardens, though you have to pay separately to get into the latter. They were laid out by 'Capability' Brown in 1760 and a pleasant walk through them takes you alongside the lake and back, through shrub plantings and tall, shady trees. There are no roses to be found but there is the Great Conservatory, a crescent-shaped building with a huge central glass dome and small pavilions at either end. It was the first construction of its kind in the world and gave inspiration for the building of London's famous Crystal Palace at Sydenham.

And Flora's hairpin? A tall pillar in the garden is surmounted by a statue of the goddess, put there when Richard Forrest was 'improving' on Brown's designs in the last century. It survived for many years, but was eventually blown down in a gale and smashed beyond repair. However, help was at hand from Shepperton film studios who, with the aid of photographs of the original, constructed a fibreglass replica 3 m (10 ft) high. It was placed on the column in April 1968 but two days later was struck by lightning and burned. A new model was made, but this time Flora sported a hairpin. It serves as a lightning conductor.

Cranborne Manor Gardens

Cranborne

On B3078 9 miles north of Wimborne.
Tel. 072 54 248
Viscount and Viscountess Cranborne
Open from April to October on first Saturday and
Sunday of each month and every Wednesday.

Parts of the house at Cranborne are pre-Tudor, added to over the centuries. The gardens, too, have gone through many alterations and vicissitudes – long periods of neglect followed by spectacular revival. In the seventeenth century, for instance, they were laid out by John Tradescant and Mounten Jennings, but the basic framework of a garden, divided into a number of separate areas by walls and hedges, was there before their time. It was used skilfully by the Marquess of Salisbury and his wife, the house's previous occupants, when they took over the house to make a fresh start with the planting, following the pattern of Sissinghurst Castle and Hidcote Manor. Lady Salisbury is one of the keenest and most knowledgeable gardeners in the country with a particular love of the old roses, which is still reflected everywhere you go at Cranborne.

Entry (and even more strategically from the point of view of sales, the exit) is through a very extensive plant centre and then along a path with a field on one side and a tall sculptured yew hedge on the other. Through shoulder-high openings in this you can catch tempting glimpses of, in succession, the Herb Garden, the Chalk Wall Garden and the Green Garden, all of which you explore in due course, but eventually you come out into the main drive with its double avenue of beech trees and the house is ahead of you through an arched gateway as you turn to the right. There are wild flowers (including orchids) in the grass on either side of the drive where it nears the gate, and you walk through this into the South Court. In beds all round are roses, including 'Cantabrigiensis', 'Gloire de Dijon' and R. ×

highdowensis, a Moyesii seedling raised by Sir Frederick Stern in his garden at Highdown near Worthing. It forms a much more bushy, and in many ways more satisfactory, garden plant than its parent and even if the colour of its single flowers is less vivid and striking, its hips are perhaps even better than those of *R. moyesii*. 'Lawrence Johnston' grows on one wall with 'Gardenia' and 'Desprez à Fleurs Jaunes' as nearby companions. Below them 'De Meaux', already classed as a dwarf Centifolia reaching perhaps 1 m (3 ft), has been clipped to a cushion of pink, no more than 45 cm (18 in) high.

Through an archway at the western corner of the house you reach the Knot Garden, but a yellow Banksian rose (*lutea*) climbing up to the eaves immediately on the right distracts the eye from everything else until it is caught, perhaps, by the soft-pink flowers of 'Cupid' just beyond it. The West Lawn is now to the left and beyond it the Mount Garden, one of the original John Tradescant features still remaining. Central to this is the mound that gives the garden its name and was a fashionable feature of Jacobean gardens. Yews clipped to the shape of tall drums surround it and there are lavender beds with box edgings and, at one end, a large planting of pink Scotch roses together with paeonies and irises.

From the Mount Garden a long yew *allée* leads to the balcony overlooking the North Court, to which steps lead down through an opening in the stone balustrade. *R. longicuspis*, 'Seagull' and an unidentified white rose of great beauty cover the walls, together with 'Sanders' White Rambler', 'Paul's Lemon Pillar' and 'Bennett's Seedling', one of the Ayrshire roses descended from *R. arvensis*, a species native to the United Kingdom. 'Gloire de Dijon' frames the steps on either side.

The North Court itself contains many roses. 'Nevada' is there, almost as ubiquitous in rose gardens as 'Kiftsgate', *R. moschata* 'Grandiflora' climbs up a pillar (a rose that originated, I think, from the old Murrell nurseries but whose origin is uncertain), *R. sericea pteracantha*, *R. pimpinellifolia altaica* (a much neglected but very lovely, pale yellow early-flowering rose with larger blooms than most of the others and certainly far better hips), while *R. filipes* and 'Seagull' scale trees. At the far end, through a wrought-iron gate framed with huge plantings of the 'Double White' Scotch rose, the River Garden can be glimpsed (and visited if you wish) or you can, if you are single-minded enough about roses, move straight on to the stable block, on one wall of which is the climber 'Breeze Hill'. Directly opposite, a robust climber with huge double crimson flowers is the old Hybrid Perpetual 'Hugh Dickson' in terrific form – better than I have ever seen it before, as it is such an ungainly grower used in any other way unless firmly pegged down, and is not normally considered as a climber.

From the stable yard, turn left into the Pergola Walk – a long, cobbled path lined with London Pride, backed by lilies on one side and irises on the other, and with roses overhead and on the pergola pillars. A huge holm oak shades a lawn to the right while ahead and to the left the spire of Cranborne church rises up against the sky. There are wisteria and clematis on the pergola as well as roses, but the latter predominate; 'Emily Gray', 'Champney's Pink Cluster' (from which all the Noisette roses are descended), *R. moschata*, *R. moschata* 'Narrow Waters', 'Cooperi', 'Paul Transon', 'Mme Alfred Carrière', 'Blush Noisette', 'Fellemberg' and 'Aloha' are some of them, so you will see that it is by no means an everyday collection. At the far end on a wall 'Albéric Barbier' mixes with a pink single I was unable to identify – a pity as it was a striking rose.

The Church Walk and the Kitchen Garden are nearby and here again there are climbers on the walls, including the climbing Tea rose 'Sombreuil' and, at the far end, numbers of the David Austin English roses are planted, outstanding among them, to my mind, being 'Dapple Dawn'. They are underplanted with pinks and violas.

Beginning to retrace your steps you now move through the Green Garden which was glimpsed earlier. This leads to the Chalk Wall Garden where the most notable rose is labelled 'L'Heritiana' (a name discussed in the account of Mottisfont Abbey gardens on page 26). Its thornless stems confirm that it is a Boursault rose, probably 'Amadis', as the rich crimson double flowers are most distinctive. In the middle of the Herb Garden, which is reached next through an arch in the yew hedge, there are honeysuckles grown in standard form surrounding a sundial plinth, sadly without its sundial. On the walls are 'Wedding Day', once again that rather strange rose with its solitary white flowers and shiny leaves called 'Cooperi', 'Blairii No. 2' in magnificent form (and those who know it will know what that means) and finally, *R. cerasocarpa*, a rose completely new to me, which has small semi-double white flowers with yellow stamens in large corymbs, followed by deep-red hips. It comes from China. Some plants of the Labrador Rose, *R. blanda*, and a hedge of Penzance Briers (all 'Meg Merrilies', I believe, though I have not actually seen it in flower) complete the rose picture as far as it is possible to do in so short an account. But visit Cranbourne and see it for yourself to find out just how many roses I may have had to pass over in this wonderful garden. If my account tempts you to go, that is enough.

The Manor House

Hinton St Mary

One mile north-west of Sturminster Newton on B3092. Next to church in Hinton St Mary, up turning to right off main road.
Tel. 0258 72519
Mr and Mrs A. Pitt-Rivers
Open under the National Gardens Scheme.

The grey stone façade of the house looks out over long, sweeping lawns with a distant view of hills many miles away. The original buildings at Hinton St Mary, set in the heart of the Blackmore Vale, were thirteenth century, but the stables are all that now remains relatively unaltered. Rebuilding of the house in its present form began in 1650; the east and west wings were added later. Up until the end of the last century, the vast Tithe Barn was still in use, surrounded by small paddocks. However, in 1929 George Pitt-Rivers, father of the present owner, carried out extensive restoration work and converted the Tithe Barn into a theatre.

Over the last six years the main emphasis has been on developing the garden and all the beds have been replanted. Gardening at the Manor is certainly on the grand scale for it covers 2 hectares (5 acres), but it is carried out with great discernment. A love of roses is evident everywhere and they are blended into their surroundings with great skill.

The rambler 'Albéric Barbier' on the forecourt wall of The Manor House, Hinton St Mary.

The gravel drive opens out into a wide fore-court with a long wall down one side on which the climbers 'Gloire de Dijon' and 'Albéric Barbier' grow and flower in fine form, their buff-orange and white flowers and deep-green leaves contrasting strikingly with the old stone-work. Directly ahead, over a stretch of lawn, is a long double border with a broad grass path down the middle. Here more than one hundred old roses in great variety are skilfully mixed with other shrubs and small trees, many Moss roses including the tall-growing 'William Lobb', with 'Honorine de Brabant', 'Tour de Malakoff', 'Fantin Latour', *R. glauca*, 'Nevada' and *R. elegantula persetosa* among the more familiar, and the modern shrub 'Dentelle de Malines', *R. webbiana*, 'Violacea' and 'Hoccombe Mill' among the much less com-mon. The avenue is broken at its mid-point by a paved area with a central urn and a planting of lavender. As the double avenue continues, you find more roses, together with paeonies, weigela (in various forms) and an enormous range of other shrubs.

Bearing left across the grass and down wide stone steps with honeysuckle on either side you come to a vast sunken rose garden. It is 45 m (50 yds) or more in length and almost as wide, with a long formal pool running down the middle, surrounded by paving and then grass. In the centre a plinth carries a graceful bronze heron, while all round, between the grass and a surrounding yew hedge, are raised rose beds with cool, grey, stone facings. In them are planted hundreds of Hybrid Teas and Floribundas, revealing a catholic taste: a place where you can admire the latest modern roses as well as the best of the old. A number of the roses here were planted before the Pitt-Riverses came to Hinton St Mary in 1970 and these include 'Peace', 'Frensham' and 'Iceberg'. More recent additions are 'Anne Harkness', 'Alec's Red', 'Beryl Bach', 'Just Joey', 'Olive', 'Princess Alice' and 'Anisley Dickson'. A Hybrid Musk 'Moonlight' in each corner and four ornamental grey-leaved willows planted in the grass complete the picture.

Up the steps at the western end of the rose

garden, you cross an avenue of pleached limes and go down steps once more to another stretch of lawn. A hedge of the striped Gallica 'Rosa Mundi' stretches away both to the left and the right, while across the grass ahead the part of the Tithe Barn not hidden by two huge and immaculately trained 'Kiftsgate' roses with 'May Queen' between them can be seen. White 'Mme Alfred Carrière' shows over a wall that joins the barn at its nearest corner, and on this wall you can find a fine selection of other roses and clematis: 'Rose Marie Viaud', *R. multiflora*, 'Violetta', 'Amethyst' and 'Zéphirine Drouhin' are among them, and there are yet more when you pass through a wrought-iron gate in the wall into another grassy area beside the barn. Here, the ground-cover rose 'Swany' has been planted in the hollow stumps of two trees and trails out over them in a most entrancing fashion.

Make your way next to a tall yew arch in the corner nearest the barn. Over and through the yews that form this, some 4.5 m (15 ft) or so high, have scrambled two vast plants of 'The Garland', creating an exquisite, soft, scented, white cloud, made up of myriads of tiny double flowers.

Through the arch, you arrive back on the drive. If you turn right towards the house, you can look over a wall into the depths of a large triangular ornamental pool with yellow flag irises reflected in the clear water. On the far side are the species rose 'Canary Bird' and white Rugosas, while a little further along the drive on a wall to the left grows 'Lady Hillingdon' with its immaculate orange, Tea rose blooms. On this side, too, a large planting of 'Roseraie de l'Hay' can be seen with the tower of the Hinton St Mary Church behind it, and then you come to the front of the house once more.

To the east of the house is a long border with many Hybrid Musks as well as other roses and shrubs underplanted with hardy geraniums and *Alchemilla mollis*. Colour early in the summer is given by some of the early-blooming, single, yellow-flowered species and the Scotch rose hybrid *R. × harisonii*.

This border runs out in line with the front of the house but after a while turns at right angles away from it. Near the corner a gap in the yew hedge that backs the border leads through into the orchard with an enormous bush of white, four-petalled *R. sericea pteracantha* standing sentinel on either side of the way. The ground then slopes away gradually among the trees and a little exploration downwards is rewarded in full measure by tree-climbing roses – 'Paul's Himalayan Musk', *R. longicuspis*, 'Rambling Rector', 'Sanders' White' – and a veritable plantation of Rugosa hybrids. These include 'Roseriae de l'Hay' reaching 2.4 to 3 m (8 to 10 ft) tall, 'Scabrosa' only a little less, and both *Rugosa alba* and 'Fru Dagmar Hastrup' at least one and a half times the size they ought to be. Various other roses, including one or two species, grow among the trees too, and with them regretfully comes the completion of the tour.

East End Farm

Pitney

Take B3153 Langport–Somerton road to Pitney, turning at Halfway House Inn. Once through village, farm is last thatched house on right.
Tel. 0458 250 598
Mrs A. M. Wray
Open under the National Gardens Scheme; also by appointment in June and July.

As you approach Mrs Wray's house down the lane through the village, roses are the first things you see: they are clambering up the wall of the old stone barn on one side of the garden of East End Farm. Both house and barn date back many hundreds of years, intriguing buildings framing a fascinating garden. The latter was at one time the farmyard and the stone walls show off the many climbing roses to perfection, giving the garden a timeless appeal.

The front garden is quite small and one of the first roses to be seen is the thicket-forming, double, yellow Scotch rose. This can be extremely invasive as its suckers run through the earth with the speed of underground trains but with much less discipline as far as direction is concerned. In fact I am not really sure that it is possible to control Scotch roses, but they make up the most diverse family (*Pimpinellifoliae*), whether in their yellow, pink or white variants, or even in the crimson-purple form of the variety 'William III'. Their decorative, fern-like leaves make them attractive even when the flowers have gone, and they seem to be great favourites in the West Country for everywhere you go you see them in profusion. Perhaps in

*The front garden at East End Farm in Pitney features a fine display
of old shrub, climbing and rambling roses.*

this part of the world they never lost, as they did elsewhere, the great popularity they enjoyed in the early 1800s. They hybridize among themselves freely and the seeds come up in a multitude of flower forms and colours. At one time Scottish nurserymen were offering over 200 varieties, though how distinctive they were from one another is open to question. And even today, with the comparatively few forms you see in modern gardens, positive identification is an almost impossible task.

However, Scotch roses are not the only kinds to be found at East End Farm. The front of the house carries 'Paul's Lemon Pillar' and 'New Dawn' and the barn, itself a massive building, nearly manages to dwarf a large 'Kiftsgate' covering one side, together with 'Albéric Barbier' and one or two others. Stroll down the garden and there is an avenue of shrub roses of every kind to be enjoyed. You will find, among many others, 'Charles de Mills', 'Blanc Double de Coubert', 'Jenny Duval', another 'Kiftsgate' trained on an enormous, locally made, umbrella some 3 to 4.5 m (10 to 15 ft) high, 'William Lobb', 'Russelliana' (of uncertain par-

entage but of no uncertain vigour and sometimes known as 'Russell's Cottage Rose'), 'Duchesse de Montebello' and the ramblers 'Albéric Barbier', 'Goldfinch' and 'Emily Gray', grown up trees or pillars. 'William Allen Richardson' finds the warm, sheltered spot it needs to show off its buff-to-apricot flowers on one wall of the barn and 'Blush Rambler', an almost thornless favourite of the Edwardians, displays its massed soft-pink flowers nearby. Everywhere you look there are roses in abundance, for this is a connoisseur's garden created by someone who knows and loves their old roses. Mrs Wray was responsible for saving the lovely but rare, and sometimes temperamental, dark velvety-red and sweetly fragrant Hybrid Perpetual 'Eclair' from virtual extinction by sending it from her garden to Peter Beales for propagation. Any gardener who can claim to have saved a plant of great beauty from oblivion has assured for themselves a niche in gardening history.

This is not a large garden but one of distinction in which the setting and atmosphere play an important part in one's enjoyment of it.

Watermeadows

Clapton

On B3165 2½ miles south of Crewkerne; 300 m (yds)
beyond Clapton Court.
Tel. 0460 74421
Raymund and Laura Gawen
Open under the National Gardens Scheme.

Watermeadows is full of character, the house formerly having been one of the old watermills of the Crewkerne district. Later, in Victorian times, it became a farmhouse, but the Gawens moved there only about eleven years ago when what is now their garden was a field, difficult though this may be to believe. There are fields beyond it still, in which picturesque Jacobs' sheep graze on the lush grass.

The Gawens claim that their garden is weed-free and it really is, as the result of a long campaign to prevent weeds from seeding themselves anywhere and through the judicious use of ground-cover plants.

Moving out into the garden from the courtyard at the back of the house on the right you see, scrambling over the remains of an old lime tree, what I hope I may be forgiven for describing as the inevitable 'Kiftsgate'. Other climbers and ramblers nearby, climbing through a line of conifers that separate the garden from the road, include pink 'Paul's Himalayan Musk Rambler', the very beautiful 'Desprez à Fleurs Jaunes' with its fruity scent and double flowers in blends of peach and yellow, 'Félicité et Perpétue', 'Bleu Magenta' and at the far end, rampaging around as if determined not to be outdone by 'Kiftsgate', is *R. longicuspis*.

However, I have jumped ahead a little. Moving down the drive from the road, on the right there is the ever eye-catching 'Marguerite Hilling', which, in full flush, distracts from the more discreet beauties of nearby 'Sealing Wax' and *R. cantabrigiensis*. Past them, turn right onto a grass path and under rustic poles with 'Goldfinch', 'Allen Chandler', 'Compassion' and the semi-climbing Bourbon 'Blairii No. 2' twined about them. To the left is the beginning of what must be one of the longest Rugosa hedges in the country, with alternate plantings of *R. rugosa alba* and 'Rubra'. It is a marvellous sight at almost any time of year with fresh green leaves, flowers and then hips. After a short distance you pass through this hedge, which continues on your right for a considerable length, but just before this point the path divides at a particularly fine and bushy plant of the nineteenth-century Gallica 'Hippolyte' with its exquisitely formed magenta-purple flowers.

Through the hedge now and backed by it on the right is a small tadpole pond fed by a little stream. *Iris laevigata*, double buttercups, primulas and astilbe line the banks, as you follow the path up a gentle slope to a planting of hybrid Rugosas among which pink 'Belle Poitevine' is outstanding. *R. alpina* (*R. pendulina*), though a native of Europe, is not often seen in gardens, but there is a fine one here as you turn the corner at the top of the slope. It never grows very tall and though it can be spreading, it is a species to be considered for a small garden with its almost thornless reddish-purple stems, deep-pink single flowers and a good show of hips to follow.

Mr Gawen is an enthusiastic taker of cuttings of roses and these now appear on the right in incredible profusion and in various stages of development in a bed devoted entirely to them. He seems to be successful with most kinds.

The end of the Rugosa hedge is now behind you and the grass path you have been following leads gently down once more towards the house. Vegetables rather than roses are on the right, at least for a while, but a rose lover's eyes will turn automatically the other way. Here is a nicely varied selection of many of the best of the old roses and some more modern varieties too. Numbered among them and picked at random are 'Rose de Rescht', white 'Boule de Neige', 'Tuscany Superb', 'Archiduc Joseph', 'Prosperity', 'Baron Girod de l'Ain', 'Souvenir du Docteur Jamain', *R. × dupontii*, 'Honorine de Brabant' and 'Raubritter'. The 'Dainty Bess' seedling 'White Wings' of 1947 vintage is one of the most modern, though opposite it David Austin's 'Shropshire Lass' of 1968 grows on a pillar. This, a cross between the Hybrid Tea 'Mme Butterfly' and the Alba 'Mme Legras de St Germaine', has 12 cm (5 in) single blush-pink flowers that are richly fragrant.

Most of the roses have now been seen but back at the house the Hybrid Musk 'Kathleen' scales one wall. Though normally a vigorous bush this can climb pretty strongly and is one of the parents of 'Francis E. Lester' which will scramble up anything. The latter has also inherited the fine, glossy foliage of 'Kathleen'.

A rectangular lawn leads down from the

house to the fence bordering the meadow where the sheep graze. Flowerbeds surround it and some of the roses to be found there are 'Crimson Conquest', 'Buff Beauty', *R. californica* 'Plena', 'Belle Amour', 'Tour de Malakoff' and the double white Scotch rose. In an oval bed in the centre the fragrant pink China rose 'Hermosa' has been underplanted with *Viola cornuta* (from the Pyrenees), which makes a most attractive combination.

Broadleas Gardens

Devizes

South of Devizes, turn off A360 at Potterne.
Tel. 0380 2035
Lady Anne Cowdray
Open from April to October on Sundays, Wednesdays
and Thursdays.

A steep drive takes you up through trees from the road until barns appear on the right with open fields beyond them and to the left you see a water tower, its stilt-like legs half-submerged by a great thicket of *R. virginiana*. Brer Rabbit's Briar Patch to the life, it makes an eyecatching mound of pink blooms in early summer, to be followed by the glorious sunset tints of its leaves in autumn. However, it is the spectacular hedge of roses on the left hand side that really catches the eye. Some 1.8 m (6 ft) or more tall and as much across, it contains, amongst other varieties, 'Belle Poitevine', 'Nevada', 'Roseraie de l'Hay', 'Blanc Double de Coubert', *R. rugosa* 'Rubra', 'Complicata', 'Marguerite Hilling', at least four plants of *R. californica* 'Plena', 'Felicia', 'Fritz Nobis', 'Constance Spry', 'Bloomfield Abundance' and the climber 'Zéphirine Drouhin'. A marvellous mixture of both old and comparatively new, it is also a mixture that keeps on flowering, for the majority of the roses are recurrent. At its peak, it really is quite outstanding.

The rose hedge is the most spectacular and concentrated rose planting at Broadleas, but there are many roses elsewhere. From the forecourt of the house, overlooked by two classical statues in niches on either side of the porch, you move through an opening in a stone balustrade and turn left along the side of the house. The immensely tall blue-green shutters for the windows make a striking contrast with the rich

coppery-orange of the flowers of a climbing 'Mrs Sam McGredy', the deep pink of 'Mme Grégoire Staechelin' and the soft mauve of wisteria on the walls, while on the left are smooth, undulating lawns and very handsome trees. From here you can see where the ground begins to fall away in the middle distance to The Dell.

However, before exploring this – for there are roses in it – you come to a left turn at the corner of the house. Here an arch in the mellow brick wall, half-hidden by a striking mauve clematis, leads you down some steps and past a white abutilon to the sunken rose garden. To the left, at the foot of the steps, is another clematis, this time the extremely rampant winter-flowering *Clematis balearica*, or Fern-leaved Clematis, from the Balearic Islands, through which the China rose 'Mutabilis' wends its way up the house wall. The rose garden itself is paved, the four main beds set symmetrically in it with a sundial as the central point. Each bed has a different colour scheme – orange, yellow, pink, red – which especially with the orange kinds (in terms of shrub roses rather thin on the ground) has produced some rather strange bedfellows.

All round this central feature, at a higher level, has been planted a mixture of old and new shrub roses, an 'Iceberg' that can only be described as vast, 'Tuscany', 'William Lobb', the seldom-seen 'Clair Matin', numerous Gallicas, the Hybrid Musks 'Penelope' and 'Cornelia', *R. glauca* and a good many more. More steps, which you climb this time, lead out of the rose garden through a large pavilion and back onto the long gravel path or terrace that runs along one side of the house. You are now some distance from it, however, and you can wander into the shade of an enormous acer or among other trees and shrubs, where there are more roses, two of the most unusual being the semi-double pink Bourbon 'Adam Messerich' and, on a wall, *R. bracteata*. This is the Macartney Rose, brought back by Lord Macartney from China late in the eighteenth century. Though it has something of a reputation for tenderness, it will flower quite happily on a north wall, producing its pure white single flowers intermittently throughout the summer.

In The Dell rhododendrons abound, as well as many fine trees and shrubs. 'Kiftsgate' climbs a pine and the other roses include 'Fantin Latour', 'Belle Poitevine', *R. elegantula persetosa* and a *R. sericea pteracantha* placed so

that the rays of the mid-day sun glow through the gigantic, ruby-red thorns on its new shoots. Described many times in print, there are few gardens where this phenomenon can actually be seen as it can here.

Corsley Mill

Corsley, Nr Warminster

Between Warminster, Westbury and Frome, off the B3298 at Chapmanslade. An enormously long, single-track lane leads from Corsley village to Corsley Mill.
Tel. 0373 88270
Mr and Mrs Charles Quest-Ritson
Open under the National Gardens Scheme.

Corsley Mill (not, in fact, the original mill, which no longer exists) is an attractive Queen Anne brick manor house or large farmhouse dating from 1700. The 1.6-hectare (4-acre) site is open and fairly exposed and slopes gently down to a small stream and trees at the bottom of the garden. The Quest-Ritsons have only been at Corsley for four years and, though the garden is far from complete, it already houses, in addition to the National Collection of European Primulas and numbers of unusual plants of many kinds, what must be one of the most comprehensive old rose collections in the country, and one that is growing yearly. By no means all the roses are fully grown as yet, but with the Quest-Ritson brand of enthusiasm behind them they will, presumably, mature in a much shorter time than usual.

What adds especial interest to the collection is the number of the roses that Mr Quest-Ritson has raised himself. He believes very strongly that modern rose breeders are not using properly the great bank of genetic material available to them from the wild or species roses and many of the hybrids to be seen here, if not yet full proof of his ideas, are very definite steps along the way. The visitor to Corsley Mill will certainly see many other unusual roses of other people's raising, though there are hundreds of varieties that are more familiar. Many, however, can be seen in this garden only.

'Ramona', the deep-pink, almost red sport of the 'Anemone Rose' (*R.* × *anemonoides*) on the wall near the front door of the house is an indi-

cation on arrival that there is a treat in store and from there you walk towards Rodden Brook at the bottom of the garden. Beside it is a long line of interesting roses, most of them (and this applies throughout) on their own roots. There appears to be none of the lack of vigour often experienced with roses grown in this way, but it is probably the more highly bred Hybrid Teas and Floribundas that most resent having to support themselves without the help of a briar. 'Rose de Rescht' is in this border, as is the 'Portland Rose' itself, the Hybrid Musk 'Francesca', Kordes' 'Frühlingszauber' (which has the same parentage as 'Frühlingsmorgen' but much stronger colouring – a cerise-scarlet with the same yellow centre on opening, but fading), 'Paul Ricault' which may or may not be a Centifolia, 'Raubritter' and others more commonly seen. Further on is a most interesting series of crosses carried out by Mr Quest-Ritson – 'Arthur Hillier' × Moyesii crosses ('Arthur Hillier' itself being a hybrid between *R. macrophylla* and *R. moyesii*) and a number of experiments with *R. glauca* (*R. rubrifolia*) all showing *R. glauca* influence in their foliage, but with flowers of varying sizes and intensity of pink. A most interesting cross involves the Damask 'St Nicholas' which was discovered in the garden of that name in Richmond, Yorkshire, belonging to the Hon. Robert James, after whom the rambler 'Bobbie James' was named. It was found as recently as 1950 and has been crossed here with another new/old rose, David Austin's 'Chianti' of 1967. The flowers are double and deep pink, with a Damask influence showing in the leaves.

If you begin to move up the slope towards the main rose planting between wide beds set in grass, you find that they are filled with every rose imaginable, a number of them great rarities. Such a one is a hybrid of *R. canina*, from 1910, called 'Kiese', which has semi-double, bright red flowers, inheriting their tones no doubt from the other parent, the Hybrid Perpetual 'General Jacqueminot'.

After 45 m (50 yds) or more the pattern of beds changes to concentric circles with four paths radiating out from the centre. In these and other beds at the perimeter of the garden are Gallicas in profusion, 'Charles de Mills', 'Gloire de France' and the rest, 'Nevada' and 'Marguerite Hilling' forming centrepieces to other plantings, Albas, Bourbons (including

Opposite: The deep pink of 'Mme Grégoire Staechelin' and the coppery orange of 'Mrs Sam McGredy' make a striking contrast with the blue-green shutters of the windows at Broadleas Gardens.

the double pink 'Blairii No. 1', which is slightly more remontant than the more frequently seen 'Blairii No. 2'), 'Martha', a sport of 'Zéphirine Drouhin' and intermediate in colour between it and its other sport 'Kathleen Harrop', and so it goes on, surprise after surprise. In how many other gardens do you see 'Abbotswood', a double pink chance hybrid of *R. canina*, or 'Serratipetala' ('Rose Oeillet de Saint Arquey'), which is similar to *R. chinensis semperflorens* but has fringed edges to its crimson petals like some of the Grootendorst varieties? Then there is a huge triangular bed of Scotch roses on the slope, beds with more Quest-Ritson hybrids of *R. glauca* and *R. multiflora*, seedlings of 'Bobbie James', a comparatively compact 'Complicata' seedling called 'Becket', several forms of *R. nitida*, which seems to be a very variable species and not just in this garden, and a *R. fedtschenkoana* cross, small, shrubby and with small white flowers and small leaves too.

These are just some of the highlights of this garden for those who like the unusual. But the more familiar are here in plenty with all their richness of flower form and colour, even if the garden needs a little more time to reach its full glory. In horticultural terms it is new and, if parts of it are still uncultivated, one can only admire what the Quest-Ritsons have achieved in a comparatively short space of time. When their work is finished – not that in one sense it ever will be – they will have around them an unmatched collection of roses and will be able to claim, as few other garden owners can, that many of them they have created themselves.

Heale House

Middle Woodford

In between A360 and A345 5 miles north of Salisbury.
Well signposted.
Tel. 072 273 207
Major David and Lady Anne Rasch
Open from Easter to end September, Monday to
Saturday, and first Sunday in each month.

It was Francis Bacon who said that a garden is the purest of human pleasures, a remark that could easily have been inspired (though there is not the least evidence that it was) by Heale House, which was in existence in his time. The western end of the house was built in the latter part of the sixteenth century, but it has gone through many changes since then, including a two-thirds reduction in size after a disastrous fire in 1835. It was then bought by the Hon. Louis Greville, great-uncle of the present owner, and restored to its former glory. It is now a magnificent building of mellow brick with stone quoining, in many places bearing the Greville crest: a swan seated on a coronet. And the setting on the banks of the river Avon is superb, a garden of stone walls and terraces leading down to the water's edge, and of smooth lawns, pergolas and graceful trees, of river walks and the calling sounds of moorhens. To the south-west of the house the water is spanned by a Japanese tea-house, brought back by Louis Greville from Tokyo. It forms the pivot of the Japanese water garden that surrounds it and has blended with remarkable ease into this most English of surroundings.

On entering the garden from the car park one of the first things to catch the eye, particularly of a rose lover, is a number of Rugosa bushes on the far side of the quietly flowing stream, leaning out so far over the water that you fear for their foothold on the grassy bank.

From this point there are several ways you can go, turning right down the bank towards the tea-house or crossing the stream further on by a brightly painted small replica of the famous Nikko Bridge. To see more roses it is better to continue on to the pergola that runs across the bottom of a walled garden. On this grow 'Easlea's Golden Rambler', 'Blairii No. 2', 'White Cockade', 'Félicité et Perpétue' and others, while below the path that runs through the pergola is a yellow border with 'Allgold' roses mixed with tobacco plants, yellow snapdragons and hypericums. Nearer still to the river are trees with climbers in them, 'Wedding Day' for one and the shiny leaves of 'New Dawn' matching those of a walnut.

In the walled garden itself the roses are mainly confined to the perimeter border and the walls, 'Mme Alfred Carrière' on one, 'Paul's Scarlet' on another and 'Climbing Spek's Yellow' mingling with a vine on yet another. In the narrow outer beds are 'Iceberg', 'Little White Pet', 'Honeymoon', 'Fleur Cowles', 'Chinatown', 'Apricot Nectar', 'Pink Chiffon', the rarely seen 'Yellow Queen Elizabeth' and a small pink American rose called 'Lilibet' which, though a Floribunda, much resembles a China. Apple tunnels (double lines of apple trees trained over curved supports so that they form leafy tunnels) lead towards the centre of the garden where clipped yews form the focal point. Another tunnel, this time of figs, is in the north-east corner, where they mingle with the strong growths of the Hybrid Perpetual 'George Dickson'. Squirrels unfortunately get most of the figs but at least they ignore the rose's deep, glowing, red blooms.

Leaving the walled garden at this corner takes you to the top terrace, from which a long paved path leads to the west face of the house. Both to the left and to the right along the terrace are roses, closely planted and growing into each other and also intermingling with the other shrubs. Here you will find 'Frühlingsduft', *R. soulieana*, *R. glauca*, 'Golden Wings', 'Mme Hardy', 'Bourbon Queen' and 'Fantin Latour' and the Gallicas 'Du Maître d'Ecole' and 'Belle de Crécy' supported in wooden frames and so tall as to be scarcely recognizable. Along the parapet on each side of the steps that lead down to the path below are 'Raubritter' and a selection of Rugosas. Flanking the steps themselves are 'Wedding Day' and 'Rambling Rector' on pillars.

Moving on towards the house, on the walls of which the most important rose could be said to be Lady Rasch's favourite, the climbing Tea 'Paul Lede', its yellowish-buff flowers flushed scarlet, you come to a wide paved area with a sundial in the middle and a lily pond on either side. Ahead and to the right, at the corner of the house, steps lead down towards the croquet lawn. A balustrade beside them is half hidden beneath the massed blooms of rambling roses, the identities of which are, for the most part, lost in the mists of time, though I picked out 'Phyllis Bide' among them.

A seedling of the rose 'Arthur Hillier' raised by Charles Quest-Ritson of Corsley Mill.

Between the lawn and the house is a paved area, made infinitely attractive by inter-plantings in the paving of *Alchemilla mollis*, rue, sisyrinchium, stonecrop and mimulus and with two *Magnolia grandiflora* flanking the french windows. Another 'Paul Lede' is beyond them, but turn away from the house and across the lawn to the lower terrace, where one of Heale House's most famous rose features, its hedge of Hybrid Musk roses, is to be found. Here 'Penel-ope', 'Cornelia', 'Moonlight', 'Felicia' and 'Buff Beauty' have been trained on a fence of rustic poles and, planted closely in groups of three and five, make a sight when in full flower that no one who sees it will forget.

Beyond this, steps lead down to the lower lawn, at the far side of which the river winds through the trees. However, turn right along a border filled with plants mainly for summer and early autumn interest and with a few roses for contrast. Beyond this, flanked on three sides by walls (one of them the wall of the stable yard) is the sundial garden. Here, under the walls, are broad beds with many shrubs and roses, predominantly the old French varieties such as 'Cardinal de Richelieu', 'Charles de Mills' and 'Camaieux', together with 'Chaucer' and a vast 'Constance Spry' from David Austin and *R. × cantabrigiensis*.

The way now leads back towards the point from which you started your tour of this memo-rable garden and house, a romantic place in which, in 1651, King Charles II found refuge for six nights before riding on to Shoreham and sailing for France. Parts at least of the house may not have changed much since his day, but the garden will certainly have done so, if not its wonderful setting. It is designed now, as all large gardens must be, for ease of maintenance, with shrubs and perennial plants that need the minimum of looking after, but those that *are* there are kept at the peak of perfection.

In the walled garden at Kellaways herbaceous plants perhaps take pride of place, but there are roses, too, like 'La Noblesse' shown here.

Kellaways

Chippenham

Take A420 north from Chippeham, turn first right through Langley Burrel on East Tytherton road. From Exit 17 on M4 follow signs to Sutton Benger and then right to East Tytherton.
Tel. 024 974 203
Mrs D. Hoskins
Open under the National Gardens Scheme.

Lush is a word that comes readily to mind when thinking of the garden at Kellaways. All the plants, whether the riot of herbaceous perennials and roses of every shape and form in the walled garden to one side of the house, or the roses and other shrubs and trees beyond, seem to merge into one another. Twice as large as they should be, such is their vigour, they leave little room for weeds to grow.

You approach the grey stone manor house, which dates from 1500, down a long gravel drive with a paddock to one side in which horses graze. The first rose you see is 'Complicata' and then the front of the house comes into view. To the left, the white rambler 'Félicité et Perpétue' climbs a tree and to the right, 'Blanc Double de Coubert', about 2.1 m (7 ft) in height, fills a corner formed by the house and a wall that runs out at right angles to it.

To see the garden in the order in which I saw it, move to the left of the house across a lawn towards a small coppice with many shrubs growing in among the trees, kolkwitzia which flowers for so many weeks in incomparable beauty just before midsummer, philadelphus, the Damask Moss rose 'Blanche Moreau' with its dark, spiky moss, a 'Fritz Nobis' of a size you would more usually associate with 'Scarlet Fire' and finally the striped mauve and crimson Bourbon 'Honorine de Brabant' on the other side of the overgrown path. Nearby, along the side of a barn, 'Meg' and 'Climbing Ophelia' show only too clearly that they could do with more sunshine and less shade from the trees, but at the end of the barn is another rose, R. californica, that ought to be suffering in the shadow of a large cherry and instead seems to revel in it. But then it is notoriously tough and will produce its multitude of bright pink flowers in most situations.

Leaving the barn, a left turn takes you along a part of the drive that has the paddock on one side and the spinney you have just made your way through on the other. In other words, you are now making your way back towards the house, passing a venerable specimen of R. × hillieri (R. × pruhoniciana) with its deep, deep red Moyesii flowers.

A wrought-iron gate at the corner of the house by the giant 'Blanc Double de Coubert' leads through into a walled garden where the herbaceous plantings take pride of place, though there are roses in the beds, too, and many more on the walls. Among these are 'Mme Alfred Carrière', 'Climbing Pompon de Paris' and 'Seagull', while in the beds among the huge and glorious heads of paeonies and a wealth of other plants can be found R. sericea pteracantha, R. ecae (a bush of buttercups in May, though a rather untidy one), 'Officinalis', R. roxburghii, 'Général Kléber', the deep-red modern Rugosa hybrid 'Robusta' from Kordes in Germany and quite a few Hybrid Teas.

'Allen Chandler' climbs beside you as you go through a gate and turn along a new path. Forming a background to the right are huge bushes of R. × alba 'Maxima', 'Fantin Latour' and a number of Rugosas, while nearer to the path yellow Scotch roses abound together with smaller Rugosas such as 'Fru Dagmar Hastrup' and 'Sarah Van Fleet'. Others are 'Charles de Mills', 'Ispahan', 'Highdownensis', 'Reine des Violettes', 'Maréchal Davoust' and a very tall 'Chianti', while the clematis 'Victoria' with its soft heliotrope-coloured flowers covers an arch as you near the greenhouse ahead.

An opening in the wall takes you to the swimming pool. A stretch of grass and then mellow stone walls surround it and at one end is what must at one time have been an open-sided barn or cart shed but is now an attractive patio-cum-summerhouse overlooking the pool. The rich red of 'Soldier Boy' is on one wall and there is a huge shrub of 'Cornelia' against another, with fig trees trained on a third. Beyond the walls lie green fields and the open countryside.

From the swimming pool you retrace your steps and then take another path from the greenhouse. A rather wilder part of the garden opens up but with plenty of roses – the Damask 'Ville de Bruxelles', a R. nitida which is, believe it ot not, 1.8 m (6 ft) tall, 'Scabrosa', 'Henri Martin', R. forrestiana and, as a complete contrast, Clematis spooneri shows its usual abandon in covering an immensely tall frame built especially for it from the remains of a dead tree.

A little further on the enormously vigorous and strangely-named rose, 'Wickwar', goes hand-over-hand up a tree. I have gradually been assembling snippets of information about this variety, having first seen it at Sissinghurst Castle, as something completely new to me. I eventually unearthed the fact that it was a seedling, perhaps of 'Kiftsgate', discovered by a Mr Steadman, nurseryman in the village of Wickwar in Gloucestershire, but never very widely distributed.

And that, I thought, was that, especially when I saw another 'Wickwar' in the garden of Mr and Mrs E. H. Gwynn at Minchinhampton, which I understood actually came from the nursery in the village of Wickwar, close by. There it was again, mountainous and white-flowered, but then by chance, in checking on something else, I saw an entry for the rose in Peter Beales' *Classic Roses*. A 'short to medium, dense-growing climber', he says, with 'clear pink flowers', a 'seedling of *R. soulieana*', which it could very well be from its leaves.

> I cannot tell how the truth may be;
> I say the tale as 'twas said to me.

wrote Sir Walter Scott. Who is right, I wonder?

Whatever the answer is, it is time the naming of virtually indistinguishable seedlings of the so-called climbing Musk roses like 'Kiftsgate' is stopped. There is enough confusion already about the identity of many of these white ramblers-cum-climbers without adding to it unnecessarily, though this does not mean, of course, that 'Wickwar' is anything but a very good rose. Enough, however, is enough, though not in this lovely garden, for nearby up another tree is yet another rambler seedling of similar dimensions and habit.

Heading back towards the front of the house now, you pass through a stable yard where the horses look out over the half-doors, perhaps admiring the immaculate pink flowers of 'Complicata' against one wall. As you round the house towards the front once again, there is one more rose to be seen, the lovely soft-yellow climber 'Leverkusen' that should be grown in many more gardens. On the wall of Kellaways, it simply bursts with vigour and health, as do so many of the plants in this wonderful garden created by Mrs Hoskins. She says, modestly, that it is the house as a background that has helped to create the whole. True, but a good deal more was needed and she has provided it with great flair.

Sheldon Manor

Chippenham

From A420, 1½ miles west of Chippenham, turn south at Allington crossroads; also signposted from A4.
Tel. 0249 653120
Major M. A. Gibbs
Open under the National Gardens Scheme and from April to early October on Thursdays, Sundays and Bank Holidays.

Sheldon Manor has been a family home for 700 years, but as with most houses of that age it has had its ups and downs. Major Gibbs lived there as a boy, but after a long absence returned after the Second World War to find much of the garden a wilderness. He and his wife set about the massive task of regeneration with great determination, and worked long and hard to restore much of it to its former glory. They also made changes and improvements that would make maintenance easier as in the old days a dozen gardeners were needed on an estate of this size. They concentrated, therefore, on trees and shrubs that require the minimum of looking after. Over the years they have assembled a remarkable collection of shrub roses, climbers and ramblers, as well as many other interesting and unusual plants.

The house is of warm grey stone with darker tiles topped by tall, square chimneys. In front are broad grass terraces, dominated by gigantic yew trees at the top and divided half-way down by a wall with wide steps in the middle flanked by massive pillars for the wrought-iron gate that leads up to the front door. To the right, as you face the house, is a thirteenth-century chapel and farther away to the left a long barn has been converted into a tea room. Everywhere there are walls in the same pleasing grey as those of the house, some of them dry-stone, and all might have been especially designed for the display of roses and other climbers.

The long drive divides as it reaches the house and a right turn will take you to a court-yard and the side door, a good place to start an exploration of the garden. From the courtyard the drive continues up a gentle slope past an old thatched granary standing on staddle stones, which is now used as an apple store. If you turn left off the drive and round to the back of the house there are a few old roses there, including an 'Albéric Barbier' rambler which has been in place since 1911, one of a small number of roses it has been possible to trace as having been planted at that early date, long before the Gibbs' return. Other roses are 'Maiden's Blush', 'Mme Hardy' and the Gallica 'Charles de Mills' but, beautiful as they are, there are even greater treats in store if you retrace your steps and cross the drive, taking a flagged path directly opposite into the old orchard.

R. hillieri, *R. macrophylla doncasteri*, 'Nevada', 'Scabrosa' and the rumbustious Rugosa hybrid 'Vanguard', which came from America in 1932, are among the first roses you see there, but everywhere you look there are others in bewildering variety, either growing as free-standing shrubs in the long grass or climbing trees. There are many shrubs other than roses there, too, and taken as a whole this is a most remarkable collection of woody plants. As there is no

One of the magnificent buttressed stone walls, festooned with roses, in front of Sheldon Manor.

defined path to follow, you wander as the mood dictates among such a wealth of beauty. From all the roses there it is possible only to pick out a few for mention.

'Alister Stella Gray' climbs one cherry tree and the warm, yellowish-buff blooms of the climbing Tea rose 'Paul Lede' show among the leaves of another. Other climbers and ramblers are 'Léontine Gervais', the Noisette 'Rêve d'Or', 'Lady Hillingdon', 'Alexandre Girault' (up a mulberry), 'The Alchymist', another Noisette 'Clair Jacquier', 'Bobby James', 'Toby Tristram', and the Danish rose 'Lykkefund' (Lucky Find). Away across the orchard, beyond a tiled and moss-covered dovecote on a long pole, the warm, rich-pink, double blooms of the Kordes climber 'Karlsruhe' can be seen against a background of trees and I can only imagine that it is the rather awkward name (from the British point of view) which has caused this fine rose to be so neglected. It is a real beauty that I have seen only recently for the first time, though it dates from 1957.

The shrub roses you can see among the trees of the orchard (in which fruit trees have largely been replaced by exotics, such as *Cornus kousa chinensis*, and shrubs like *Syringa villosa*) include 'Agnes', 'Baronne Prévost' (about the earliest Hybrid Perpetual still in commerce), 'Lady Hillingdon', the Pimpinellifolia hybrid 'Williams' Double Yellow', *R. sweginzowii macrocarpa*, which is the best garden form of this species of the fearsome thorns, bright pink flowers and showy hips, *R. woodsii fendleri*, 'Eugenie Guinoisseau', the double, marbled Sweet Brier 'Glory of Edzell', which is one of the first roses each year into flower, 'Duc de Fitzjames' (a lovely dark-pink Gallica), 'Goldbusch', and the Penzance Brier 'Anne of Geierstein', with its striking, fragrant dark crimson flowers.

At the bottom corner of the orchard nearest to the house a climbing form – as if this was needed – of 'Scarlet Fire' flashes its dazzling red blooms from a tree to the left as you make your way back towards the house and take a short detour of 90 m (100 yds) or so down the drive to see many more roses, both to the left and to the right. This part of the drive is, in fact, bordered on both sides by hedges of what look like one or other of the many multiflora hybrids, and you pass from this area out onto the wide lawn at the front of the house. The stone walls of the terraces are on your right and a tall yew hedge lies ahead, but before you

reach it there are more roses to see. Along one terrace wall 'Max Graf' spreads itself and cascades down in the way it should be used, rather than as a somewhat inefficient ground-cover plant, and nearby are such other shrubs as the white-flowered *Poncirus trifoliata* (known for some reason as the Japanese Bitter Orange) and a double form of 'Canary Bird'.

A gate in a wall leads from here into another open grassy space with yet more roses, dominated by the massive trunk of a fallen elm which must be all of 2.1 m (7 ft) in diameter and which, from a ring count that he carried out, Major Gibbs calculates must be some 250 years old. Roses here include several very old *R. moyesii*, probably dating from 1935, many Moss roses, plus 'Jenny Duval', 'Boule de Neige', 'Buff Beauty', 'La Mortola', the creamy-white flowered Damask 'Botzaris', 'Rose de Rescht', *R. roxburghii* and a whole lot more. Also in this part of the garden is a collection of magnolias, including the magnificent *Magnolia liliiflora* 'Nigra', a Japanese variety with flowers larger than the familiar *R. soulangeana*, deep purple outside and paler within and borne in succession right through the summer.

An opening in a hornbeam hedge takes you into the area which contains the swimming pool, a conversion that Major Gibbs carried out from the old water garden. The two halves of the lawn here are on different levels and it is in this wonderful setting that pageants are staged in the summer months. The upper lawn forms a natural stage and the lower one the auditorium.

This is about the only part of the garden – a comparatively small one – where there are no roses, but more can be seen as you move back towards the house and up wide steps in the terracing towards the front door. To the left is the old barn with 'Lawrence Johnston', 'Mme Alfred Carrière' and 'Maigold' on the walls and other climbers nearby; some on the house walls are 'Lady Sylvia', 'Emily Gray', 'Zéphirine Drouhin', 'Ramona' and 'Cupid'. The China rose 'Comtesse du Cayla' grows by the front door and the Abyssinian Gallica *R. sancta* (*R. richardii*) is in a corner by the chapel at the far end of the terrace.

Sir George Sitwell could very well have been summing up this garden when he wrote: 'Let climbing roses drop in a veil from the terrace and smother with flower-spangled embroidery the garden walls . . . and the dusty gold of the sunshine shall mingle with the summer snow of the flying petals'.

The Old Rectory

Burghfield

*Exit 12 off M4 onto A4, then south at sign to Burghfield
village. In village, turn right after Hatch Gate Inn,
house entrance on right.*
Tel. 0735 29 2206
Mr and Mrs R. R. Merton
*Open, garden only, under the National Gardens Scheme
and by written appointment.*

'I think the roses have climbed and climbed and
climbed until they hang from the branches and
walls and creep over the ground like a strange
grey mist . . . when the summer comes there
will be curtains and fountains of roses.' The
description of Frances Hodgson Burnett's
secret garden is apposite here as a lot of the
glory at The Old Rectory, for rose lovers at
least, is to be found 6 or 9 m (20 or 30 ft) or
more above the ground. Up and through every
tree a climbing or rambling rose scrambles with
exuberant abandon, and the sight of them all in
full bloom in June and July is almost over-
whelming.

The rectory itself has a Georgian façade
added to an older building. You do not immediately see many roses from the drive, but if
you walk round to the back of the house there is
a sheltered courtyard with a sink garden for
Alpines with the climbing rose 'Breeze Hill' on
the wall behind. Beyond it is what is perhaps
the most incredible rose in the garden, a plant
of *R. helenae* of such a size that the multiple
shoots at ground level are like the trunks of for-
est trees. *R. helenae* is a climber that came to us

The tree-climbing R. brunonii *and 'Breeze Hill' in the courtyard at The Old Rectory.*

from China in 1907, a member of the *Synstylae* group and named after the wife of the plant collector, E. H. Wilson. It flowers comparatively early for this kind of rose, in mid- to late June, with huge corymbs of white single flowers, followed in early autumn by clusters of small red hips that are just as decorative in their way. In most gardens it would be put up a tree, but the Mertons planted it against a wall which it rapidly scaled and then arched out from, making a tunnel through which you have to walk to reach the vegetable garden.

To do that you would have to turn right, but on the left there is an old stable building and its surroundings to explore first. 'Kiftsgate' covers one end of it and others on the walls and round about are 'Adélaide d'Orléans', 'Bleu Magenta' (the largest and latest flowering of the purple ramblers), 'Veilchenblau' to keep it company, 'The Garland', the climbing Tea rose 'Mrs Herbert Stevens', 'Lawrence Johnston' and a rose that has baffled the owners of many old gardens seeking its identity. This is 'De la Grifferaie' introduced by the French raiser, Vibert, in 1845. It has fragrant, fully double, magenta-pink flowers, not unattractive, but its presence here, and in most of the other gardens in which it is found, is most likely due to its use at one time as an understock. On the back of the barn is the modern climber 'Compassion' and a sturdy seedling of 'Kiftsgate' is emerging through a crack in the concrete path there. Beyond the barn is the orchard with a number of shrub roses planted in the grass among the trees.

Returning towards the house you pass on the left a rose with the rather quaint name of 'Little Compton Creeper'. However, the name does not refer to the size of the rose but to the fact that it was raised in America by the Brownells of Little Compton, Rhode Island. The parentage is not known but the glossy leaves suggest *R. wichuraiana*. The flowers are coppery-pink.

A gate in the wall by the sink garden leads to a part of the garden where a vista of lawns and tall trees opens up on the right while to the left herbaceous plants grow under a long wall on which, of course, there are roses: 'The Alchymist', creamy-white 'Saga' doing its best to emulate the climbers, 'Phyllis Bide', *R. multiflora*, 'Climbing Cécile Brunner', 'Aloha', 'Blairii No. 2', 'Alister Stella Gray', 'Mme Grégoire Staechelin', 'Parkdirektor

Riggers' and the Gallica 'Cardinal de Richelieu', like 'Saga' used as a climber, among them. In the bed itself and not against the wall, mixed with the other plants, are more roses including two species, the St Mark's Rose and the grey-leaved *R. fedtschenkoana*, the white flowers of which, almost alone amongst the wild roses, appear throughout the summer and early autumn.

Beyond this long border, towards the farther end of the garden, are the tall trees that carry 'Bobbie James' and all the other invasive climbers and ramblers to such impossible heights. Here, too, surrounded by shrubberies and small open spaces, each one a miniature garden in itself, is a large pool in the middle of which is a statue of Antinous, favourite of the Emperor Hadrian who, despite this (or, who knows, because of it), drowned himself in the Nile. There is, of course, a wealth of moisture-loving plants in every shape, size and colour.

From the pool one moves across the bottom of the garden towards the tennis court. A short pergola at one end, known in the Merton family as The Bus Stop, has *R. longicuspis* climbing over it. But it has emerged that the rose sold by most nurseries which we have been happily growing for years as *R. longicuspis* is, in fact, *R. mulliganii*, which has much smaller hips. The true *R. longicuspis* is, it appears, something of a rarity, so bear this in mind when you read of it appearing in a number of the other gardens. I have never had the chance to compare the two side by side and I have a feeling that the same will apply to most of the owners of the gardens in which it grows. They may well have *R. longicuspis*, but the odds are on *R. mulliganii*.

But the roses are not just in the vicinity of the pergola. They are all round the tennis court and of particular interest is a fine selection of ramblers, a number of which are of unknown origin. By that I do not mean that Mrs Merton does not know where she got them from, but that she knows nothing of their ancestry or what their names may be.

Mrs Merton would certainly echo the sentiment expressed in a quotation from Somerville and Ross's *Some Irish Yesterdays*: 'In the amenities of gardeners, as in love, the advice to "Take me while I'm in the humour", is sound, and a cutting in the hand is well worth six in or on the bush, when the bush is another's.' For she has the knack, as she will tell you, of spotting unusual roses in wayside hedges or

Opposite: 'Adélaide d'Orléans', another of the magnificent ramblers at The Old Rectory, on the stable block.

gardens and the most engaging habit of stopping and taking or asking for a cutting wherever she may be, in this country or abroad. Her skill as a propagator and plantswoman, which is evident in every corner of the garden at The Old Rectory, does the rest. This method of plant acquisition must inevitably result in there being a number of unknown varieties in her collection, but to me this gives them added interest.

'Blushing Lucy' was one Mrs Merton did know that I had never heard of before, an enchanting, fragrant, pale-pink rambler raised in Horsham, Sussex, by Dr A. H. Williams in 1938. *Modern Roses 8* classes it as a large-flowered climber, but it does not look like that to me. However, there are other more easily recognizable ramblers about which there is no real doubt – the always pristine 'Sanders' White', 'François Juranville' and 'Félicité et Perpétue'. Also in the tennis court area are *R. webbiana*, arguably the most graceful and dainty of all species roses with flowers of the most delicate lilac-pink, followed by urn-shaped hips, 'Poulsen's Park Rose', 'Constance Spry' and 'Stanwell Perpetual'.

This is a garden that you leave with a deep admiration for the owners' unflagging enthusiasm and for their profound knowledge of plants. A picture of that white magic cascading from the tree-tops remains in the mind's eye long after the visit is over.

Great Barfield

Bradenham

On A4010 from High Wycombe to Princes Risborough, turn off at Red Lion Inn for Bradenham. At village green turn right. House down lane past cul-de-sac sign.
Tel. 024024 3741
Mr Richard Nutt
Open, garden only, under the National Gardens Scheme.

When a garden is described as a plantsman's garden, as this one rightly should be, the average gardener can be daunted. There is an implication that all the plants will be too exotic for an amateur to grow. And if, as here, there are two National Collections as well – of *Iris unguicularis* and of *Ranunculus ficaria* – those whose gardens hold only the National Collection of ground elder may feel overawed.

But it does not have to be so. A true plantsman's garden, as Great Barfield is, means that although there are many fascinating rare and unusual plants, they are blended skilfully in foliage, flower and habit of growth with more mundane cousins so that you are aware only of an overall harmony and not of strange exotics that look out of place and unhappy in their surroundings.

At Great Barfield there are some interesting roses in the front of the house where the drive sweeps in between raised grassy banks. 'Kiftsgate' wanders up through a tall pine tree, but the rose to note, weaving in and out of a large holly, is 'Sir Cedric Morris'. This, according to Peter Beales who introduced it, was a chance cross between *R. glauca* (*R. rubrifolia*), which gives the rose its plum-purple young leaves and shoots, and *R. mulliganii*, as it was discovered in a bunch of *R. glauca* seedlings and the other rose was nearby. *R. mulliganii* is very similar to *R. longicuspis*, so it is from this side of the family that the vigorous habit and the great sprays of sweetly scented flowers presumably come.

Other roses nearby, at the top of the bank along one side of the drive, are the ground-hugging 'Max Graf', *R. × paulii rosea*, which I feel has much more character than *R. × paulii* itself, and a variety that has been identified as *R. kordesii* but to me looks rather too light a pink. On the house itself at the front is 'Souvenir de Claudius Denoyel', producing masses of its fragrant, cupped scarlet flowers even though it is on a north wall and has a reputation for being difficult to grow. On the walls at the sides and back are: 'Lady Hillingdon', 'Cooperi', with its polished leaves, the seldom-seen Pimpinellifolia hybrid 'Williams' Double Yellow' (which has the same parent on one side as 'Harison's Yellow' [*R. foetidea*] and is very like it except for the green carpels in the flower centres in place of yellow stamens), 'Gloire de Dijon', the Bourbon 'Blairii No. 2' and 'William Allen Richardson', a Noisette.

Looking out from the terrace at the back of the house there is a long vista of lawn with trees at the far end. This is broken up by island beds containing many small trees, shrub roses and other shrubs, including a notable collection of viburnums with the large-leaved, white-flowered *Viburnum ceanothoides foetidum* and *Viburnum plicatum* 'Pink Beauty' among them. One of the tallest trees, a fir, has the rampant 'Diany

Binny' almost coming out at the top, but much more important and remarkable is that the rose has grown so that its fragrant white flowers appear on all sides of the tree, not just on that nearest the sun. Roses in the island beds include a number of species: *R. webbiana*, *R.* × *cantabrigiensis*, *R. nitida*, *R. majalis* (probably better known as *R. cinnamomea*, an early-flowering European species with pink flowers and greyish leaves), the low, spreading *R. richardii*, *R. virginiana*, *R. primula* and *R. willmottii*. Another bed has, among others, 'Headleyensis', the soft pink Damask 'Mme Zoetmans', another form of *R. nitida* with less shiny leaves, a number of Rugosas, and the single-flowered soft-orange Hybrid Tea rose 'Mrs Oakley Fisher'.

Trees line the western border of the garden and there is a small grove of them at the far end of the lawn. Under all these (and up them) are so many roses that only a few can be picked out for mention. The climbers and ramblers, some of them trained on frames, include 'Alida Lovett', 'Amadis' (a Boursault), 'Violette' with *R. longicuspis* growing up a pine tree behind it, 'Goldfinch', 'Helen Knight', *R. multiflora* and 'Debutante'. Shrub roses include 'Duc de Guiche', 'Arthur Hillier', *R. fedtschenkoana*, *R. forrestiana*, the *R. macrophylla* seedling 'Master Hugh' with rose-pink flowers and huge flagon-shaped hips, and 'Gipsy Boy', showing its customary lack of restraint.

On the return journey towards the house up the eastern border of the garden, following the line of a flint wall that has seen better days, there are more climbers, 'Souvenir du Docteur Jamain', 'Sombreuil' and *R. wichuraiana* among them. The fiercely thorned and spined *R. sweginzowii* is on the left just before you come to the main planting of old garden roses in a wide bed along the wall. All the main families – Gallicas, Damasks, Albas, Centifolias and so on – are to be found there, grouped together, and there is one Macrantha hybrid, 'Lady Curzon'. This makes an arching shrub with dark green leaves and very large, fragrant, pale-pink single flowers with crinkled petals. Other roses thereabouts include the Burgundian Rose, *R.* × *centifolia parvifolia*, which, in addition to these two, has been given more names in its time than it has seen hot summers.

A lane borders much of the east side of the garden with corn fields on the farther side. Along this Mr Nutt has planted, between trees that were already there, many hazel bushes

and, for the benefit of passers-by on country walks, quite a few Moyesii varieties, including 'Eos' and the fiery red 'Eddie's Jewel', which arose from a cross between a Moyesii rose and the old floribunda 'Donald Prior'. 'Seagull' and 'Wedding Day' clamber up two of the trees.

A plantsman's garden? Yes, in the best possible sense of the term, and one not to be missed by anyone who wishes to see how all plants, not just roses, should be grown to best advantage.

The Manor House

Bledlow

Off A4010 or B4009 near Princes Risborough, signposted Bledlow Village. Manor House in the village. Tel. 084 44 3499
The Lord and Lady Carrington
Open, garden only, under the National Gardens Scheme and by appointment from May to September. Lyde Garden always open.

The Carringtons have two gardens at The Manor House, the first an extensive and fairly formal one round the house itself, while the second, the Lyde Garden, lies across the road. The creation of the latter is a remarkable achievement. Planted on the steeply sloping sides of a small ravine where the coming together of the waters of some thirteen or fourteen springs forms the source of the Lyde river, roses and other shrubs and plants provide a solid bank of colour at the height of the season, a truly remarkable and breathtaking sight. Paths wind downwards to an extensive wooden walkway over watercress beds and bog gardens beside the stream and then upwards again on the farther side. Bledlow church can be glimpsed through trees at the top.

The roses on show include 'Nevada', 'Fred Loads', 'Wilhelm', 'Golden Wings', *R.* × *alba* 'Maxima', 'Dorothy Perkins' (used as a sprawler like its parent, *R. wichuraiana*, rather than as a climber), 'Cantabrigiensis', 'Scabrosa', *R. glauca*, 'Complicata', 'Marguerite Hilling', 'Scarlet Fire', 'Buff Beauty' and many more – all renowned for their profusion of bloom. This the Carringtons call their Village Garden and it is open at all times, free of charge.

Back across the road, wide lawns shaded by majestic old trees border the drive as you approach the house from the road, in this open part of the garden. Much of the rest is divided into compartments enclosed by high yew hedges, each garden within a garden having its own style and theme. In one the yellow and white Floribundas, 'Korresia' and 'Iceberg', are planted in company with lavender, though the chalky soil of the Chilterns means that they have to struggle to be at their best. 'The Fairy', planted in enchanting combination with santolina and day lilies by the swimming pool, does not seem affected by the chalky soil and, both here and in the area round the croquet lawn, there are a number of shrub roses that seem much more able to cope with the chalk than the more highly bred Floribundas and Hybrid Teas. (The same thing was very noticeable at Humphrey Brooke's garden at Claydon in Suffolk and at Hambleden Manor.)

Some of the roses that are doing well at The Manor House include 'Paul's Himalayan Musk Rambler', grown up an apple tree, and 'Wedding Day', scrambling through a lilac, while the rambler 'Adélaide d'Orléans' is successful as a lax, free-standing shrub. Others include 'Marguerite Hilling' – a great favourite here – 'Trier', 'Penelope', the Apple Rose, *R. pomifera*, which, despite its name, has gooseberry-like hips that follow the single pink flowers, *R. rugosa* 'Alba' and *R. rugosa* 'Rubra'. These are all to one side of the house but fronting it, some distance away and rather in the shade, are more shrub roses, 'Commandant Beaurepaire', 'Vick's Caprice', 'Boule de Neige', *R. californica* ''Plena' and the semi-double form of *R. pomifera*, 'Duplex' (or Wolley-Dod's Rose). It has rather better flowers than the type but fewer hips and both have the same attractive grey-green, rather downy-looking foliage. There is also a rose labelled 'Esther Baird' which I have not seen in flower and about which I can find nothing.

An enclosed garden beside the house as you make your way towards the tennis court has more roses and on the stop netting of the court itself are the ramblers 'Veilchenblau' and a much greater rarity, the American-raised 'Apple Blossom'. The huge heads of flowers do resemble apple blossom but, rather more surprisingly, it has that famous old Hybrid Perpetual, 'Général Jacqueminot', with its large, double scarlet flowers, only one generation back in its parentage. Nearby is a paved garden with a lily pond and roses abound once more in its neighbourhood. This is, in fact, a garden where roses crop up at every turn and there is no actual rose garden as such.

The Manor House

Hambleden

From A4155, Henley to Marlow road, follow sign on north side to Hambleden. House on right at end of village; no name plate.
Tel. 0491 571 335
The Viscount and Viscountess Hambleden
Open, gardens only, under the National Gardens Scheme.

You do not need to be told that the soil in this garden is chalky and flinty: the garden wall on the right as you turn in at the gate is of flint and the house walls are flint-faced, as are those of many buildings in the village. Older roses do not seem to mind chalky soil nearly as much as the more highly bred moderns, which perhaps accounts, in part, for the success of Hambleden Manor's rose garden. I say 'in part' because the roses are grown in what was once the vegetable garden, which means that barrow loads of manure and compost over the years have left the ground in good heart.

However, the rose garden does not confront you as you enter through the gateway from the village street. As you approach the house, you see first a magnificent copper beech, which the drive encircles on its way to the forecourt of the house. The wall on the right supports an enormous 'Scarlet Fire' and 'Mme Alfred Carrière', while *R. longicuspis* comes over the top of it from the other side. To find the roots of the latter you must pass through a gate in the wall to the area surrounding the swimming pool, where you can see that it covers a pavilion as well as the wall. However, if you really want to appreciate the flamboyant beauty of all three roses, look down on them from the raised lawn that runs along the east side of the house and slopes down towards the pool.

Continuing round the house, you can look into an intriguing garden room with a domed glass top, and then you come across some shrub roses planted in the grass further up the slope towards the tennis court. These, however, have not thrived and are on the list for removal some time in the not-too-distant future. So retrace your steps back to the front of the house, where a wide lawn stretches away on the far side of the copper beech to another tall flint wall. In front of this is a wide border with many shrubs and roses in it, 'Golden

Wings' and a number of Rugosas among them. On the wall itself is another gigantic 'Scarlet Fire' and 'Easlea's Golden Rambler', while 'May Queen' garlands a small metal pergola in the centre.

The rose garden proper is on the far side of this wall. Roughly square, probably 45 by 45 m (50 by 50 yds), it typifies the unbelievably vast vegetable gardens of earlier times. Admittedly, when the house was built, there was probably a large staff of servants to feed as well as the family, but it is by no means the biggest that I saw. Many have, like this one, been converted to other uses, but others, depressingly, lie derelict and forgotten.

The rose garden was laid out to the design of Peter Beales and is full of interest. Gravel paths separate the many beds, most of which are devoted to one of the families of old roses, though there is often more than one bed for each group and quite large numbers of each variety included.

As is to be expected, with Peter Beales as the inspiration behind the garden, there are some unusual varieties. Thus among the Bourbons, along with the familiar 'Boule de Neige', 'Commandant Beaurepaire', 'Coupe d'Hébé', 'Mme Lariol de Barnay' and so on, there are the rare and very thorny, strong magenta-red 'Vivid' introduced by Paul in 1853 and 'Mrs Paul' with its loosely formed flowers in pale blush-pink, from the same raiser, forty years later.

The Centifolias include 'Pompon de Bourgogne' ('Parvifolia') with closely packed, narrowly tapering leaves and rosy-purple flowers, while the Damasks take in the Portland group in the varieties 'Jacques Cartier' and 'Comte de Chambord', understandably so as the Portlands were once known as Perpetual Damasks and are closely allied to them. It seems pretty certain that a Damask rose, probably the 'Autumn Damask', was one of the parents of the original Portland, together with a Gallica which passed on its relatively short and compact growth.

The family was named after the second Duchess of Portland whose life spanned a good deal of the eighteenth century. She was a keen rosarian and one story has it that it was she who organized the passage of Mr Kennedy, of the Hammersmith nurseries of Lee and Kennedy, to France during the height of the Napoleonic Wars to take roses to the Empress Josephine's garden at Malmaison. According to Jack Harkness's book *Roses* (Dent), these roses were

named 'Portlands' by André Dupont, gardener to the Empress, after they reached France from England, though it is believed their origin was in Italy. At any rate, the Portlands, like the Bourbons which they preceded by a few years, were the first of the recurrent rose families to be raised in the West.

The round central bed of the garden has an interesting grouping. As a pivot for the whole there is a standard of the *Sempervirens* rambler, 'Félicité et Perpétue', and round it are planted bushes of the Polyantha, 'Marie Pavie', which dates back to the last century and has attractive double white flowers in clusters, plum-purple canes and dark green leaves. It is not too unlike the better-known 'Yvonne Rabier' and I am not sure that it is in quite the right place, as it is rather dwarfed and hidden by an outer ring made up from bushes of the original Portland rose, here labelled 'Paestana', which it seems to have been called when it first arrived from Italy. The bright red flowers, opening flat, clearly show Gallica influence, probably that of 'Officinalis', which they much resemble.

Round this central bed there is an area of low-growing varieties like the crimson China rose 'Fellemberg' (a real old Chinese name, that), the china-pink Polyantha 'Nathalie Nypels' in particularly fine form, 'Ballerina', 'Little White Pet', 'Yesterday', 'Buff Beauty' and 'Prosperity', both the latter, with their naturally sprawling habit, keeping low, as does the other and lesser-known Pemberton Hybrid Musk, golden yellow 'Daybreak'. The modern Floribunda 'Escapade' blends in very well with these and underneath them all Japanese 'Nozomi' (the accent, incidentally, on the 'i' – 'Nozom-i) does its best to cover the ground.

The beds of the larger roses are grouped all round these, while at the bottom of the gently sloping site is a fence with a wide border in front of it with more old roses, and with open fields and trees at the top of a rise as a backdrop. As there are some far-from-common varieties and species along this fence I think it would be worth while to mention what is there.

From right to left as you face the fence there are to start with *R. sweginzowii*, the Sweet Brier 'Meg Merrilies' and 'Schneelicht', a Rugosa hybrid, the pure white single flowers of which are borne all along the arching canes. This is the first of several less usual members of the Rugosa family, for apart from 'Sarah Van Fleet' which is quite common there are: the white sport of 'Conrad Ferdinand Meyer', 'Nova

Zembla', 'Mrs Antony Waterer', 'Vanguard', which has large orange-salmon flowers deriving from Pernetiana ancestry, and the fearsomely thorny 'Dr Eckener'. This has light yellow flowers opening from peachy coloured buds and growth that is probably only equalled by 'Cerise Bouquet'. It is one of the hardiest of roses and a strong recommendation for cold districts, if you have room for it.

Moving along the line of the fence you next encounter dainty 'Schneezwerg', 'Scabrosa', 'Roseraie de l'Hay', *R. pomifera* 'Duplex', *R. nutkana* from western North America with its striking spherical hips, *R. californica* 'Plena', *R. sericea pteracantha*, *R. moyesii*, *R.* × 'Headleyensis' (a hybrid of the early- flowering *R. hugonis* and, to my mind, even better), *R.* ×

dupontii (which I have enthused about elsewhere) and lastly another Sweet Brier 'Amy Robsart'. Lord Penzance, who raised so many of these roses by crossing *R. rubiginosa* (*R. eglanteria*) with other species and varieties towards the end of the last century, named a large proportion of them, as mentioned elsewhere, after characters in Sir Walter Scott's novels. Hence 'Amy Robsart', 'Catherine Seyton', 'Edith Bellenden', Flora McIvor', 'Julia Mannering', 'Jeannie Deans', 'Lucy Ashton', 'Meg Merrilies' and so on, a number of which it would be very hard to find nowadays. They are not, of course, roses for small gardens. With many of them the flowers are very fleeting and they were grown as much for their scented foliage as for their brief displays of colour.

Each of the beds in the large rose garden at The Manor House, Hambleden, is devoted to distinct families among the old roses.

Winslow Hall

Winslow

*On A413 Aylesbury–Buckingham road, in centre of
Winslow itself.*
Tel. 029 671 2323 (house)
Sir Edward and Lady Tomkins
*Open, house and garden, all Bank Holidays, except
Boxing Day. Also open 1 July to 15 September daily,
except Mondays, and from 15 to 30 September,
weekends only. Open Sundays in May and June by
appointment only. (Ring 029 671 3433.)*

Although set quite close to the busy main road through the little town of Winslow, Winslow Hall becomes a haven of peace once you have passed through the gates. Traffic noise vanishes and you are aware only of smooth green lawn, merging into trees in the distance, planted with a fine range of unusual shrubs and roses.

The massive frontage of the Hall faces the garden and it is one of the few houses designed by Sir Christopher Wren to have survived virtually unchanged since it was built between 1698 and 1702 for Sir William Lowndes. Between the house and the lawn is a brick-paved forecourt flanked by beds of modern roses, predominantly in amber and yellow tones, 'Arthur Bell', 'Troika' and 'Peace' among them and with the white of 'Iceberg' to set them off. To the left a wonderful collection of named varieties of violas in every imaginable colour grows under a spreading *Prunus*, while others effectively carpet the ground beneath a standard wisteria.

An opening in a low brick wall leads out of the forecourt on to the lawn. Two standards of the Polyantha rose, 'The Fairy', guard the opening like twin sentinels, and a whole bed of the same variety runs right along the far side of the wall, its soft pink complemented by a bush of the floribunda 'Pernille Poulsen' at each end. Until very recently 'the Fairy' was considered a sport of the rambler 'Lady Godiva', but Jack Bentall now suggests that it was actually bred by his mother, Mrs Bentall, in Essex from the Poly pompon 'Paul Crampel' and the Walsh rambler 'Lady Gay' in 1932.

On your left as you come out on to the grass is a bed of 'Iceberg' set against a high yew hedge. Across the way, in round beds cut into the turf, are various shrub roses including

'Nevada', 'Marguerite Hilling', some Albas, 'Canary Bird', 'Ferdinand Pichard', 'Golden Wings', 'Penelope' and a very new rose from Germany, 'Kordes Robusta', which is a most unlikely-looking Rugosa hybrid with glowing deep-scarlet single flowers. 'Temple Bells', an American rose sometimes classed as a climbing miniature and sometimes as a ground cover rambler, is used here for covering the ground under a *R. moyesii*. Two other much more recent ground-cover roses, this time from Poulsen of Denmark, 'Pink Bells' and 'White Bells', are featured in another bed. They really do cover the ground, too, unlike so many of the roses catalogued as such that fail dismally to do so.

Moving on up the lawn there are curved informal rose beds with a wide range of shrubs and specimen trees in between. Dark red 'Intrigue', a great favourite of the Tomkinses though a stranger to me, 'Just Joey', which is everybody's favourite, and 'Fragrant Delight', which will be as popular as any when better known, are some of the roses featured, while among the shrubs and trees are *Aralia variegata*, a tulip tree and witch hazel, the biggest exochorda I have ever seen, the Japanese crab, *Malus floribunda*, an amelanchier and a *Rubus tridel*, and an oak tree over 200 years old. Pink oxalis covers the ground under a *R. glauca* (*R. rubrifolia*) and there are beds of Hybrid Musks, 'Frühlingsgold' and pink 'Aloha', this time underplanted with that other climbing miniature, 'Nozomi'. Further along there is a bed of that gay performer in geranium-red and yellow, the Meilland raised 'Cocktail' which you see all too rarely but which at its best (without black spot) will brighten up any garden. 'Nymphenburg' and the Damask 'Ispahan', under trees to the left, seem to do reasonably well in the semi-shade.

At the top of the garden, which occupies some 1.2 hectares (3 acres) altogether, there is a fenced-off paddock and beyond that is the Winslow Bowling Club on land belonging to the Tomkins and on which they have planted yet more roses. Where the paddock adjoins the garden there is a tall fence across its full width against which an assortment of Rugosa roses grows and some of the traditional ramblers such as 'Dorothy Perkins' and 'American Pillar'. Also a modern climber, the fragrant red 'Dublin Bay', which has a reputation for being somewhat reluctant to climb, seems to be doing all right here.

A great clump of the Kordes Sweet Brier hybrid 'Sparrieshoop' is to the right as you begin to turn back towards the house, its fragrant single flowers a rosy salmon pink with a lighter centre. There are yet more rose plantings against the wall now on your left, beyond which lies the extensive vegetable garden. There are roses there, too, but they are mainly for cutting for the house or are new varieties that the Tomkins are trying out before planting them in the main garden.

The range of species roses and varieties at Winslow Hall may not be said to be as great as some, but they are used attractively with other plants and demonstrate well how to use roses for ground cover. And, of course, there are other fine shrubs and trees which should on no account be missed. An original touch that combines the best of both is where *Cotoneaster horizontalis* has been encouraged to mound up to something over 1 m (3 ft) and through it to great effect weave both clematis and rambling roses such as 'Albertine'. The latter flowers first and then the clematis. What could be better?

Alderley Grange

Alderley, Wotton-under-Edge

Two miles south of Wotton-under-Edge. Turn north-west off Bath–Stroud road (A46) at Dunkirk.
Tel. 0453 842161
Mr Guy and The Hon. Mrs Acloque
Open under the National Gardens Scheme.

The house here is Jacobean, dating from 1608, with a walled garden divided into a number of areas. Each one is different, but you become aware of the strong link between them almost immediately, for this is above all an aromatic garden. Every herb and other kind of aromatic plant hardy in the British Isles, and many not normally so, are to be found in the Acloques' collection and almost every one releases its own very individual aroma into the air around it if the leaves are plucked or brushed against, or even if left to its own devices on a warm, humid afternoon.

This is no simple herb garden with plants grown to add spice to dishes for the table. Instead, they are used most skilfully in the plantings for the sheer individual beauty of their foliage and, in some cases, the flowers.

The soft blues, greys and greens of the leaves are blended with consummate skill, with here and there a lemony green and other tones to give contrast to point up the overall effect.

But what about the roses? The Acloques believe, quite rightly, that all roses, and especially the older ones which they favour, should not be isolated in beds but should be mixed and blended in with other plants. A few roses, *R. primula* and some of the Sweet Briers, have aromatic foliage, but most of the old ones have scented flowers. And what goes better with the white, maroon, pink and purple of the old rose blooms than the silvery greys and grey-greens of many herbs? If proof were needed that they blend together to perfection, this is the garden to provide it.

However, I have jumped ahead a little, for there is a 'Paul's Himalayan Musk Rambler' and a *R. primula* near the front door to enjoy before you even leave the forecourt of the house. Then through the gate and you are amongst the roses, albeit perhaps not at their best at this particular spot, for they are rather starved of light, sandwiched in between the house wall and another one to the right of the path. Where the area opens up some of the first varieties to come into view are 'Rose d'Amour' (*R. virginiana* 'Plena'), *R. glauca*, 'Empress Josephine', 'The Alchymist' on the wall, and a massed bed of the lovely modern floribunda 'Iceberg' which many people have discovered fits perfectly into any scheme with roses, old or new.

'Prince Charles' and the rambler 'Minnehaha' are off to the left near a variegated holly. It is difficult to believe that M. H. Walsh, of Massachusetts, the leading American breeder of ramblers at the turn of the century, used the Hybrid Perpetual 'Paul Neyron' with its enormous, paeony-like blooms as one of the parents of 'Minnehaha'. Its slightly fragrant flowers are small and pink, fading to white, and are carried in large clusters – what one might expect, of course, from the other parent, *R. wichuraiana*. 'Paul Neyron' seems to have vanished without trace.

The garden now opens out with a venerable catalpa and a gnarled, geriatric mulberry with propped-up branches shading the lawn. The mulberry is reputed to have been planted when the house was built in the reign of James I. He was anxious to promote the silk trade in this country and issued an edict to the Lords Lieutenant of various counties instructing them to

The garden at Alderley Grange blends aromatic plants with the old roses in the most enchanting fashion.

distribute 10,000 mulberries, so that virtually every garden of any size should have at least one. The price was six shillings a hundred trees, and while it is difficult to believe that there is no truth in this story, considerable doubt was cast by Alan Mitchell in an article in *The Garden* on the age to which mulberry trees are reputed to grow. If he is right, this one could not be nearly 400 years old, but I prefer to believe that it is. It certainly looks it. Beyond is an equally impressive *Magnolia grandiflora*.

Following round the walls you see the rambler 'Alexandre Girault', the crimson Boursault 'Amadis', assorted Scotch roses, 'La Belle Sultane', the almost single Gallica (also known as 'Violacea') and, at the first corner, a great mound of honeysuckle and 'Albéric Barbier' intertwined. So far at any rate, neither is victorious in its struggle for supremacy.

A gentle slope now leads down past the rather angular 'Château de Clos Vougeot', with 'Rambling Rector' on the wall and a planting of the dwarf Centifolia 'Petite de Hollande' surrounding a maple. In front is the bottom wall of this part of the garden and you turn left along it beside a broad bed of aromatic plants of every kind with roses, of course, amongst them. The roses include such as 'Rose Marie Viaud' (a seedling of 'Vielchenblau'), 'Blairii No. 2', the Setigera hybrid 'Souvenir de Brod', and the much more modern American rose 'Aloha', which, like 'Iceberg', is at home in any company with its magnificent, scented, old-style flowers. A line of 'The Fairy' also merits mention out of a vast selection that would read like a rose *Who's Who*, and always in the air is the drifting fragrance of the aromatics, a heady, all-pervasive mixture of scents that it is impossible to describe.

Through an opening in the wall an avenue

of pleached lime trees lies ahead and a paved path to the left takes you past more roses. In the lawn to the right, a grey-leaved willow casts its shade across the late-flowering Centifolia 'La Noblesse', the rosy-red Penzance Brier 'Greenmantle', 'Highdownensis', 'La Noblesse', various Rugosas and others, while on the other side of the path are 'Hunter' and a hedge of the fragrant, deep plum-crimson Sissinghurst Rose, 'Rose des Maures' (see also page 44).

An armillary sphere on a pedestal forms a focal point at one side of the path you now stroll along through a series of rose arches and you can see as you go, by way of a change from so much charm and beauty, the three most poisonous plants in the British list, henbane, monkshood and hemlock. They fit, of course, into the pattern of herbs and plants, used by the old-time apothecaries, which are still grown by the discerning. Woad is here, too, with its yellow flowers, and the elegant pink and white spikes of dittany (*Dictamnus*), cultivated since Roman times.

At the far end of this path is the square Bee Garden. The geometric pattern of beds has been planted entirely with herbs, the different foliage colours forming their own patterns within the whole. Four standard privets with clipped, ball-like heads give height to what otherwise is a very low-level planting, while along the end wall are the white Centifolia 'Blanchefleur', 'Belle Amour', a seedling intermediate between the Albas and the Damasks with semi-double, fragrant soft pink flowers and yellow stamens, and 'Direktor Alphond' which came direct from the Berlin Rosarium, via Peter Beales.

Finally, a left turn takes you back towards the house past 'Gloire des Mousseux', living up to its name as one of the most beautiful of Moss roses, 'Fimbriata', 'Mme Isaac Pereire' (what scented garden should be without it?), 'Quatre Saisons', tall, rangy 'William Lobb', the globular, deep-pink 'René d'Anjou' with its bronze-tinted moss and sweet scent, and finally a hedge of 'Ispahan' as you approach the greenhouse.

Sweet Williams, straight out of the cottage gardens of the past, cover the ground below the roses and, with their associations with other times, somehow symbolize what has been seen. Already acclaimed for the skill with which they have used aromatic plants, the Acloques deserve equal fame for their roses.

Hidcote Manor

Hidcote Bartrim, Chipping Campden

Three and a half miles north of Chipping Campden. Take B4081 and turn east at junction with A46 to Hidcote Bartrim. Well signposted.
Tel. 038 677 333
The National Trust
Open daily, except Tuesdays and Fridays, from April to end October

Hidcote Manor set a fashion in gardening almost by accident. Major Lawrence Johnston, who created the garden from 1905 onwards, started with a bare and windswept site on the edge of the Cotswold Hills. Windbreaks were needed but he had the imagination to make these into the predominant feature of the garden, not simply surrounding the whole with tall trees or hedges but using the hedges, mainly of beech and holly, to divide it into a series of garden 'rooms' of varying size, each with a different planting theme. The garden was not open to the public until it was taken over by the National Trust, but Major Johnston had many gardening friends who saw and admired what he had done and adapted his ideas elsewhere. Vita Sackville-West was one and you can see the influence of Hidcote very markedly at Sissinghurst Castle.

Hidcote is big enough to be able to accommodate many kinds of garden within its boundaries and once the trees and hedges had grown and provided the much-needed protection, it became possible to open out many areas. Woodlands with appropriate shade-loving plants in the damp, peaty soil alternate with long vistas as in the Lime Avenue, the Beech Allée and the Long Walk, so that there is plenty of variety.

Major Johnston was a lover of the old varieties of roses, and began to collect them together at Hidcote long before it was fashionable to do so. He realized how well their soft mauves, purples and pinks, and their informal habit of growth, would blend in with and enhance plantings of other shrubs and flowers, so everywhere you go in the garden they are to be seen in ones and twos, and in small clumps. Even in the otherwise rather gloomy entrance courtyard 'Violette' and that old favourite 'Gloire de Dijon' do their best to brighten up the walls.

Once inside the garden, of course, any gloom vanishes. It is difficult to set a course to follow as paths lead off in all directions, but the official guide has a good map. The garden yard, right by the entrance and the shop, has the Noisette rose 'Rêve d'Or' on one wall and, if you decide first of all to make for the Old Garden, dominated by its great Cedar of Lebanon, you will find in the beds and on the walls fine specimens of 'Complicata', *R. californica* 'Plena', *R. glauca*, 'Felicia', 'Buff Beauty', 'Vanity', 'Lavender Pinocchio', 'Magenta', 'Texas Centennial', which was a sport of the old Hybrid Tea 'President Herbert Hoover' that occurred in 1935, 'Frau Karl Druschki', 'Natalie Nypels' and, of course, right along one wall, a number of plants of that marvellous yellow (but once-flowering) climber 'Lawrence Johnston'.

In his fascinating book *Climbing Roses Old and New* Graham Thomas tells how the raiser, Pernet-Ducher, produced two varieties from the same cross in 1923. The parents were 'Mme Eugène Verdier' and *R. foetida persiana* and one of the resulting roses was 'La Rêve', which Pernet-Ducher preferred, and put on the market. Major Lawrence Johnston saw the other rose and thought it the better of the two. He bought the only plant for Hidcote and called it 'Hidcote Yellow', the name it continued to bear until, in 1948, Graham Thomas asked if he could exhibit it at the Royal Horticultural Society, where it won an Award of Merit, and Mr Thomas persuaded Major Lawrence to agree to change its name to 'Lawrence Johnston'. The original plant is still at Hidcote and both it and the others of that ilk more than justify his faith in it.

At the entrance to the Tea Rooms are the climbers 'Souvenir de Claudius Denoyel' and 'Mme Caroline Testout' and if you move on to the White Garden you will find low-growing 'Gruss an Aachen' and an anything but low-growing 'Frau Karl Druschki' among other white flowers, spring and summer bulbs, *Anaphalis triplinervis*, *Campanula latiloba*, *Fuchsia magellanica* 'Molinae' and many more.

As I have said already, everywhere you go roses appear: 'Golden Wings', 'Penelope', 'Cupid', 'Frühlingsgold', 'Iceberg', 'Bobbie James' scrambling through a holm oak, 'Francis E. Lester' on a pine, *R. hugonis* and *R.* × 'Hidcote Gold', a hybrid between *R. hugonis* and *R. sericea*, which was raised at Hidcote in 1948 and has single, canary-yellow blooms. In the Pine Garden are Rugosas and a hedge of the Hybrid Musk 'Cornelia' with, arching above them, the long shoots of *R.* × 'Highdownensis' spangled with velvety crimson flowers. And from the Pine Garden you can pass straight into the Old Rose Walk which, from the point of view of the rose lover – and for others, too – is the high point of a visit to Hidcote.

It consists of a long straight path with wide borders on either side in which an enormous variety of the old French roses mixes enchantingly with lupins, paeonies (to give colour in May before the roses), day lilies and Japanese anemones, with hardy pinks and geraniums, various forms of sage and penstemons ('Hidcote Pink' is one of them) for edging, all with a tall backing of French hybrid lilacs, up which some of the roses wend their way.

You enter the Rose Walk through an opening in a yew hedge with various Moyesii varieties on either side and the soft-pink blooms of 'Stanwell Perpetual' sheltering under one of them. A short avenue of clipped Portuguese laurels comes next, and then you are among the roses. And what do you find there? Picking out only a selection there is 'Francofurtana' (which I prefer to call by its other name of 'Empress Josephine'), 'Surpasse Tout', 'William Lobb', 'Marcel Bourgouin', 'Mme Zöetmans', 'Fru Dagmar Hastrup', 'Chapeau de Napoléon', 'Zigeuner Knabe', 'Nuits de Young', 'F. J. Grootendorst', 'Oeillet Panachée', 'Charles de Mills', 'Pompon Parfait', *R.* × *alba* 'Maxima', *R. multibracteata*, 'Lanei', *R. elegantula persetosa*, 'Cardinal de Richelieu', 'Petite Lisette', 'St Nicholas', 'Louis Gimard', 'Maiden's Blush', 'Fantin Latour', 'Sissinghurst Castle' ('Rose des Maures'), 'Félicité Parmentier', 'Tuscany Superb', 'President de Sèze', 'Mousseline' ('Alfred de Dalmas'), 'Baronne Prévost', 'Mme Plantier' and finally, its huge, arching, almost thornless canes mixing with other shrubs, a beautiful specimen of the species *R. setipoda*. This rose, coming from Western China, will reach some 2.7 by 2.7 m (9 by 9 ft), as it does here, and has enchanting single flowers in loose corymbs that are pale pink, fading to white in the centre and with deeply notched petals. They are fully 5 cm (2 in) across and are followed by rather hairy, flagon-shaped hips. Only its size when fully grown can account for the fact that it is rarely seen in modern gardens, but there are two here and another one if you turn left at the end of the path, together with a planting of *R. rugosa* 'Alba', and 'Blanc Double de Coubert', 'Nevada' and silver-leaved plants such as the Scots thistle *Onopordum acanthium* and *Rubus deliciosus*.

The garden then opens out to a newly created orchard, the young pear and apple trees by no means fully established so that you can see through them, at the far side of the grass, a hedge of the striped Gallica rose 'Rosa Mundi', surrounding two sides of the vegetable garden. I paced this out and found that it is something like 108 m (120 yds) in length and is spectacularly beautiful in full bloom. It owes its origin, I believe, to the similar but earlier hedge at Kiftsgate Manor nearby.

It remains only to walk back along the outside of the Old Rose Walk, between it and the 'Rosa Mundi' hedge, and to pick out a few of the varieties that have been planted so far back in the rose borders that they may have been missed. Two such are the Bourbons 'Mme Lauriol de Barny', with its full, quartered, silvery-pink flowers, and a vast, sprawling bush of 'Bourbon Queen' which, judging by its size, finds Hidcote Manor garden as much to its liking as the visitors do.

Kiftsgate Court

Chipping Campden

Take B4081 3½ miles north of Chipping Campden and turn east to Hidcote Bartrim at junction with A46. Just up road from Hidcote Manor, so follow Hidcote National Trust signs.
Tel. 038 677 777
Mr and Mrs J. G. Chambers
Open, garden only, from April to end of September, Wednesdays, Thursdays and Sundays. Also open on Bank Holiday Mondays.

Kiftsgate Court was built in the late nineteenth century by Sydney Garves Hamilton, who owned the Manor House in nearby Mickleton. The Georgian front of the latter, with its high portico, was actually moved bodily to the new site on a specially built light railway and used in the new building, forming a most impressive façade. In 1918 the house was bought by Mr and Mrs J. B. Muir (the lovely single white shrub rose, *R. sericea* 'Heather Muir', was named after Mrs Muir) and has been in the

same family ever since. The Muirs' daughter, Mrs Binny, now looks after it for her own daughter and her husband, the present owners. She has all of her mother's talent for choosing the right plant for the right place and for blending harmoniously not only the colours and forms of flowers but those of foliage as well.

The house is most spectacularly sited high on the northernmost spur of the Cotswold Hills, although it is not until you are well into the garden, beyond the house and a band of trees, that you realize that it is built on a shelf of land and that the land falls away steeply below you. There are glimpses of magnificent views through the trees and Broadway Tower is on the distant skyline. Winding paths lead down the slope to the lower garden and the semicircular swimming pool but descent is steep and there are not many roses there. The same cannot be said, however, for the rest of the garden. The worst you will have to contend with are a few steps, and there are roses everywhere.

From the drive you enter the garden through a small wicket gate and a gravel path leads round the side of the house to a paved area on several levels. Immediately below to the left is a large bed with roses predominantly in shades of red, including the McGredy Floribunda of 1960 called 'Sherry', aptly named for its rich, dark coppery-red colouring. This is in one of four beds that go to make up the Four Squares garden, the others containing roses such as 'Lavender Lassie', 'Magenta', 'Mme Pierre Oger', and the Tea rose 'Rita' in blue-mauve, not to be confused with the rich pink Floribunda of the same name which came from Fryer's nurseries in 1960. To one side a paved half-circle is backed by a hedge of the Hybrid Musk 'Felicia' and other roses in the area are *R. elegantula persetosa*, magenta-crimson 'Russeliana' sprawling over the terrace wall at one corner, 'Cramoisi Superieur', 'Cosmopolyte', 'Crimson Conquest', 'Dusky Maiden', 'Frensham', 'Maid of Honour' (a Kordes 'Crimson Glory' cross with large, fragrant, single, salmon-pink lowers in trusses), another Kordes variety, the Hybrid Musk 'München', 'Red Favourite', 'Robert Le Diable' and 'Scarlet Fire' on a wooden frame.

Standing with your back to the house wall all these can be seen from the terrace round the house, where *Magnolia delavayi* with a trunk like a tree and *Lonicera* 'Splendide' are trained

Opposite: *Roses below the first terrace at Kiftsgate Court. The China rose 'Mutabilis' scales the wall behind, reaching undreamed of heights.*

against the mellow Cotswold stonework. But by far the most remarkable climbing plant on the house walls is the rose 'Mutabilis', normally considered to have done well if it reaches 3 m (10 ft). Here it is up to the eaves, which means that it has climbed something like 9 m (30 ft), and with its multi-coloured blooms it is a sight to remember.

Moving down from the terrace and past the sundial in the middle of the Four Squares garden, that enchanting pink Sweet Brier 'Manning's Blush', which has been in cultivation since before 1832 (when it was first recorded), is on the left of you by a further flight of steps. At the bottom, paving gives way to grass paths and a gleaming white rose growing on a frame just ahead catches the eye. On closer inspection (and with a little help from Mrs Binny) this turns out to be the singularly beautiful 'Una', introduced in 1900 by George Paul. Probably a hybrid between a Tea rose and R. canina, it has inherited its hooked thorns and dull-green, serrated leaves from the latter, but its flowers are its glory. Semi-double, fully 7.5 cm (3 in) across and primrose-scented, they open from creamy-yellow buds. They are reminiscent of the flowers of 'Nevada' but there is a difference which is difficult to define, and I think the blooms of 'Una' are, if anything, the lovelier of the two. It will make a strong climber up to about 3 m (10 ft) but is not recurrent.

Ahead to the left, with the steep drop down to the lower garden just beyond them, are several plants of 'Frühlingsgold', 'Blush Damask', 'De Meaux' and a few others, but at this point you turn right onto a path with herbaceous plants in beds on either side, interplanted with roses. These include R. willmottiae, the Polyantha 'Natalie Nypels' and its cousin 'Nypels Perfection', 'Petite de Hollande' and 'Empress Josephine', one of a number of roses planted at Kiftsgate pre-war. 'Centenaire de Lourdes', a rose from 1958, with a good deal of 'Frau Karl Druschki' in its parentage and semi-double, soft rose-pink flowers, is there too, against the background of the huge, Greco-Cotswold pillared portico of the house. To the right are R. californica 'Plena', a vast 'Cerise Bouquet', 'Mutabilis', 'Pompon de Paris' and R. moyesii 'Geranium'.

A left turn through wrought-iron gates takes you into the White Garden, with an octagonal pool and a fountain in the middle of the paved area. This, Mrs Binny explains, is basically a spring garden but there are roses to give later colour, even though they are predominantly white. It is here that R. sericea 'Heather Muir' is to be found. There cannot be many other gardens where there are roses named after two members of one family, as there are here, the other being, of course, 'Diany Binny', a vigorous, tree-climbing variety which Mrs Binny herself feels could flower rather more profusely than it does. R. soulieana adds its white flowers and grey-green leaves to the overall white theme, together with R. × alba 'Semi-plena', and up steps ahead is the single-flowered Hybrid Tea 'White Wings'. Along a paved path, R. brunonii 'La Mortola' provides a splash of white against a high wall and two fine specimens of Cornus kousa chinensis are immediately ahead beside the path. Cooper's Burmese Rose (R. cooperi) and the rambler 'Lady Godiva' adorn another wall as you make your way towards an opening in a beech hedge that crosses this part of the garden. And it is at this point that the trumpets sound for, as you pass through it, you come into the daunting presence of the famous, or perhaps almost infamous, Kiftsgate Rose (R. filipes 'Kiftsgate').

Originally brought to the garden as a R. moschata seedling (I believe from the Royal Horticultural Society garden at Wisley) its size is staggering. It has already brought down one or more oak trees and is at the moment slowly swallowing an enormous copper beech. It flowers late in July, and though this is still spectacular, its shoots grow 4.5 m (15 ft) or more in a year, and, as Mrs Binny points out, by the time that flowering occurs they have developed to the extent that they tend to hide the huge panicles of bloom. In one panicle alone, 410 flowers have been counted, so to count the total number of flowers on the plant would be a thankless task. The rose is a phenomenon that has spread its progeny far and wide, but none of them has so far equalled the Kiftsgate Rose for sheer size.

'Kiftsgate' has thus far diverted and held the eye, but it has strong competition in late June and early July from the long double hedge of 'Rosa Mundi' that runs past it along both sides of a wide grass path. At its peak, this is as striking in its own way, but it is not a garden feature to be adopted without careful consideration in a small or even a medium-sized garden. When out of flower, and particularly in the latter part of the season, Gallica foliage is far from beautiful and mildew can be a problem, something that is almost unnoticed in a garden the size of Kiftsgate Court, but an eyesore for a large part

The beautiful white 'Una', a rose featured at Kiftsgate Court but seldom seen elsewhere.

of the season in a more limited space. At Kiftsgate, however, for the sheer gaiety of its few weeks of flowering, it is something not to be missed, and even though there is apparently considerable reversion from the pink-and white-striped flowers of 'Rosa Mundi' to the deep pink of the parent 'Officinalis', the overall effect is scarcely diminished.

Behind the 'Rosa Mundi' hedges are wide borders of shrub roses and other shrubs and plants. Another path runs behind the left-hand border and rejoins it after a while. Along it one can find 'Mary Rose', 'Nypel's Perfection', *Deutzia* 'Rosalind', 'Chianti' (on a bamboo frame, as are many of the others), 'Stanwell Perpetual', 'Mme Ernst Calvat', 'Mme Hardy', 'Cardinal de Richelieu', 'Honorine de Brabant' and the very beautiful, fragrant, soft-pink Centifolia 'Gros Choux d'Hollande' where the two paths merge once more. There, too, is a white deutzia and the rose 'Una' once again, at the point where you walk under a carefully trained arch of grey-leaved *Sorbus lutescens* into a small fernery. There the fronds of a multitude of different ferns form a striking contrast to what has gone before.

From the fernery a gravel path leads back along the edge of the drop down to the lower garden, where 'Nevada' roses alternate with *Philadelphus coronarius* 'Aureus' along the edge, making a striking combination. Down some steps to the right and there is a grey border on your left before the path leads you out onto a small lawn and the wicket gate through which you entered the garden.

Many people, I am sure, visit this garden just to see the Kiftsgate Rose, but though this is perhaps the star attraction, it is a garden of many other delights and with a fine range of plants of many kinds. And all, of course, in a dramatic setting.

John Mattock Roses

Nuneham Courtney

In Clifton Lane (B4015) off main Oxford–Henley–Maidenhead road, A423. Signposted.
Tel. 086 738 265
The Display Garden of John Mattock Limited
Open every day.

It could be argued (particularly by the owners of other nurseries) that the nursery display gardens listed in this book should not be there. However, if they form rose gardens in their own right I think that they do deserve a place, as they serve a useful purpose when they are used to show off many of the old roses and particularly the species. In the ones I have chosen you do get a very wide range, bigger by far than you would find in most gardens, and for someone new to growing them it is possible to see what they will look like in maturity. It is difficult to visualize, looking at first-year plants in the nursery itself, what the final size and sheer bulk of some of the more rampant growers may be.

At the Mattock nursery the display garden is next door to the garden centre shop. Along one

The grass path, flanked by shrub roses of every kind, leading to the small fernery at Kiftsgate Court near Chipping Campden.

side of this over a long terrace is a wooden pergola-type canopy that supports white-flowered 'The Garland', growing with its usual enthusiasm. In front of the terrace and leading away to the right is a large rectangular area of grass with nine beds cut in it that contain a wide variety of Hybrid Tea and Floribunda roses, including such varieties as 'Benson and Hedges Gold', the McGredy rose 'Rocky' in bright red, 'Congratulations', 'Simba', 'Olympiad', 'Keepsake', 'Tranquillity' and so on, but as these will be changed periodically for newer varieties, it is best perhaps to say simply that there are bedding roses there.

From this part of the garden, move down the grassy slope at one end and turn left at a small wooden pavilion round which are clustered three large bushes of *R. californica* 'Plena' while another stands off to the right. Ahead of you now is a long bed of shrub roses and a shorter one to the left. In both there is a great mixture of varieties, some modern, some old garden roses and some species, while here and there are small clusters of Floribundas which, although looking rather dwarfed by the others, are there to give greater continuity of colour. Of the modern shrubs (listing only a few examples) there are yellow 'Lady Sonia', 'Kathleen Ferrier' and 'Fountain'; of the old garden roses 'Tour de Malakoff', 'Honorine de Brabant' and 'Mme Hardy'; and of the species 'Helen Knight' growing as a shrub and not as a climber, *R. forrestiana* and *R. sweginzowii*, the hips of which resemble nothing so much as small, highly polished carrots. Another rose I was glad to see was 'Kazanlik'. I have myself grown what I believe to be the very old Damask rose 'Trigintipetala' for many years, which the books say is the same as 'Kazanlik'. For my money, the latter is much darker in the colouring of both its flowers and leaves, and certainly 'Kazanlik' in the Mattock garden seems to confirm this – assuming, of course, that what I have got is, in fact, 'Trigintipetala', as mine came from a cutting of a rose found in Greece. The name 'Kazanlik' comes from the town of that name in Bulgaria where for centuries the rose has been grown for the production of Attar of Roses.

At the far end of the rose garden, a number of varieties are planted in the grass as free-standing shrubs, again a mixture of different kinds, and after seeing them there is a choice of paths back. You can go either between further long beds or down a broad grass area where there

are rustic frames on which climbers grow, mostly modern ones like the McGredy trio named after Irish bays – Dublin, Bantry and Galway – with the rambler 'Bobbie James' as the odd-man-out. If you take the other route, past more shrub roses, you will find, as before, a good if a fairly conventional selection, though two roses I spotted are not often seen. One that was a real newcomer to me was the Kordes-raised 'Lichtkönigin Lucia', which is of medium size and has bright yellow flowers and very good foliage. I was even more surprised to find that it was introduced twenty years ago. Golden-orange 'Westerland' (Kordes again) was the other.

Planted among the roses and giving them an added attraction are many flowering cherries, *Prunus avium* 'Plena' and *Prunus* 'Kanzan' among others, and also dark-leaved *Acer platanoides* 'Crimson King'. *Berberis thunbergii* 'Atropurpurea' forms a hedge down one side of the garden.

Oxford Botanic Gardens

Oxford

Rose Lane, Oxford.
Tel. 0865 242737
University of Oxford; Superintendent: Mr J. K. Burras
Open every day.

This is the oldest botanic garden in Britain and the second oldest in Europe. It was founded in 1621 on the banks of the river Cherwell with the intention of cultivating plants for herbalists and apothecaries. It is highly likely that roses were among the plants grown, for their main value in those times was as medicinal rather than decorative plants. In fact, a number of the varieties that can be seen in the garden now, such as 'Rosa Mundi' and 'Quatre Saisons' (the Autumn Damask), date from at least the fifteenth century if not earlier, so it is at least possible that they have been growing there ever since, although not necessarily in the same beds.

You enter from the High Street, just beside Magdalen Bridge, and immediately to the right, with only railings separating it from the street, is a rose garden dedicated to the research workers of Oxford University who discovered the clinical importance of penicillin. Box hedges of varying heights enclose the beds in which can be found a rather unpredictable mixture of old garden, species and modern roses which do not, to my mind, always go very well together. Thus 'Mme Isaac Pereire' rubs shoulders with the 'Peace' sport, 'Kronenbourg' ('Flaming Peace'), *R. multibracteata* with 'Chinatown', various Hybrid Musks with 'Fountain', 'Scarlet Fire' with 'Celestial' and so it goes on. At the far end there is a planting of *R. glauca* (*R. rubrifolia*), hardly at its best as it is in the shade of some trees.

Things improve when, leaving this first garden behind, you pass through a small gate beside the impressive main entrance (designed by Inigo Jones) into the Botanic Garden proper. A long gravel path leads straight ahead and to reach the first of the roses, follow this to the point where the second of two intersecting paths crosses it. Turn left and you will see roses on your right.

These are arranged in four beds in a line and they should be seen in sequence (from the other end) for they illustrate the main stream of the story of the rose and also explore one or two interesting byways. Thus the first bed in the line shows what are usually termed minor species and their variants, like the Dog Rose, the Sweet Brier and the Scotch roses that are native to the United Kingdom. From the colder parts of the USA and Northern Europe there is *R. acicularis* (pink-flowered and sometimes known as the Arctic Rose), while the important China group includes Rugosas, *R. bracteata*, *R. roxburghii*, *R. banksiae* and *R. moyesii* 'Geranium'.

The second bed shows first known crosses between species, for instance *R. rubiginosa* × *R. foetida* producing the Sweet Brier hybrid 'Lady Penzance', *R. rugosa* × *R. wichuraiana* producing 'Max Graf' and *R. pimpinellifolia* × *R. foetida* producing 'Harison's Yellow'. The same bed also shows hybrids away from the main lines of

A superb bloom of the very fragrant Bourbon rose 'Mme. Isaac Pereire'.

breeding such as the Grootendorst Rugosas with their frilled petals, the climber 'Mermaid', 'Nevada' (which may or may not have a Moyesii seedling in its veins) and the Boursault roses in the form of 'Amadis', here given the disputed prefix R. × lheritierana, which is discussed in the account of Mottisfont Abbey.

The third bed parades the main ancestral species and their varieties – from the East, R. moschata, R. chinensis, R. multiflora, R. gigantea and R. wichuraiana, and from the West, Gallicas, Damasks, Centifolias and Moss roses, with R. foetida from the Middle East. In each case, sample roses of these progenitors are shown.

The fourth bed starts with hybrid varieties from 1800 to 1880, which, of course, includes the Bourbons, Noisettes, Hybrid Chinas, Hybrid Perpetuals and Tea roses, showing very clearly what an important eighty years that was in the long history of the garden rose. The story from 1880 onwards comes next: more Hybrid Perpetuals and Teas, the Pernetianas, the Wichuraiana ramblers, the Polyanthas and Floribundas, the Hybrid Teas and, almost, it seems, as an afterthought, the Hybrid Musk roses.

There were gaps in the beds when I saw them last owing to an exceptionally severe winter and it is to be hoped that replacements for the more difficult roses will be found. The roses on the surrounding walls, however, of which there are no fewer than thirty-three varieties, had more protection and seemed not to suffer, even such tender beauties as R. × hemispherica (R. sulphurea or the Sulphur Rose) and R. × anemonoides surviving unharmed.

If you carry straight on after the historical beds and cross the main central path, you come to another path which curves to the left following the line of an immensely long shrub rose border. A lot of the roses in it are inevitably familiar but there are many that are less so. For instance, pink-flowered 'Glory of Edzell' (possibly a Pimpinellifolia hybrid) and the very lovely 'Mannings Blush', a Rubiginosa hybrid as is 'Amy Robsart' nearby. Among the species are R. acicularis again, R. 'Macrantha', R. forrestiana, R. multibracteata (which has mahogany-coloured prickles and lilac-pink flowers sheathed in grey-green leafy bracts), R. macrophylla, 'Golden Chersonese', R. woodsii fendleri and the Burnet rose 'Blushing Bride', as well as a number of other Scotch roses. It is a very impressive collection and it is a pity that it suffers, as any garden must that is open all the

time to the public, especially in or near a big town, from the absence or misplacing of labels. Fortunately there is a label on a real rarity, 'Allen's Fragrant Pillar', a climbing Hybrid Tea from 1931 with large double flowers, cerise-pink, flushed yellow. 'Paul's Lemon Pillar' was one parent and 'Souvenir de Claudius de Denoyel' the other.

We started inside the gate with one oddity. Here is another: some of David Austin's English roses, such as 'Mary Rose', 'Abraham Darby', 'Emmanuel' and 'Fair Bianca' – none of them tall growers – appear to have been recently planted behind roses that will reach three or four times their size. Nevertheless, there are some wonderful things to enjoy in this garden.

Ivy Lodge

Radway

Take A41 north-west of Banbury and then B4086. Turn left just before Edgehill. Drive leads past a number of cottages before reaching house.
Tel. 029 587 371
Mrs M. A. Willis
Open under the National Gardens Scheme.

The garden here was just a field when Mrs Willis came to it thirty years ago, difficult though it is to believe this now. It is still, however, a very open site with a view from the house of wide lawns gently stepped up every 27 m (30 yds) or so as the ground rises slightly. On the second step is a pond with the white flowers of R. × paulii framing it. Down both sides of the garden large island beds with trees, roses and other shrubs break up the expanse of green. Beyond the garden the land rises steeply towards the ridge of Edgehill and the monument can be seen amongst the trees at the top marking the spot where King Charles I looked down on the first battle of the Civil War in 1642. It was actually fought over the land where Ivy Lodge stands today, but the house itself is eighteenth century with later alterations. Among these are the crenellated parapets overlooking the forecourt added by Mrs Willis herself and the wide paved patio at the back. This has a low stone surround, beyond which are flowerbeds.

Two square tubs on the patio contain the azalea 'Beauty' and outside the French windows the pink blooms of 'The Fairy' are underplanted with campanulas. Hardy pink geraniums abound and in a bed to the right are self-sown foxgloves, the ever-faithful 'Iceberg' and the American rose 'Apricot Nectar', with its pinky-apricot blooms some 11 cm (4½ in) across and its strong, fruity fragrance. Away to the left is a small summerhouse with 'Bobbie James' scrambling up an almond tree nearby. Further over is what Mrs Willis refers to, very aptly, as her 'tapestry hedge' with its blended leaves of differing colours.

Moving out from the house along the right-hand side of the garden, you find a planting of the China rose 'Mutabilis' in one of the first of the island beds. Thorn trees and hollies line the boundary and both here and in many other places throughout the garden the snowy white blossoms of philadelphus scent the air in June and early July. There can be few trees or large shrubs that do not have a climbing or rambling rose in them and 'Rambling Rector' and 'Bantry Bay' are two of the first you see. Nearby is the unusual 'Harry Maasz', a spreading, trailing rose rather than a climber, with large, semi-double flowers in cherry-red, paling towards the boss of orange stamens in the centre.

A garden of this size can quite happily accommodate large thickets of native wild roses, the Dog Rose and the rest, and they are there in plenty at Ivy Lodge. In some cases they were originally the rootstocks of other roses, but they are no less beautiful for that and Mrs Willis welcomes them and lets them have their head. Equally strong-willed is a 'Paul's Himalayan Musk Rambler' (supported by an ilex) which must be about 12.2 m (40 ft) tall by about 6 m (20 ft) across the base. Its leaves literally vanish beneath the tens of thousands of pale pink flowers, while close by there are large beds containing 'Cerise Bouquet' (for once not dwarfing its surroundings), 'Zéphirine Drouhin', 'Stanwell Perpetual', R. soulieana, 'Marguerite Hilling' and three bushes of 'Maigold' used as a shrub rather than a climber. 'Seagull', 'Rambling Rector' and 'Max Graf' are climbers nearby.

There is a spinney at the top of the garden, each tree with its rose or roses, and as one crosses to the other side and turns towards the house there are large plantings of 'Nevada' and 'Marguerite Hilling' and 'Maigold' once more, which give a marvellous splash of concentrated colour. It would be difficult to think of three roses that put on a more glorious display in June each year and two of them do have some flowers later. They have 'Kassel', R. longicuspis, 'New Dawn', 'Frühlingsgold' and various Rugosas for neighbours, while not too far away 'Kiftsgate' is taking on the challenge of a large oak tree. And 'Max Graf' is again used here as a climber, rather than for ground-cover, logically enough as it is after all a hybrid of R. wichuraiana.

A narrow stream leads back in the general direction of the house, and you can now see a meadow, enchanting in early summer with wild flowers. Each year Mrs Willis plants tulips to mingle with them in a most delightful way, provided the badgers do not dig them up first. (This problem has only been solved with the installation of a low-slung electric fence.)

You pass 'Nathalie Nypels' and 'Nypels' Perfection' as you make your way towards an avenue of espaliered limes with a large urn from the old Crystal Palace as its focal point.

A double line of fruit trees, underplanted with strawberries, leads on towards the house, and past it you turn left towards the swimming pool and the summerhouse. As usual, roses crop up all the time, R. × paulii, 'Wedding Day', 'Mme Alfred Carrière', 'Little White Pet', 'Ballerina' and many more, while Kordes' pink and very fragrant 'Sparrieshoop' hides an old stump.

There are more roses to be seen at the front of the house, where a path leads between low box hedges from the forecourt out onto a wide grass path between two long beds. Thatched cottages can be glimpsed over the walls that border this part of the garden.

The beds contain some old roses but also many modern ones, together with lavender and purple-leaved berberis. 'Gruss an Aachen' is there, as is 'Dearest', 'Plentiful', 'Lady Lindsay', 'Kronenbourg' (much admired by visitors apparently but not, understandably to my mind, by Mrs Willis), 'Magenta', looking much more robust than usual and less in need of crutches, 'Kassel', and finally 'Aloha', equally at home as a shrub or climber. At the end of the path is a sundial, cheerfully hiding the frustration of being almost entirely in the shade of a very large willow.

But then most things look happy in this garden. They are allowed plenty of room to spread themselves, and have air and sunshine (any that is going) in abundance.

Warwick Castle

Warwick

In the centre of Warwick.
Tel. 0926 49521
Open all year.

The origins of the first Victorian Rose Garden at Warwick Castle date back to 1868. It was then that George Guy, the fourth Earl of Warwick, commissioned Robert Marnock, designer of the Royal Botanic Society's garden in Regent's Park, to introduce some flower gardens into the castle grounds. They were already attractive, for the landscaping of them had been one of 'Capability' Brown's earliest commissions. However, by the second half of the nineteenth century something more than long vistas of parkland with lakes and venerable oaks and beech plantations was wanted, as flowers had become fashionable once more. The excellence of Marnock's design for the rose garden, 'a charming and secluded rosary', according to *The Gardeners' Chronicle* of the day, has probably never been surpassed.

The original rose garden vanished long ago, but in 1979, quite by chance, Paul Edwards, the castle's landscape and garden consultant, came across two of Marnock's drawings in the Warwickshire County Record Office and recognized at once the historical importance of the discovery. Accompanying the drawings was the original design for much of the decorative architectural ironwork used to support the rambler and climbing roses.

With such information available, as well as the original site, it was decided to start on a re-creation of the garden. Brambles and weeds had to be cleared away, as well as the remains of a 1930s tennis court, and then new topsoil was brought in. Local craftsmen were commissioned to assemble the ironwork for the arbours and arches, and in the autumn of 1984 more than 700 roses were planted under the supervision of the castle's head gardener. They were given a season to establish themselves before the garden was opened to the public in 1986.

The garden is approached by a long path that passes beneath no fewer than thirteen arches, on each of which an 'Albéric Barbier' displays its creamy blooms and immaculate gleaming foliage. All round the garden are trees, including a holm oak, an enormous acacia and many others, but they are far enough away from the perimeter not to cast their shadows over the roses, except perhaps early and late in the day. Through them you catch glimpses of the castle towers and the spires of nearby churches, while to one side is another feature resurrected from the past. Paths lead upwards past a shady pool into which water flows over ancient stones in a small cascade so that the gentle sound of the falling water pervades the garden at all times.

The rose garden itself is geometric in design with island beds, some linked by gravel paths and some with grass round them. Everywhere there are metal arches, pillars and bowers, and the boundary of the rose garden itself is one continuous bed backed by a metal framework, broken only in a few places by arches over which roses like 'Adélaide d'Orléans', 'Félicité et Perpétue' and 'May Queen' are trained. Twenty-four iron tripods, set in the grass at intervals, in keeping with the overall geometric design, are almost hidden from view under the massed blooms of 'The Garland', but it is in the perimeter bed that the unusual use of a number of the old roses occurs. Many of the Bourbons and more particularly the Hybrid Perpetuals are leggy and ungainly growers if left to their own devices. Here they are trained in continuous lines on metal posts linked by curved rails, rather in the manner of a catenary. The roses chosen are 'Boule de Neige', 'Baron Girod de l'Ain', 'La Reine Victoria', 'Commandant Beaurepaire', 'Gruss an Teplitz' and 'Variegata di Bologna', and it is an admirable way of keeping them under control. They are beautifully grown and obviously cherished; I have seldom seen such sturdy specimens with such fine foliage and sumptuous blooms.

'De Meaux' and 'Little White Pet' are used as weeping standards and there are beds of, amongst others, 'Old Blush', 'La France' and 'Mary Rose'. The latter, with its lovely, many-petalled pink flowers, seems slightly out of place in a Victorian rose garden, since it was introduced in 1983 and named to mark the recovery of Henry VIII's flagship from the Solent! I suppose you could say the same about the lovely soft-purple 'Warwick Castle' that fills the central bed under four linked arches of the rambler 'Aimée Vibert', but it was raised and named especially by David Austin to celebrate the rebirth of this lovely rose garden, and as such more than justifies its place.

Duxford Mill

Duxford

Duxford signposted at junction 10 of M11 and A505,
the Royston–Newmarket road. In Duxford, turn left
down Mill Lane. House on right.
Tel. 0223 832325
Mr and Mrs Robert Lea
Open under the National Gardens Scheme.

Duxford Mill has a garden that gives the lie to the belief that you can only plant trees for posterity. Practically every tree in this garden, over a thousand of them, has been planted by the Leas since they bought the mill just after the last war, and many have reached or are approaching maturity. It is difficult to imagine that they have not always been there.

The mill itself, a building of great attractions, is part white-painted weather boarding and part brick, with a mansard roof, and dates back to Norman times. Reference to a mill on this site is made in the Domesday Book survey of 1080: 'One Mill here worth 12s. It is broken and can be repaired' was how it was described, though this may perhaps have been a slightly earlier building on the same site. Oliver Cromwell was a frequent visitor, as was Charles Kingsley who, it is claimed, wrote at least a part of *The Water Babies* here.

In front of the mill today a wide gravel terrace overlooks the mill pool and stone steps lead down to a smaller, lower terrace which is almost at water level. Standing on the upper one, if you can draw your gaze away from the giant trout loafing in the crystal clear water at your feet, you look down almost the full length of the garden. In the foreground is the pool and beyond it what is actually an island in the River Cam. On it, like a sentinel, stands what is reputed to be the tallest weeping willow in England, some 23 m (75 ft) high and unusually upright for its kind, while on either side of the garden two huge curved rose borders catch the eye with their blaze of colour. A small classical temple is in the distance and behind it, against the skyline, the Leas have planted a frieze of

ornamental trees to give the maximum variety of outlines, texture and leaf colour.

At one side of the house is the old mill sluice and if you take the path past it, you climb a grassy slope beside a stream on which swans glide in an idyllic setting. Below you to the left is the tennis court and beyond it are the flood gates, where the waters of the river divide to form the island on which part of the garden stands. A small footbridge takes you to an area of grass where there is a wired-off enclosure with a pond for ornamental waterfowl. Beyond this you encounter the first rose of the garden to be seen at close quarters, a rose that Mr Lea knows as *R. lucens*, though it is perhaps better known by its alternative name of *R. longicuspis*. Bear it in mind, as it will shortly appear again in the story of this garden. At this point it is happily climbing a tree.

R. lucens came to us from China in 1915, but there are not, in fact, very many old roses in this garden as the Leas believe that their plants should give colour over as long a period as possible. However, there is (inevitably) 'Kiftsgate' (in a rather subdued mood) and a little further on, past a spring water garden with primulas, marsh marigolds, hostas and astilbes, the rose 'Treasure Trove', a 'Kiftsgate' seedling that was raised in 1961 at the Worcestershire home of John Treasure, the clematis specialist. It has loosely double flowers of a yellowish-apricot colouring and the same coppery coloured young shoots and vigour as its parent. Here it is growing up a large walnut tree and not too far away are two specimens of the 'fossil tree' *Metasequoia glyptostroboides* which were grown by Mrs Lea from cuttings from the first tree sent to this country by the Arnold Arboretum in 1948.

By now we are moving along the river bank once more where, rather improbably, roses like 'Canary Bird' and another *R. lucens* (which was up a poplar that blew down) were being swamped when I saw them by the lush growth of the immensely tall Indian Balsam (*Impatiens glandulifera*), a cousin of the familiar Busy Lizzie. Ahead lies an area where vegetables and flowers for cutting are grown, and beyond that are several island beds with many shrub roses in them, grown as much for their foliage effect as for their flowers, *R. glauca* prominent among them.

It may not seem very much like it from the description so far, but there are some 2000 roses in the garden altogether and about 250 varieties. And what gives many of them a particular fascination (not to say merit) is that they have been bred by the Leas themselves. I discovered that I must, without realizing it, have seen some of them before, for when a number were sent for trial to the Royal National Rose Society (RNRS) Trial Grounds I must have assessed them for a possible award. None have so far been successful, but looking at some of them in the Leas' own garden, one wonders why they have not shown up quite so well at St Albans. However, Mr Lea, who does the rose hybridizing, is not really interested in their commercial potential: an award would be a pleasant bonus and a considerable achievement but no more.

The first bed of mixed Hybrid Tea and Floribunda roses that you come to – and it is a very big bed indeed – is almost entirely made up of Lea varieties, though there are a few others such as the so-called ground-cover roses 'Rosy Cushion' and 'Red Blanket' and the very lovely 'Grace Abounding' raised by Jack Harkness, the flowers of which change from soft pink in the bud to cream as they open. In smaller beds nearby, *R. lucens* comes back into the picture for Mr Lea has used it quite extensively in his breeding programme even though it is reputed to be not quite hardy. There is a marvellous-looking white 'Pascali' × *R. lucens* cross which has fine coppery foliage, and ('Pascali' × *R. lucens*) × 'Ballerina' has given 'White Ballerina'. The original apple-blossom pink 'Ballerina' and also 'Marjorie Fair' are close by for comparison.

Nearby, the brilliant scarlet 'Dorothy Wheatcroft' fills a bed with its huge trusses of bloom intermingled with the purplish foliage of *Rhus cotinus coggygria* to great effect, and as you begin to walk back towards the house you pass on the right a winter border with coloured stems and foliage.

And so to the biggest rose planting, the longest rose border of all, that has some Lea varieties in it but also many from other raisers as well. As you approach it your eye is caught

Looking across the water at Duxford Mill to where roses surround the small classical temple.

first by another plant of the ground-cover rose 'Red Blanket' climbing a tree, which is a pretty extraordinary start. The rest are mixed Hybrid Tea and Floribunda varieties: 'Lilli Marlene', 'Escapade', 'Rusty Marge' (called that by the Leas because of its colour), 'Tradition', which is a very good scarlet-crimson Hybrid Tea from Kordes that you do not see often enough for its merits, 'Priscilla Burton' (in this garden appearing not to lose all its leaves by mid-June through black spot), the pretty multi-coloured 'Letchworth Garden City' and 'Regensberg'. 'Princess Alice', rapidly making a name for itself as one of the best new yellow Floribunda varieties, is there, too, as is 'Anne Harkness' which is also gaining a reputation as one of the best roses for cutting and for exhibition, and 'Firecracker', whose lovely rose-pink colour has never been matched by another rose since it was introduced in 1965.

To continue: 'News', 'Fred Loads' at the back and a good many miniatures of mixed vintage at the front, 'Strawberry Ice', which seems to do better here (and at St Albans) than it does in many other gardens, several of the so-called 'blue' roses including 'Intermezzo', 'Eye Paint' and the bilious-looking 'Greensleeves', and 'Saga', which, though usually grown as a fairly small shrub, does a good job here of helping to clothe the fence at the back of the border with its creamy white flowers, and is not even eclipsed by 'Maigold'. Nearby is another Lea variety called, in view of its bright orange-red colouring, 'Cheerful Charlie'. On the Miller's cottage, to the right at the end of this bed, an unpruned bush of the fragrant red American grandiflora rose, 'Carrousel', climbs to something like 3 m (10 ft).

Another large rose bed, this time reached by crossing the terrace in front of the house and

A bed containing many seedling roses raised by Mr Lea at Duxford Mill.

turning left instead of right as you did before, has another very varied selection, but I will only mention one of them, another Lea rose. 'Fragrant Cloud', crossed with *R. lucens*, has produced rather an unlikely offspring, a variety with most attractive semi-double flowers in pale pink and with fine dark leaves to set them off. Such a cross requires imagination, abundantly present in the Leas' garden at Duxford Mill. The stream and island give enormous natural advantages to the garden but the Leas have put them to excellent use.

Elton Hall

Peterborough

Five miles north of Oundle on A605. Well signposted.
Tel. 08324 468
Mr and Mrs William Proby
Open on Bank Holiday Sundays from Easter to August,
on Wednesdays from May to August and on Sundays
from July to August. Also by appointment.

Elton Hall, an imposing Gothic mansion, stands on a site on which there has been a house since the time of the Norman Conquest. It has been the home of the Proby family for over 300 years, since Sir Peter Proby, Lord Mayor of London and Comptroller of the Royal Household, was granted land and property at Elton by Queen Elizabeth I. His grandson, Sir Thomas Proby, completed the main house in 1666, incorporating the existing medieval chapel and gatehouse. Succeeding generations of the Proby family, particularly in the eighteenth century, enlarged and altered it so that the house seems now, at a superficial glance, to be less old than it is. Dominated by turrets, towers, tall chimneys and castellations, it looks rather austere as you approach it down the long drive from the road, but much less so as you move round to the south face. Here the high, arched windows look out over lawns and a parterre, while away to the right you get a glimpse of the rose garden.

The gardens as a whole are now being restored and something like a thousand new roses were put in during 1983 and 1984 under the supervision of Peter Beales, who drew up the planting plan for the rose garden and suggested what should go in the nineteen beds. It makes an impressive list.

The layout is formal, on the Victorian pattern, with beds set in the grass, but the planting is a mixture of formal and informal. There are, for instance, several beds containing only Hybrid Teas, like 'National Trust', 'Alec's Red', 'Blessings' and 'Shot Silk', but of the less formal plantings the roses in perhaps one sample bed will give the flavour of the whole: 'Cornelia', 'Mutabilis', 'Yvonne Rabier', 'Mme Hardy', 'Mme Legras de St Germain', 'Irene of Denmark', the fragrant pink Hybrid Perpetual 'Comtesse Cécile de Chabrillant', 'Charles de Mills', 'Duke of Edinburgh', 'Jacques Cartier', 'Cornelia', 'Comte de Chambord', 'Louise' (a cerise-pink Hybrid Tea from 1924) and 'Fabvier'.

Of the less frequently seen roses in some of the other beds here is a sample: 'Mme Elisa de Vilmorin' (Hybrid Tea of 1864, dark carmine), 'Lewison Gower' (a deep-pink sport of 'Souvenir de la Malmaison' discovered by Arthur Wyatt), 'Dr Edward Deacon' (another old Hybrid Tea, this time from 1926), 'Mme de Tartas' (reputed to be one of the parents of 'Cécile Brunner'), 'Le Havre' (a vermilion-red Hybrid Perpetual), the Tea Rose 'Mrs Campbell Hall', very fragrant and with golden-orange flowers, and rosy-red 'Mme Wagram' from 1895, the parents of which are unknown.

Towards the top of the garden the ground rises slightly and here are big, curved beds, two of them planted informally. The largest of the three, in the centre, contains 'Fragrant Cloud' and a rose of Peter Beales' own raising, 'Everest Double Fragrance', which has a mixture of attractive coral-pink and cream double flowers. Behind these beds is another that runs the whole width of the garden, backed by a hornbeam hedge, with an orchard beyond. In this bed, apart from a further number of old garden roses, there is a fair selection of species, although nothing particularly unusual: *R. californica* 'Plena', *R.* × *cantabrigiensis*, *R. virginiana*, *R. moyesii*, *R. glauca*, *R. sericea pteracantha*, 'La Belle Distinguée', 'Manning's Blush', 'Golden Chersonese', *R. webbiana* and 'Canary Bird', together with some Hybrid Musks.

There are plenty of seats in the garden, so that you can sit and admire the roses and let their scent drift over you, or you can take a break from them and stroll along the colourful herbaceous border that runs along the northern side of the rose garden. But the roses will draw you back irresistibly. They make a wonderful display.

Glazenwood

Bradwell

On A120 Braintree–Colchester road, 2½ miles from Braintree, turn south at Bradwell sign. Beyond village turn right and then right again. Glazenwood drive on left.
Tel. 0376 83172
Mr and Mrs D. A. H. Baer
Open under the National Gardens Scheme and certain other Sundays for charities, from April to mid-July. Also by appointment, May to July.

Glazenwood has botanical associations going back a long way, for it was from there that Samuel Curtis published the *Botanical Magazine*, started by his father-in-law and cousin, William Curtis, in 1787. The plates were hand-coloured by his numerous daughters.

Curtis bought the house and 20.8 hectares (52 acres) of land in 1819 and planted something like 12,000 fruit trees of various kinds, later adding a collection of many of the finest flowering shrubs and other plants, including 1200 varieties of rose. Among his other activities, he was commissioned by the Duke of Newcastle to lay out Clumber Park in Nottinghamshire (now a National Trust property) but, despite a growing horticultural reputation, he was not a rich man and conceived the idea of opening his grounds to the 'Nobility and Gentry' for an annual subscription of two guineas. For this they were also entitled to copies of his publications as well as shrubs, roses and fruit from the garden. Though it may seem that they were getting too much for their money, the scheme was a success.

After Curtis's time the house and grounds went through many vicissitudes and when the Baers bought it little of what Curtis would have known remained. Only the north end of the house was habitable. Major restoration of both house and garden followed and over the years it has once more become a place of great beauty, containing a fine range of shrubs and other plants, blended together with great skill, and meticulously maintained. Among these there are many roses, though no formal rose garden, which is not to say that there are no borders in which the planting is predominantly of roses. Most of the varieties have been picked for their known garden value rather than for their rarity. There are many Hybrid Musks,

used in massed plantings to tremendous effect, and tree-scaling climbers and ramblers such as 'Kiftsgate' abound in the more wooded parts of the garden.

You will find one rose of considerable rarity here: 'Beauty of Glazenwood', growing on the south wall of the house. Curtis recorded it in his *Botanical Magazine* and presumably gave it this name, though it is perhaps more generally known as 'Fortune's Double Yellow', introduced by Robert Fortune from China in 1845. Although not a particularly strong grower, it has the most eye-catching flowers, loosely semi-double and a bright coppery-yellow, flushed scarlet. Like the Banksian roses, it should be pruned immediately after flowering – if at all – as it only flowers on the old wood.

The east side of the house looks out over a wide lawn, bordered at the far end by tall trees, almost every one with its own rose, so that at midsummer they become a magical curtain of white blossom with their scent drifting in the air, as is the way with the *Synstylea* roses. But leave these for the moment and take a path nearer the house that leads away into the shade of oak trees and between massed plantings of the Rose of Sharon, which is used most effectively for ground cover in many places in the garden.

Soon, however, you take a zig-zag course between high hedges with every so often glimpses of shrubs, the Hybrid Musk 'Felicia', philadelphus, variegated weigela, escallonias, white-flowered buddleia, eleagnus and many others, until a wall can be seen ahead with 'Albertine' and 'Pink Perpetue' peeping over from the far side. Turn along this, past more shrub roses, until you come out into a sundial garden surrounded by potentillas, the plinth of the sundial being formed from a baluster from the old London Bridge.

The wall runs along one side of a swimming pool and between it and the pool is a long line of the rose 'Pink Perpetue' (already glimpsed from the other side), grown as a shrub rather than a climber. Opposite, on the other side of the pool, is a hedge of the fuchsia 'Mrs Popple' and in the background are the huge, papery-white, poppy-like flowers of *Romneya coulteri*.

Ahead is a wide rustic arch leading to the tennis court over which grows *Clematis* × 'Jackmanii', its deep-purple flowers contrasting strikingly with the small white blooms of an unidentified rambler. On the wires all round the tennis court the climber 'New Dawn' has been trained, together with about half-a-dozen of the bright scarlet 'Parkdirektor Riggers'.

Turning along the side of the tennis court, you pass many more roses among the plants on either side: Hybrid Musks, a big planting of well-grown 'Queen Elizabeth', 'Blanc Double de Coubert', 'Leverkusen' and 'Nevada'. Yet another path lies ahead, flanked this time by full rose borders. Among the varieties here are 'Scarlet Queen Elizabeth', the lovely, scented, yellow 'Chinatown', 'Iceberg', 'Queen Elizabeth' and a group of the Hybrid Tea 'Rose Gaujard' rivalling it for height. At the end are tall eucalyptus trees. A left turn takes you across the top of the kitchen garden, passing many interesting shrubs on the way and the roses 'Buff Beauty' and 'Cornelia', underplanted with Lamb's Ears (*Stachys lanata*). The tall spiky heads of teasels form a striking contrast nearby.

At this point you can walk onto the lawn and follow the great curving line of trees that were first seen from a distance, with the house itself, white-painted and with a grey slate roof, away across the grass. Alternatively, you can turn left once again down the far side of the kitchen garden, along a path lined on one side by *Geranium endressii* 'Wargrave Pink' and on the other by *Geranium* 'Johnson's Blue', backed by a hedge of 'Buff Beauty', a most effective combination.

From this point you can wander at will through areas of semi-woodland with winding paths and open spaces for shrubs and other plants that do not thrive in the shade. Here you will find hydrangeas of many kinds, potentillas (which are a great feature of this garden), a great mass of the glaucous-leaved *Sedum* 'Autumn Joy' with a white escallonia behind it, agapanthus, tree-climbing roses, including *R. filipes* 'Kiftsgate' scaling some semi-derelict pear trees of Curtis vintage, 'Complicata', 'Rosa Mundi', 'Moonlight', *R. glauca*, various Rugosas, 'Marguerite Hilling', 'Canary Bird', 'Maigold', *R. moyesii*, 'Golden Wings', and, above all, many other Hybrid Musks.

Everywhere you go you wonder at the immaculate way in which all these are grown and beautifully cared for. There is not a weed to be seen which is no mean achievement in a garden of this size. Twenty years or so is not long in gardening terms, but the feeling of maturity and permanence that the Baers have achieved in such a relatively short time speaks volumes for the imagination of the original planting and their skill in carrying it out.

Hyde Hall Garden

Rettenden

Towards Chelmsford on the A130, through Rettenden village, left at The Bell Inn, then left again into Buckhatch Lane. Hyde Hall can then be seen up hill to right.
Tel. 0245 400256
Dr and Mrs Dick Robinson
Open (garden only) every Wednesday, from April to September inclusive. Also open one Sunday each in April, May, June or July under the National Gardens Scheme. Also by appointment.

My first visit to Hyde Hall was a revelation. When asked which are the outstanding rose gardens in the country, particularly for old roses, most people would probably answer 'Castle Howard' or 'Sissinghurst Castle'. They might mention some of the other National Trust properties but the list would not go very much beyond that. Although I have known Helen and Dick Robinson for some years, I had no idea what was in store for me as I drove for the first time through the flat Essex countryside and turned into the long drive that leads to the top of a low hill on which stands Hyde Hall and the wonderful garden that surrounds it.

The house, which dates back to the seventeenth century, is a typical Essex farmhouse, with a timber frame and lath and plaster construction. The Robinsons bought it in 1955 for farming but gradually the garden assumed greater and greater importance and belts of trees were planted to give some shelter on the exposed hilltop site. The garden today is the result of some twenty-five years' gradual development. It has evolved rather than been planned from scratch, and is a garden for all seasons, for there is a profusion of plants there other than roses and a wide variety of ornamental trees, including the National Collection of *Malus* (flowering crab apples).

The minute you leave the car park you are among the roses. To the left of the path is a miniature rose garden with a tiled central area on which stand old wine jars with a succession of plants in them to suit the season. The miniature roses are in raised brick beds all round the paved area and include a wide selection of varieties, among them yellow 'Rugul', 'Magic Carrousel', 'Mr Bluebird', 'Little Buckaroo' and the tiny 'Maid Marion', deep cerise with a white eye and my idea of what a miniature rose should be. Crossing the original miniatures with the larger Floribundas to increase the colour range brought about a gradual change in size, too, so that many modern so-called miniatures are nothing of the sort.

On the left is a broad sweep of grass sloping down gently away from the house. In this, beds have been cut out for many of the best modern and not-so-modern bedding roses, 'Escapade', 'Trumpeter', 'Silver Jubilee', beetroot purple 'News', 'Deb's Delight', 'Dearest' and 'Tombola' to represent an older generation of Floribundas, 'Typhoon', 'Troika', deep-red 'Rubella' from de Ruiter (new to me), and many, many more. You can either wander among these beds picking out the varieties and, incidentally, noticing how well they are grown, or you can move on down the slope past a group of prostrate conifers and then beds of herbaceous plants until you reach the end of a long double catenary. This runs right across the bottom of the garden and displays an almost unbeatable collection of climbing roses.

But the catenary here is not as others are. Those you see at Regent's Park or Wisley Garden are massive structures with the uprights between which the ropes are suspended probably 3 to 3.7 m (10 to 12 ft) tall. At Hyde Hall they are no more than 2.4 m (8 ft) and your eye is on a level with the roses when the long shoots are tied in to the ropes. This training is, of course, much easier to do when they are low down and all the varieties, especially the less vigorous ones, are much better displayed in consequence.

In the main I want to avoid long lists of plant varieties, but I cannot resist mentioning them here as the number and range is so remarkable. It includes 'Sympathie', 'Mme Grégoire Staechelin', 'Crimson Descant', 'Dreaming Spires', 'Etude', 'Karlsruhe', 'Raymond Chenault', 'Zitronenfalter', 'Compassion', 'Parade', 'Seagull', 'Schoolgirl', pale pink 'Santa Catalina', 'Fugue', 'Chaplin's Pink Climber', 'Cupid', 'Albéric Barbier', 'Bantry Bay', 'Climbing Iceberg', 'Dortmund', 'Swan Lake', 'Pink Perpétue', 'Morning Jewel', 'Climbing Blessings', 'Grand Hotel', and the very new 'Summer Wine' which has single coral pink fragrant blooms. What a collection and, as if that was not enough, growing up through all of them are clematis with bush roses in the beds between the pillars that support the ropes.

To walk between these two lines of roses is quite an experience on its own but at the end you are greeted by great banks of shrub roses: the icing on an already very rich, and very delicious, cake. They begin before the south-east corner of the garden is reached, turn the corner and then continue in incredible profusion halfway up the eastern boundary in a wide bed that gets wider still as it approaches the house.

Opposite the first of these roses is the Lower Pond with willows, dogwood, astilbes, primulas and other plants that relish the damp soil. The pond is overlooked by a seat backed by a hedge of the pink Hybrid Musk 'Felicia' and there are miniature roses in front of it: a place to pause and rest, where you can gaze at distant views over the level countryside and enjoy the scent of roses from all around. Back once more to the eastern rose border, you can pick out a few of the varieties that catch the eye for one reason or another.

The clusters of small white flowers of 'Trier' will have already been spotted as you left the catenary and turned up the slope, and nearby are the very fragrant Kordes variety 'Erfurt' and the same raiser's modern Moss rose which was introduced in 1960 from a cross between a traditional but unspecified red Moss and his Floribunda 'Independence'. The same Floribunda was used by Mattock to produce the Rugosa hybrid 'Hunter', whose very double crimson flowers can be seen nearer the back of the border, vying with 'Autumn Fire' and 'Cerise Bouquet' for size and *joie de vivre*. Pink 'Poulsen's Park Rose' is another big rose and you carry onwards from it up the slope, wondering at the sheer profusion of bloom in the blends of pink, white, maroon, purple and crimson, so typical of the old roses, the Albas, Bourbons, Gallicas, Damasks, Moss roses, and all the rest until you are confronted by the startling scarlet and yellow bicoloured blooms of 'First Choice', like a vivid, tropical bird. (It could, I feel, have been placed to better effect elsewhere.) Then follow the more restrained pinks of the Damask 'Marie Louise', 'Mme Lauriol de Barny', a Bourbon, and the fragrant 'Omar Khayyam' which was propagated from a rose growing on the grave of Edward Fitzgerald at Boulge in Suffolk, purported, in turn, to have come from a rose growing on Omar Khayyam's grave in Nashipur. The tiny centifolia 'De Meaux', 'Vick's Caprice', 'Chianti', 'Souvenir de la Malmaison' and 'Baron Girod de l'Ain', its dark blooms edged with white, are just a very few I have chosen to single out from the wealth displayed.

'Constance Spry' is a modern rose with the look of an old one, happy as a shrub or short climber.

If you can tear yourself away, there are more delights to come. Near the top of the slope turn to the left and the Top Pond is on your right, with modern bedding roses on your left. Flagged walks surround the pond and water plants abound, the moisture-loving *Alchemilla mollis* to the fore. Rounding the western end, you follow a curved bed of that 1957 Hybrid Tea and Gold Medal winner in its day, 'Dorothy Peach'. An offspring of 'Peace', it is, some people say, a better rose in some ways, although hardly obtainable these days. The bright pink climber 'Bantry Bay' is on a wall behind.

There now comes a pause from the profusion of roses, although there is still a jewel or two to be picked out every so often. For instance, at the entrance to a small individual garden near the house where the predominant colours are blue and white are bushes of the modern shrub rose 'Angelina' whose flowers rather resemble, on a smaller scale, those of 'Complicata' in that they are the same combination of pink and white. And behind the house, on a path leading to the vegetable garden, 'Paul's Lemon Pillar',

'Mme Edouard Herriot' (The Daily Mail Rose) and 'Mrs Sam McGredy' are trained on a wire fence. More climbers surround the vegetables.

If you backtrack now and return round the front of the house to the yard, you pass on the way a garage, the contents of which will certainly be imprisoned one day by a vast plant of the 'Kiftsgate' seedling 'Toby Tristram' (see also page 20). Equally rampant specimens of *R. gentiliana*, *R. longicuspis*, 'Wedding Day' and, on a slightly smaller scale, 'Sanders' White Rambler' scramble over the walls and roof of a huge barn that forms the whole of one side of the yard, the bricks of which indicate Elizabethan origin. *Clematis montana* competes with the roses every step of the way, while behind the barn is another yard where the slightly tender, white-flowered 'Cooperi', scaling yet another roof, shows that, given the right place to grow, it can be quite at home in the climate of the United Kingdom. Although it suffered a setback in the harsh winter of 1985–6, it is rapidly recovering and should soon reach 9 m (30 ft) from stem to stern once more.

A drive leads downhill from the yard. Follow this a little way and then turn left into what is known as the Pig Park, which is now home for great banks of 'Nevada' and 'Golden Wings' and a fine group of shrubs from the Moyesii family, including pink *R. holodonta* and the Hillier-raised pair *R.* × *highdownensis* and *R.* × *hillieri* (*R.* × *pruhoniciana*) with very striking deep red flowers. The main part of the *Malus* collection is to be found here and there are many other trees and shrubs of outstanding interest planted either in groups or singly in the gently sloping grass. You could wander for an hour here without seeing everything.

There are many familiar shrub roses among the plantings and some less common ones, such as the Hybrid Musk 'Autumn Delight', which was one of those put out by the Bentalls in 1933. It has clusters of white flowers, as does, not too far away, an enormous 'Kiftsgate', trained on a metal frame into a gigantic igloo.

A fitting note on which to finish comes as you walk from the Pig Park towards the car park. On a tall wall to the left is 'La Mortola', one of the Far Eastern climbers that are such fantastic tree-scalers, named after the famous Italian garden in which it was found by Sir Thomas Hanbury. The single flowers are white and comparatively large for this type of rose and the leaves very long and pointed, with a distinctive and attractive grey-green sheen. The rose survives and appears in several of the gardens described in this book but, at the time of writing, the future of the wonderful garden it came from is, sadly, still very much in doubt.

Capel Manor

Waltham Cross

Two and a half miles north-east of Enfield. Leave M25 at junction 25 and turn south on A10. Almost at once turn right at traffic lights into Bullsmoor Lane. Entrance on right.
Tel. 0992 763849
London Borough of Enfield Education Department
Open every day from March to October.

Capel Manor is primarily an educational establishment, running many courses on different aspects of horticulture, on flower painting, botanical illustration and allied subjects, and the gardens, grouped round an old eighteenth-century manor house, demonstrate the wide range of subjects taught. The Historic Garden shows gardening styles and plantings used in the sixteenth and seventeenth centuries and includes a knot garden (introduced from France in the late fifteenth century) and a medicinal herb garden, where plants are grown that were recommended for use in the old herbals. Gerard, perhaps the most well-known author of one of these, was actually superintendent of the gardens of Theobalds Palace, in part of the grounds of which Capel Manor now stands.

The eighteenth-century is personified by open parkland, bounded by a ha-ha, and among many fine trees is included perhaps the oldest and largest copper beech in the country.

Representing more modern times are the walled garden, originally designed to provide vegetables and fruit for the house, the Rock Garden, a concept dating from about 1830, the Wild Garden based on William Robinson's ideas, Theme Gardens based on the pioneering work of Major Lawrence Johnston at Hidcote, a garden for the disabled and a Trial Garden where plants are tested for the Consumers' Association. The old stables and part of the grounds are leased to the Horses and Ponies' Protection Association.

The main collection of old roses is to be found in the Walled Garden, at one end of which stands a range of glasshouses for the more tender commercially-grown plants such as sugar cane, bananas and so on. From the paved centre with its sundial, six paths radiate outwards, the two nearest to the glasshouses covered by wooden pergolas on which grow a wide range of climbing plants, though no climbing roses. Old roses do, however, line the other paths, 'Duchesse de Verneuil', 'Souvenir du Docteur Jamain', 'Mousseline', 'Vick's Caprice', 'Du Maître d'Ecole', 'Duc de Guiche', 'Paul Ricault', 'Ipsilanté', 'Félicité Parmentier', 'Honorine de Brabant' and 'Mme Pierre Oger' among the old ones and 'Constance Spry', 'Dame Prudence', 'Lavender Lassie', 'Magenta' and 'Wife of Bath' representing the more modern hybrids that blend so well with them.

In one corner is a group of short – or comparatively short – growers, including 'Hermosa', 'Perle d'Or', and the two dwarf Centifolias, 'De Meaux' and 'Petite de Hollande', while, at the other extreme, a vast plant of *R. brunonii* almost covers the whole of the end wall. Mingling with the roses and greatly enhancing them are plants such as rosemary 'Mrs Jessop's Upright', *Campanula persicifolia* 'Alba', Japanese anemones, *Iris germanica* 'Moonlight Sonata', *Alchemilla mollis*, violet-purple *Campanula glomerata* 'Superba', the Chinese sacred bamboo, *Nandina domestica*, and the Italian jasmine, *Jasminum humile*, while there are pink and grey-leaved bedding plants in beds in the grass.

The long wall down one side of the garden has a mixture of shrubs such as *Weigela florida* 'Variegata', its leaves edged creamy-white, abelia, *Erigeron* 'Pink Jewel' and the two herbaceous clematis, *C. integrifolia* 'Hendersonii', with deep-blue bell-shaped flowers and *C. heracleifolia* 'Campanile', together with a number of Hybrid Musk roses (including Lambert's 'Trier') and some of David Austin's earlier English Roses, 'The Yeoman' and 'The Friar'.

All the different gardens are well signposted so that there should be no problem in finding the Historic Garden, where there is a number of old roses, such as the 'Autumn Damask' and its white mossed sport 'Quatre Saisons Blanc Mousseux', 'Celeste' and *R. foetida* and its bicolor sport, grouped round a sundial, while away to the left in a grassy area under the trees a few species roses are planted.

Most of the garden is peaceful and a delight to walk through, but the Trial Grounds are, unfortunately, subject to the constant roar of traffic from the M25. However, I suppose that trial grounds could be considered as places for work and not for relaxation. The ones at Capel Manor are certainly of interest, with, at the time of writing, three different rose trials going on, for dwarf Floribundas, hedging roses and modern, scented ones. Since rose growers are always on the lookout for the latter, here is a complete list of them. They are: 'Scented Air', 'Fragrant Delight', 'Southampton', 'Sheila's Perfume', 'Arthur Bell', 'Korresia', 'Margaret Merril', 'My Choice', 'Harry Edland', 'Escapade', 'Deep Secret', 'Ena Harkness', 'Blue Moon', 'Prima Ballerina', 'Paul Shirville',

A fragrant modern Floribunda rose of great distinction, 'Southampton' makes a striking hedge.

'Double Delight', 'Alpine Sunset', 'Fragrant Cloud', 'Wendy Cussons' and 'Alec's Red'.

However, without wishing to pre-empt the trial results, I do not want it to be thought that I endorse all these without qualification. 'Ena Harkness' is an old rose now and, apart from a tendency to hang its head, there have always been two strains, one scented and one not. 'Prima Ballerina' is a martyr to mildew in most gardens, as is 'Double Delight' which makes a pretty poor plant anyway in most situations, even if the flowers can, at their best, be lovely. The others present no problems, though 'Harry Edland' may be difficult to find.

The Gardens of the Rose

St Albans

Leave M1 at Junction 6 or leave M25 at Junction 21 and follow signs to St Albans. At Noke Hotel, fork left. Gardens are signposted about a quarter of a mile on left up Chiswell Green Lane.
Tel. 0727 50461
The gardens and trial grounds of The Royal National Rose Society (RNRS).
Open every day from early June to October.

These gardens also house the Society's headquarters and administrative offices in what was, and still is (as far as external appearances are concerned), a fairly large country house that was originally a farmhouse. The RNRS moved there in 1960 and began to lay out the 4.8-hectare (12-acre) gardens.

It is not, on the face of it, the most promising of sites, as it is on comparatively high, flat ground and is very exposed. It has only a thinnish layer of loam over a gravelly subsoil, which needs large quantities of organic matter added to it if the roses are to thrive. That the roses flourish so magnificently, making this one of the leading rose gardens in the world, is a tribute to the skill and dedication of the small gardening staff. A lot of hard work goes into looking after the 30,000 or so roses, and even if the gardeners worked right round the clock, they could hardly produce better results.

The Society's Gardens Management Committee has a say in what goes on, too, of course; the final say, in fact. As I am a member of it, I should perhaps declare an interest before handing out any more praise. The Committee has realized that the views of some of the purists of the past, who thought only in terms of roses, can no longer prevail. Other plants are being introduced into the garden, not only because that is what the majority of people like and is the way that they garden themselves, but because in time it will make for a longer opening period and hence more visitors. At the moment, the season is from mid-June until some time in October, depending on the weather. In other words the gardens are open only when the roses are out.

Now let us have a look around. As you come through the entrance from the car park, there are two directions in which you can go. To the left is the large Trial Ground with The Queen Mother's Rose Border around its perimeter. Queen Elizabeth, the Queen Mother, is Patron of the Society and in her border are planted rose varieties to which the RNRS has given awards in its trials, though lack of space does mean that award winners from the earliest years are no longer represented. To include them all would be impossible as awards of various kinds have been presented since before the First World War.

Straight ahead as you come through the gate is The Presidents' Walk, flanked by a long double catenary on which all the best modern climbers are displayed. Follow this along the path towards the house and behind the catenary on your right you will be able to glimpse examples of the Moyesii family and other wild roses that bear splendid hips in the late summer and autumn. Also there is a fine specimen of the Gallica 'Empress Josephine', named after the wife of Napoleon I, who did so much at Malmaison to bring rose gardens into being (see also page 7).

Beyond the catenary on the other side is the main display garden, but half-way along the path you can make a start by turning right through a gap into the old rose garden. In this, in separate beds, are fine collections of all the old rose groups, the Damasks, Gallicas, Albas, Centifolias and Moss roses. These include the historic 'Autumn Damask' which was probably grown by the Romans and was one of the roses (the other being the China rose 'Old Blush'), which joined together to give the West its first robust, repeat-flowering rose family, the Bourbons. Growing beside it, and sometimes showing white and sometimes pink flowers on the

The circular pergola at the end of the President's Walk in The Gardens of the Rose, the gardens and trial grounds of The Royal National Rose Society.

same bush, is its white, mossed sport 'Quatre Saisons Blanc Mousseux' and the original 'Portland Rose' or 'Duchess of Portland' as it is sometimes called. Along the eastern border of this area is an exceptionally fine collection of Moss roses, and the western border has some of the less well-known Kordes Frühling roses, such as 'Frühlingsschnee' and that rampaging beauty 'Cerise Bouquet', carrying its massed clusters of quite small cerise-pink flowers along branches that threaten to engulf everything around them. It is difficult to imagine the demure 'Crimson Glory' as one of its parents or why Wilhelm Kordes, who (according to most of the records) raised it, should later disclaim it.

Leaving the old roses and carrying on towards the house you pass through a circular pergola enveloped in the octopus arms of the enormously vigorous *R. mulliganii*. Ahead you can see other examples of tree-climbing roses weaving their way, gipsy-like, through the branches of a number of mature cypresses. From these examples you can learn that 'Silver Moon', vigorous enough and with larger flow-

ers than most of the wild, white-flowered climbers and ramblers, is rather shy of blooming when compared to the others, and that the charmingly named 'Rambling Rector' is quite the reverse.

Beyond the house is the cafeteria and it will be worth your while to make a quick trip along the back of this to the small Courtney Page Garden to see a few Tea roses, particularly if you can catch 'Soleil d'Or' in bloom. This was the first rose put on the market by the French nurseryman and hybridist, Joseph Pernet-Ducher, as a result of his long and patient quest for bright yellow garden roses with a robust constitution and large double flowers. It was introduced in 1900, the outcome of a cross between a Hybrid Perpetual rose and *R. foetida persiana*, the latter generally considered to have a great reluctance to breed. It was followed in 1910 by the much better (and much more yellow) 'Rayon d'Or', and it was these two crosses that are held largely responsible for the handing on of black spot to so many modern varieties. *R. foetida* itself is a martyr to it, at least

A general view of the gardens looking west from the Edland Pavilion: the Floribunda 'Korresia' is in the foreground.

away from its native haunts, and over the years seems to have infected all modern rose strains.

Returning past the cafeteria once more, you can spend some time in the model gardens, designed especially to show how roses can be grown (with other plants) in a small space. Through the second of these gardens an opening in the fence leads to the Miniature rose garden. Here the Miniatures are grown in what is probably the most effective way possible, for this is a sunken garden with brick-faced terraced beds for the roses round three sides. They are much easier to see than if they were planted at ground level and the scented ones are much more accessible to those whose backs are no longer as flexible as once they were. Behind the Miniatures, along the fence, is a number of China roses, whose airy habit of growth does not overwhelm their smaller cousins. And they really are cousins, for the original Miniature came from China, too.

A short pergola, over which 'Paul's Himalayan Musk Rambler' drapes its swags of pale pink blooms in July and August, leads up and out of the sunken garden so that you find the main display area opening up before you once more, only this time from the other side. In it you can wander among bed after bed of the best of the modern Hybrid Tea and Floribunda roses, comparing the beauty (and health and weather-resistance if it comes to that) of one with another, or you can move down the western perimeter to the scented garden to compare fragrances. This particular planting is intended to show that, contrary to popular belief, a great many modern varieties have a perfume as strong as those of the past. Among the varieties growing there are: 'Just Joey', 'Arthur Bell', 'Margaret Merril', 'Fragrant Delight', 'Pristine', 'Radox Bouquet', 'My Choice', 'Pot o' Gold', 'Wendy Cussons', 'Alpine Sunset' and perhaps a dozen more.

Moving along the same path you come into the western end of a mammoth horseshoe-shaped pergola, which must be all of 72 m (80 yards) long, though its sweep is broken in the middle by a round formal pool. Up the forty-six brick pillars of this, and over the top when they

*The Polyantha rose 'The Fairy' surrounds the pool at the end of
the Princess Mary Walk.*

can be persuaded to do so, grows a wide range of climbing and rambling roses, to which clematis varieties and species, one per pillar, have been added quite recently. Growing climbing plants one scrambling up through the other, not only looks enchanting but, if carefully planned, greatly increases the period when flowers are to be seen.

The pergola is another good place in the garden to compare and try to sort out the multitudinous white, small-flowered ramblers, and 'Seagull' at the end of the first crescent near the pool is a particularly fine one to note. Beyond the pool, which is bordered by the low-growing Polyantha 'The Fairy', the pergola continues with more climbers and ramblers, including early-flowering 'Maigold', 'Sanders' White' and a very beautiful pink rambler rose called 'Ethel', which can only be admired at St Albans as it is not available commercially.

But do not leave the pool for a moment. Look instead up towards the house along the Princess Mary Walk (she was Patron before the Queen Mother). This is a paved path with long borders of mixed Floribunda roses planted in profusion on either side and so spectacular at the height of summer that it is the most photographed feature of the garden. Walk along it if you feel inclined or turn in the opposite direction to admire the modern shrub roses along the southern border of the garden. Here is a fine collection of Pemberton's Hybrid Musks (and some later Kordes ones) amongst other roses such as the lovely but neglected salmon-pink shrub 'Kathleen Ferrier'. Pemberton has been blamed for calling his roses Hybrid Musks when their connection with the Musk rose is tenuous to say the least, but he actually introduced them as Hybrid Teas. That was early in this century and it was Courtney Page, Secretary of the RNRS at that time, who saw them at a Society show and not surprisingly ruled them out of the Hybrid Tea classes. Because of their fragrance he suggested the name Hybrid Musks instead, which, although botanically and historically just as inappropriate, has nevertheless stuck.

From the eastern end of the modern shrub

rose border you can walk towards the Edland Pavilion, in the centre of the gardens. You can take one of two paths, the first leading between more modern shrubs, Rugosas and the like, and including one of great interest, R. × micrugosa, which is a cross between R. roxburghii (The Chestnut Rose) and R. rugosa, and the Bourbon and Hybrid Perpetual beds. These latter are some of the poorest in the gardens and their future development needs urgent attention, for the Bourbons and the Hybrid Perpetuals, well grown and at their best, demonstrate two very important stages in the development of the rose. A good many other plants such as delphiniums and species tulips have been mixed in with them for spring colour, but much more still needs to be done.

Taking the other path you pass on the other side of this bed with species roses of the *Cinnamomeae* group on the right. The Edland Pavilion when you reach it is ringed in front by lilac-pink-flowered 'Escapade' and has 'Climbing Iceberg' covering what would otherwise be a rather bleak south end and 'Félicité et Perpétue' on the other. Paths on either side of it lead to the Trial Grounds, separated from the Display Gardens by a flourishing hedge of the Rugosas 'Roseraie de l'Hay' and 'Schneezwerg'. Along part of the south side are more species, including a number of American ones, with the Queen Mother's Rose Border running round most of the perimeter. At the far end there is actually a gravel path behind it and on the other side of this a long wide bed filled with numerous members of the vast Pimpinellifolia (Spinosissima) family of Scotch roses and some other species.

And so to the Trials themselves. The purpose of these is to judge new varieties that are not yet on sale for their value as garden plants, rather than for their commercial or exhibition potential. This includes their use in private gardens, public parks and environmentally. They are judged over three years by a panel of sixteen judges, plus the RNRS President, and the panel is divided into four groups, whose visits are arranged so that the roses are judged every week throughout the flowering season. Marks are awarded for disease resistance, habit and vigour, form of bloom or cluster, colour purity, continuity, general effect and novelty and fragrance. Judging is done under Trial Ground numbers so that the judges can remain impartial, but the lack of name labels can be frustrating to any visitor to the gardens who takes a

fancy to a particular rose. However, it is more than likely that the roses in the trials will not have been named yet anyway and be known only by the breeders' code number. No-one is going to waste a good name on a rose that may not come up to expectations in the trials and may, therefore, never go on sale. The proportion of roses that do get awards is comparatively small, but at the end of the second year those that are thought worthy of it will be given a Trial Ground Certificate. It is only after completing the third year that other awards, such as Certificates of Merit and the even better, but much harder to come by, Gold Medals or even the President's International Trophy for something exceptionally outstanding, are given.

These trials are an important part of the work of the society and they give the visitor a unique chance to look into the future and spot a potential winner.

It may be wondered why there is a considerable area of open grass space in the trial area, unoccupied by any rose beds. This serves two purposes. First, it allows the trials beds to be moved to new ground so that newly planted roses are always put into fresh ground and, secondly, it is in this open space that the marquees are sited for the Society's annual Rose Festival in July. Visit the gardens then and you get a real bonus.

Mannington Hall

Saxthorpe

Signposted from Saxthorpe off the B1149 Norwich–Holt road.
Tel. 0263 87 284
The Hon. Robin and Mrs Walpole
Open, garden only, from May to September on Sunday afternoons; also open in June, July and August on Wednesdays, Thursdays and Fridays, from 11 a.m. to 6 p.m.

This house is of the same period and style as Helmingham Hall (see page 115), though flint, brick and terracotta have been used in the construction rather than brick alone. In the eighteenth century it was purchased by Horatio, first Baron Walpole of Wolterton, brother of England's first Prime Minister, Sir Robert Walpole, and it has been in the family ever since.

There is an air of great tranquillity about the 8-hectare (20-acre) garden. And this is not, I think, solely because it is deep in the countryside and sheltered by many fine trees from the world outside. It is a tranquillity that comes from the still waters of the moat and lake, from the smooth green lawns and a feeling of the past. It has the peace of the English countryside a century or so ago and there are roses everywhere. Greeting you as you approach is a fine specimen of *R. wichuraiana*, its long shoots starred with single white flowers as they tumble down towards the water of the moat from the wall beside the drawbridge.

The Walpoles have a working arrangement with Peter Beales Roses and it is through their joint efforts that Mannington Hall can now be considered one of the most beautiful rose gardens in the country. What you cannot see growing in the comparatively small display garden at the Beales nursery you are likely to be able to admire at Mannington. You can buy roses at both places, too.

Although there are roses to be seen everywhere the greatest concentration is in the Heritage Rose Garden. This, true to form in an estate of this size nowadays, is in what was the old walled kitchen garden, 0.4 hectares (nearly an acre) of it, and many of the fruit trees have been retained. It is divided into sections, each one planted with roses from a different period in history. The first one you see on your left as you enter the garden through a wide double door is a long bed of species roses that occupies the whole of the south wall. These are, of course, the wild kinds from which all cultivated roses are descended. Some of them, however, may also be found in one or two of the period gardens, but only because the period covers the date when they were first discovered.

On the right is another long wall bed with more species and their near relatives, the origins of the latter in most cases also being obscure. The Green Rose, *R. chinensis* 'Viridiflora', is a case in point, and though it has been in cultivation at least since the middle of the

R. wichuraiana tumbles down the wall as you approach the drawbridge over the moat at Mannington Hall.

The modern shrub rose 'James Mason', raised by Peter Beales, and the old Alba rose 'Celestial' at Mannington Hall.

nineteenth century, nobody knows its origins. *R. melina* is in this bed too, a rare dwarf native of Colorado and Utah in the United States with solitary rose-pink flowers and the brightest orange hips imaginable, set off by grey-green leaves.

Ahead and to the right, as you come through the gate, is what looks at first sight like a sheep pen. This is an understandable mistake, as you soon find out, for it is actually a reproduction of a medieval garden, surrounded by wattles. In the centre is a yew tree and round it are turf seats and the roses. These include the Gallicas 'Officinalis' and 'Rosa Mundi', 'Maiden's Blush' and 'Autumn Damask', while over the entrance, looking a little uncertain of itself historically, is 'Rambling Rector'.

A hornbeam hedge separates the Classical Garden from the rest and here you can find roses from the eighteenth and the first part of the nineteenth centuries, from 1700 to about 1836. This was, of course, an important period in the story of the garden rose when the Centifolia and Moss roses were being devel-

oped and, towards the end of the period, the raising of the first Noisette roses from 'Champney's Pink Cluster', itself thought to be the product of a China and Musk rose cross. They are an interesting group with a charm all their own and take their name from the Noisette family. A French nurseryman called Philippe Noisette, who had settled in Charleston in South Carolina, was introduced to John Champney's 'Pink Cluster' rose, probably by Champney himself, for he was a rice-growing farmer in the same area. Philippe Noisette bred seedlings from it and sent some to his brother Louis in Paris, who carried on developing the strain so that most of the best Noisette roses are of European origin. They are represented here by 'Blush Noisette', 'Aimée Vibert' and 'Desprez à Fleurs Jaunes' ('Jaune Desprez').

However, attractive as the Centifolia, Moss roses and Noisettes may be, much more important in the story of the rose were the first Bourbons, which also come into this period. They were, as I mentioned when writing about The Gardens of the Rose at St Albans (see page 102), the result of a chance cross between the recurrent China Rose 'Old Blush' and the 'Autumn Damask', a minimally recurrent Western variety and the only one in those days which even tried. This resulted in the first vigorous repeat-flowering roses raised in the West, the Bourbons.

There are Bourbons in the Classical Garden at Mannington and more come later in the Victorian Garden next door, for Bourbons were the most popular garden roses for a very long time. There is also in the Classical Garden a variety called 'Rose du Roi' or 'Lee's Crimson Perpetual', very fragrant and bright red, now considered the forerunner of the Hybrid Perpetual family, which gives strength to the argument that a good deal of their development ran parallel to that of the Bourbons and that they did not simply follow in after them.

The Victorian Garden burgeons with big, blowsy, many petalled, strongly scented blooms in pinks, reds, white, maroons and purples: 'Belle de Crécy', 'Boule de Neige', 'Mme Isaac Pereire' and 'Champion of the World', a fragrant, rose-pink Hybrid Perpetual which, if it does not quite live up to its name, is not at all bad. And, of course, there are Moss roses galore, particularly in the cottage garden at the far end, where borders of lavender set them off to perfection. There, too, is a pergola of rustic poles with climbers of the period and a number of Penzance Briers trained on them.

Across the way is the Orchard Garden where, among trees, a few shade-loving shrubs and some roses that will tolerate a certain amount of it grow quite happily and 'Paul's Himalayan Musk Rambler' reaches upwards for the light. Beyond it is perhaps the most striking feature of the Heritage Rose Garden, something from the Edwardian period of the early 1900s. It is a trellis garden created from designs by Gertrude Jekyll, octagonal in shape and with beautifully made trellis-work on all sides, up which ramblers and climbers are trained. Let into four of the sides are what are best called small bowers, round which are entwined 'Debutante', 'Dorothy Perkins', 'Minnehaha', 'American Pillar', 'Cupid', 'Silver Moon', 'Elegance' and a number of others.

The Between-Wars Garden has a formal pool and rectangular beds with varieties appropriate to the period, while the modern rose garden beyond it could be said to be more relaxed in design. It runs the full width of the walled area and has thirteen round beds in the centre for classic modern roses such as 'Iceberg', 'Peace' and 'Piccadilly' and later varieties like 'Silver Jubilee' (well on its way to becoming a classic), short-growing 'Penelope Keith', 'Cardinal Hume' and 'International Herald Tribune'. Large D-shaped beds at either end contain an interesting selection of modern shrub roses including 'Constance Spry', 'Fred Loads', 'Frühlingsgold' and some varieties of Peter Beales' and David Austin's own raising including 'Pavlova', 'Graham Thomas', 'Chaucer' and 'Mary Rose'.

This whole Heritage Garden was not complete at the time of writing. Certain areas had yet to be tackled and in others there had been losses from harsh winters with gaps still to be filled. The problem of a leaking pond needed to be solved. But all this work is in hand and may well be something to look back on by the time this book is published. And it all looks terrific even now.

How many other houses are there, I wonder, which have all four Banksian roses – the single and double whites and the single and double yellows – growing on their walls? What other house has 'Raubritter', 'La France', 'Hermosa', the Gallicas 'Conditorum', 'Belle de Crécy' and 'Jenny Duval', the Hybrid Perpetuals 'Baronne Prévost', 'Duke of Wellington' and 'Empereur du Maroc', the Moss roses 'Mme de la Roche-Lambert' and 'Louis Gimard' plus a good many others growing in the car park? All round the tea room and sales kiosk are roses. 'Bourbon Queen', the Noisette 'Crépuscule' with its creamy-orange flowers, 'The Alchymist', 'Francis E. Lester', 'Mme Plantier', 'Frühlingsgold' and R. × alba 'Maxima' are used to back the selling area, trained on wires between wooden uprights.

A stroll round the house between the moat and the lake takes you to the south lawn, and at the far side of this you will see vast curved beds of shrub roses. In one corner is a small temple and tucked away behind it, and so perhaps easily missed, is a collection of roses of the Pimpinellifolia family, or Scotch or Burnet roses as they are often and certainly more easily called. R. pimpinellifolia itself is there and, from the literally hundreds of hybrids that have been raised from it, mainly by Scottish nurserymen towards the end of the last century, included here are 'Double White', 'Double Pink', 'Mary Queen of Scots', 'Old Yellow', 'Double Yellow' and 'Marbled White'. As can be seen, the said Scottish nurserymen were either lacking in imagination when it came to names, or perhaps there were so many varieties that they simply ran out of inspiration.

From the multitude of old roses in the curved beds beyond the temple one in particular stands out, an enormous bush of 'Scarlet Fire' going hand over fist up a large tree and already most of the way to the top. From here you can make your way to the scented garden, where the beds are cut out from the turf to reproduce the pattern of the moulding on the ceiling of the dining room in the house. A tree in the centre stands in for the chandelier and the roses include the Sweet Brier *R. rubiginosa* and two of Lord Penzance's hybrids, salmon-pink 'Lady Penzance' and rosy-red 'Greenmantle', all three of which have fragrant foliage as well

as scented flowers. Other varieties are the Bourbons 'Louise Odier' and 'Mme Pierre Oger', the Centifolia 'Spong', the pinky-lilac Hybrid Perpetual 'John Hopper', an unusual white Rugosa of great charm called 'Mme Georges Bruant', and two modern roses, Peter Beales' 'Anna Pavlova' again and 'Lavender Lassie' which, in my experience and despite what all the books and catalogues say, is, for all its other fine qualities, completely scentless! Obviously the Walpoles do not agree.

I have given only a taste of this wonderful garden. There can be very few old roses in commerce today that you cannot see there and quite a few that you will not find on any nursery list. At the end of a week you would still discover corners with new treasures.

Looking back towards the house at Mannington Hall from the South Lawn.

Peter Beales Roses

Attleborough

On A11 Thetford–Norwich road just before reaching
Attleborough.
Tel. 0953 454707
Mr Peter Beales
Nursery display garden, always open.

The nursery here carries by far the largest list of old roses in the country and it contains a good many modern ones too. As with the account of David Austin's display garden, I am not attempting descriptions of the individual roses as there are far too many, but it can be taken for granted that if there is a species or old garden rose, or a climber or rambler for that matter, that you especially want to see, you will find it in Peter Beales' collection. If not in the display garden itself, with which we are primarily concerned here, it can probably be found in the nursery fields, albeit in an infant state. From the month of May onwards a number of the roses can be seen in full bloom in the polythene tunnels that run down one side of the display garden and are used to house the pot-grown roses that will be exhibited at the Chelsea Flower Show.

The show garden is quite large and is being developed further. It has been attractively laid out and has a number of other plants growing with the roses, which of course is just what will happen when roses from the nursery are sold and planted in other gardens. Few gardens nowadays grow roses and nothing else and Mr Beales believes in showing how they can be blended in with other plants to the best advantage.

To see the garden, walk from the car park into an open grassy space with beds of roses on either side and then through an arch to an area where there is an informal pool. At one side of this is a low mound which is used most effectively to display the growing band of ground-cover roses, and beyond the pool a number of beds in a multitude of shapes and sizes have been cut in the turf and are used to show off the beauties of the modern rose. The main road runs alongside the display garden and species roses have been planted in a line on that side so that in time they will help to blot out both the sight and sound of the cars and lorries passing on their way to and from Norwich.

At the far end of the modern rose garden is a double line of posts and there are more along the side of the garden away from the road. These will in time form a rose walk and pergola for climbers and ramblers, which have already been planted but have yet to show their paces. In the middle of this line of pillars, a gap leads the way, or rather will do so in the next year or two, to an area still to be developed.

Even in its formative stages, however, the garden is well worth seeing.

Lime Kiln

Claydon

Three miles north of Ipswich, turn off A45 on to B1113
at sign for Claydon. Just inside village, turn sharp right
up Claydon Hill. House up drive on left, no nameplate.
Tel. 0473 830334
Mr Humphrey Brooke
Open, garden only, from mid-June to mid-July daily.

One of the first roses you see as you go up the drive towards the house at Lime Kiln is that very attractive Bourbon 'Souvenir de la Malmaison', some 2.4 m (8 ft) across instead of its more usual 1.2 to 1.5 m (4 to 5 ft). It was named, when it was introduced in 1843, in memory of the wonderful rose garden created by the Empress Josephine, and when you meet Humphrey Brooke he leaves you in no doubt that this rose is his favourite. The large, double, very fragrant, creamy-pink flowers are singularly lovely, but unfortunately they cannot always be relied on to open well in our English climate. Mr Brooke has the answer, of course, which is to squeeze each bud gently when it first starts to show colour and he tells of an old nursery hand in days gone by who was paid 6d a day for doing just that. In the right kind of summer 'Souvenir de la Malmaison', though, may not need this form of gentle persuasion to give of its best. The climbing form almost never does.

Roses twice their normal size seem to be the pattern throughout this remarkable garden, for Mr Brooke gives all his roses their head and does not believe in pruning other than to remove dead wood as and when it occurs and a certain amount of dead-heading. As there are very few modern varieties this does not seem to matter at all. It certainly does not inhibit flowering and, contrary to the popular belief about old roses, so wide is the range of varieties grown that there are blooms in plenty to be seen from May until well into the autumn. With some of the China roses flowering goes on until Christmas or even the New Year.

Over 500 varieties altogether, many of them rarities and a number still to be identified, old and less old, grow in wild profusion, up trees and up each other, over walls and summer-houses, pergolas and arches. This is one of the great rose collections and at their summer peak it would be difficult to imagine anything more beautiful. Their perfume fills the air.

The garden was first started in the early 1920s round an old Tudor farmhouse by Countess Sophie Beckendorff, widow of the last Czarist ambassador to London. A passionate gardener, she is said to have thought nothing of ordering plants from 60 or so nurseries in the course of one year. She died in 1928 and the garden was neglected and became quickly overgrown. It was not until Mr Brooke and his wife (a granddaughter of Countess Sophie) bought Lime Kiln in 1954 that the garden came to life once more and they were able to uncover and restore a good deal of the old rose garden near the house. You can see it now with beds surrounded by stone-paved paths, and of course many of the trees, including a vast mulberry, also date from the early days of the century or some time in the 1800s.

This is not an easy garden to describe in any logical sequence. Stand at any point in it and face north, south, east or west and you will be looking at roses. They surround you and at times almost overwhelm you, but among this wealth of beauty there are some that should be singled out for special mention. Where else, for instance, would you be likely to see anything other than a few of the very hardiest Tea roses – 'Lady Hillingdon' or 'Mrs Herbert Stevens' perhaps? But here there is a considerable range of them, grown in pots, taken under glass in the winter and, with their soil changed completely every three to four years, they seem to thrive. Many of them were brought back by Mr Brooke from a visit to the East German rosarium at Sangerhausen.

In the summer they are kept mainly in the area of the old paved rose garden near the house, and there too 'Perle d'Or' and the less common but very similar 'Jenny Wren' (a 'Cécile Brunner' offspring) share a bed and the former defies all the rules by going up to 2.1 to 2.4 m (7 to 8 ft). To its right 'Ayrshire

Splendens' grows 9 m (30 ft) across with a viburnum, shoulders aching, beneath it, while nearby on a summerhouse is another rose from Sangerhausen, the rambler 'Ghislaine de Féligonde', which carries pink-tinted, yellowish-white flowers in great profusion. On the side of the paved garden away from the house is a hedge of Penzance Briers.

The mulberry tree already mentioned stands in a walled garden which is also close to the house, and here one can see the very fragrant red climbing Hybrid Tea 'Vicomtesse Pierre du Fou' on one wall and on a pergola on the far side the wonderful snowy-white Setigera climber 'Long John Silver'. In the shade of the mulberry itself is a plant of a Hybrid Tea from 1917, the almost single, very fragrant, velvety scarlet 'K of K' (Kitchener of Khartoum) which won a National Rose Society Gold Medal in 1916.

Moving on you pass outbuildings and the glasshouse in which the Tea roses winter. Over these and rapidly submerging them are 'La Mortola', 'Kiftsgate' and yet another rose with a similar all-conquering habit that originated with Hillier's of Winchester and which they called 'Lime Kiln' after this garden.

Further still away from the house is an open grassy area with species roses at the far side. These include grey-leaved R. fedtschenkoana with its usual elbows-on-the-bar sprawl, R. webbiana, and R. woodsii fendleri from North America and Mexico, which is swamping everything around it with its vigour and sending up suckers all over the grass in front of it. It has lilac-pink flowers with creamy stamens and there are very few thorns on its slender shoots. Those that there are are red.

Also in this particular line of shrubs is R. pomifera 'Duplex', R. sweginzowii which has just about the biggest and brightest hips of any species (consolation for being landed with a name like that) and a hybrid of R. canina. All of these, and the other species I mentioned, are on the very edge of a deep, overgrown hollow that was at one time a chalk pit. Many trees were cleared from it by the Brookes in the early days, but there are still enough there to support more of the wild, white, multi-flowered ramblers. However, the rose to see and wonder at in the chalk pit is a gigantic chance seedling of R. moyesii, certainly more than twice the height it should be and, though it was difficult to see its full extent sideways because of surrounding shrubs, Mr Brooke assured me (with a pinch of

*The old paved rose garden near the house at Lime Kiln, Claydon
with roses everywhere.*

agricultural salt?) that it was fully 18.2 m (60 ft) across.

Once you have scrambled down to the bottom of the depression – and it is a scramble – you can see that there are no fewer than 39 main shoots coming from the base and that these are thorny for the first 1.8 to 2.7 m (6 to 9 ft) only and then smooth. The flowers are pink as in the original wild form of *R. moyesii* and the

hips are typically long and bottle-shaped. I have not seen them but they must be quite a sight in such prodigious quantities. Nobody yet has put forward a reasonable – or should one say provable – explanation for such phenomenal growth. Mr Brooke does not know why. He has named it 'Freia'.

Other species round about once you have climbed back up to ground level are *R. sericea*

Near the house at Lime Kiln 'Ayrshire Splendens' sprawls across a viburnum, hiding it from sight.

Lime Kiln's brick walls show off the climbing and rambling roses, with geraniums an effective underplanting.

pteracantha, R. willmottiae, R. macrophylla and *R.* × 'Highdownensis', and opposite them across the grass is a line of Rugosas.

Moving on round the house, steps take you down to a slightly lower level where 'Cerise Bouquet' cascades from above in a crimson-pink waterfall with two more rarities nearby from the East German collection. One of these is the Hybrid Perpetual raised by Pernet Père in 1868 called 'Baronne Adolphe de Rothschild' (also called 'Baroness Rothschild') which has very large and double soft rose-pink blooms of great charm, and 'White Flight', a Multiflora hybrid of moderate vigour. Two of the less common Hybrid Musks are in this area, too: 'Francesca' with apricot-yellow blooms, making a leafy bush of graceful habit, and one from America with creamy flesh-coloured flowers and a fine scent called 'Bishop Darlington'.

On round the house and one comes across *R. abyssinica*, reputed to be a rather tender and considerably more prickly form of *R. moschata*, which originated in the country that gives it its name, and here, too, is the original of the rose that Mr Brooke calls 'Sophie's Perpetual' after Countess Sophie Beckendorff but which I believe is the same rose as the 'Dresden China', which appeared in the catalogue of rose growers Ernest Paul and Company in 1926. Yet another unusual rose is 'Wolverston' or the Wolverston Rose, found growing on Wolverston Church and believed to be a variety raised by William Paul in about 1860. Lime Kiln garden is full of such fascinating speculations and question marks hang in the air over many of the roses. Maybe I have been guilty of concentrating too much on the unusual, for a garden like this makes rose snobs of us all, but you would be hard put to find many of the roses elsewhere so it would be a pity not to mention them. At the same time, it is a garden where the usual become unusual, at least in size, and where the fairly common *R. californica* 'Plena' carries something in excess of 8000 blooms on a single bush.

All of this has been achieved on a chalky soil, on which it is commonly said that roses will not grow well, if at all. True, this particular *R. californica* was started off in a 1 m (3 ft) deep hole filled with topsoil, peat and leafmould with a handful of bonemeal thrown in and many of the other roses had the same good send-off, but after that they have thrived with the minimum of attention. Only the few Flori-bundas and Hybrid Teas that have been tried have not been particularly successful, so do not visit Lime Kiln if you are expecting a garden of conventional bedding roses. Nothing is conventional there. It is wild and wonderful and with the magic of a fairy tale at high summer. 'I wouldn't want to make it look like a gardener's garden, all clipped an' spick and span, would you?' as Dickon said in *The Secret Garden*. 'It's nicer like this with things runnin' wild, an' swinging' and catchin' hold of each other.'

Helmingham Hall

Helmingham

East from Stowmarket on A1120 and then south on B1079 to Helmingham.
Tel. 047 339 217
The Lord and Lady Tollemache
Open, gardens only, on Sundays from May to September, or by appointment for parties.

Helmingham Hall is one of two great moated country houses in East Anglia that have notable rose gardens. At one of them I asked rather naively if these moats were a purely ornamental feature and it was pointed out to me, most courteously, that they had been there since the time of the Wars of the Roses and that they had been dug very definitely for defensive purposes. In its present form Helmingham dates from late in the fifteenth century and the 18.2 m (60 ft) wide moat is still largely intact. You have to drive over a working drawbridge to reach the inner courtyard and the front door, though visitors to the gardens normally use the entrance near the stable shop and tea rooms.

Helmingham is perhaps unique in having two moats, one round the house and a much older one, thought to be of Saxon origin, round the walled garden probably to protect stock from marauders. The wall of the garden dates from 1745 and surrounds it on three sides only, the fourth side, which faces the house, remaining open. Here a wide grass causeway breaches the moat to give access to the garden.

The first part of this has two knot gardens, one on either side of the central grass path, in which mauve violas (*Viola conuta*) fill (or did when I saw them last) the beds which are surrounded by low box hedges. In the centre of each is an urn surrounded by white tobacco plants and all round the outside, against the walls, are wide beds in which Lady Tollemache, a skilled gardener, is building up a collection of Hybrid Musk roses. Her intention is to make it as complete as possible, which would be a bigger task than many people realize. Taking only those raised by the Reverend Joseph Pemberton, in addition to the well-known 'Penelope', 'Cornelia', 'Danaë', 'Felicia', 'Moonlight', 'Pax', 'Prosperity' and 'Pink Prosperity', 'Thisbe' and 'Vanity' there are much rarer ones, not all of which are still in commerce. They include 'Aurora', 'Callisto', 'Ceres', 'Charmi', 'Clytemnestra', 'Daphne', 'Daybreak', 'Fortuna', 'Nur Mahal' and a good many more. Then there are the quite numerous later German varieties such as 'Hamburg' and 'Erfurt', one or two American ones, such as 'Bishop Darlington', those appearing under the name of Bentall, and all this without harking back to the pioneer of the group, Peter Lambert, who preceded even Pemberton with varieties like 'Trier', a rose on which the latter based his initial breeding lines.

Pemberton was a clergyman who lived in the village of Havering-atte-Bower, in Essex. He, with his sister Florence, started in the first instance to raise plants for friends. Eventually they were doing this on such a scale that they decided to start a nursery. Their gardener was A. J. Bentall and he and his wife worked also in the nursery. On Florence's death the entire stock of roses was bequeathed to the Bentalls, who set up a small nursery on their own in the same village. It appears (and for much of this information I am indebted to Hazel Le Rougetel) that it was Mrs Bentall who was the hybridist and to her must be credited the breeding of 'Buff Beauty', the provenance of which has remained a mystery for so long. One parent at least is now known, the Noisette rose 'William Allen Richardson'.

But back to Helmingham. Passing through a wrought-iron gate in the dividing wall that bisects the moat garden, you enter what I hesitate to call, as I have used the word bisect, the larger half. This is, in turn, divided into four enormous beds for vegetables, round each of which are really spectacular herbaceous borders. Behind them, trained on wires so that they hide the vegetables, are climbing roses, crimson-purple 'Gruss an Teplitz', Ayrshire ramblers, 'Albertine', 'New Dawn', 'Félicité et Perpétue', the climbing Hybrid Tea 'Rich-mond', 'Debutante' (which is rather similar to 'Dorothy Perkins' but not as subject to mildew), 'Alister Stella Gray' which is rarely out of flower through the summer, 'The Garland' and one of its offspring, 'Blush Rambler'. This last was raised by Cants of Colchester in 1903 and is almost thornless; it has fragrant, semi-double, light pink flowers in small trusses and is quite a rarity. There are also a few other roses on the wires that nobody so far has been able to identify.

The blooms of all of these are in the old rose colours, so the flowering plants in the borders in front of them have been chosen to blend well: pinks, reds, creams and silvers. The stronger-coloured flowers – hot oranges, reds and yellows – come to the fore in late summer when most of the roses are over.

On the other side of the walls, between them and the moat, are long beds with different planting schemes. If, for instance, you walked back towards the house along the outside of the southern wall, it would be to admire the paeony and iris border and the roses that are there too. Among them are the light-crimson Hybrid Perpetual 'Captain Hayward', 'Boule de Neige', 'Desprez à Fleurs Jaunes', 'Richmond', 'Stanwell Perpetual' and a number more.

On the farther side of the house, to the east, Lady Tollemache has created an entirely new garden of tremendous charm, though this one is not normally open to the public. Brick steps lead down into a knot garden containing plants that were in cultivation before 1750, the majority of which are herbs, so there is much greygreen foliage to be seen. At the far end, right across the garden, is a double hedge of the Gallica 'Rosa Mundi' which, in full bloom, is one of the gayest sights imaginable with its pink and white striped flowers.

A gap in the centre of this hedge leads to an old rose garden where there are beds containing species and members of all the old rose families backed by a great vista of parkland beyond. Not too far away is the swimming pool and near to it are large specimens of 'Nevada', R. sericea 'Heather Muir', 'Cerise Bouquet' and 'Raubritter', while 'Bobbie James' scrambles up one of the many cherry trees.

Fortunate visitors of the future may well find even more to delight them. Lady Tollemache talks with great enthusiasm of her plans for extending the rose plantings and this is clearly a garden with a great future as well as a wonderful past and present.

Arthingworth Manor

Desborough

Five miles south of Market Harborough on A508. Take turning on left signposted to Arthingworth. Turn right on entering village and Manor is on left up long drive. Tel. 0858 86 219
Mr and Mrs William Guinness
Open under the National Gardens Scheme.

Two wings of Arthingworth Manor form a wide angle enclosing the forecourt with the front door in the middle. The soft pink blooms of 'New Dawn' are on the walls to either side and up a gentle slope ahead is a long lawn with trees and gently curving beds flanking it. In these grow a fine selection of shrubs and some roses, 'Canary Bird' and 'William Lobb' amongst them, but the soil is limy so there are no ericaceous plants, rhododendrons, camellias or lime-hating heathers. Fortunately, roses are tolerant and, though they prefer a slightly acid soil, they are perfectly happy in what they find at Arthingworth, as their exuberant growth shows, although, of course, they are very lovingly tended by Mrs Guinness.

As you move out from the house and up the lawn, immediately on the right is an intriguing herb garden divided into small brick squares, with one square for each herb except for a semi-circle at the end. Opposite is a round bed with a box edging, planted with pink and white roses, and beyond it you bear left, past a fine show of delphiniums and through an opening in a high brick wall. On this grow the deep velvety-red climber 'Château de Clos Vougeot', 'Leverkusen' and 'New Dawn', which you see everywhere in this garden, not just as single specimens but in threes and fours and more. To your left 'Gloire de Dijon' and an enormous *R. helenae* (or maybe two of them) almost cover an end wall of the house. To the right are the rather sad, half-demolished remains of the old Manor, where Mrs Guinness plans to create a ruin garden, a throwback to the days when ruins were specially built for just that purpose. However, your path now takes you across the grass towards a croquet lawn with trees and shrubs in island beds, philadelphus, *R. glauca* and 'Frühlingsgold' and the purple-leaved *Cotinus coggygria* among many others. At the far side is a retaining wall above one of the drives to the farm (Arthingworth Manor is a working farm), with open countryside beyond. *R. × paulii* is trained along the top of the wall but is not really draping over it and trailing down as it should, so another rose could be tried there – 'Raubritter' perhaps.

From this lawn you duck and weave into a secret path through the overhanging branches of shrubs and trees. Rugosas with their vicious spines grow on either side, but fortunately not too close, and after a short while you emerge once more, by the walls of the ruin. Past this and down a gentle slope, again under trees, you come to the rose garden, but one of the trees will certainly detain you first, if only briefly. A pterocarya, a member of the walnut family, it has enormous leaves and female catkins fully 30 cm (12 in) long.

The rose garden is on rising ground, positioned carefully by the Guinnesses so that a large part of it can be seen from a distance. The roses are planted in beds in great drifts of each variety, interspersed with smaller groupings. Their luxuriant growth and the sheer beauty of their multitude of flower forms are a source of wonder and envy to someone who gardens, as I do, on practically pure sand, on which most roses struggle to thrive.

'Raubritter' sprawls down a bank, covering a great deal of ground with its lovely, globular pink blooms; 'Felicia'; a great bank of star-studded *R. × paullii*; 'Fru Dagmar Hastrup', 'Henry Martin', 'Constance Spry' (rather in need of support, so great is the weight of bloom), 'Tuscany Superb', 'William Lobb', 'Golden Wings', 'Mme Hardy', 'Honorine de Brabant', 'Centifolia', 'Reine des Violettes' and many more are here. Among them the pink spikes of foxgloves make a pleasing contrast of form, with pansies used here and there for underplanting. Whichever path you take, beauty is abundant, and fragrance is in the air. This path leads past 'Penelope' and 'Scarlet Fire', another one past *R. sericea pteracantha*,

'Königin von Danemarck', 'Fantin Latour' and 'Paul's Himalayan Musk' vanishing into the trees above.

Above the rose garden you can walk once more through the long grass among trees and if you bear a little to the right there is a slope leading back towards the house on which a number of unusual roses have been grown as standards. 'Max Graf' is one admirably suited for this because of its long trailing shoots, but *R. fedtschenkoana*, *R. × paulii* and *R. glauca* are perhaps a little less successful, though in the case of *R. glauca* it looks as if the standard stem is created from one of the shoots of the rose and not an understock. I have tried this way of creating standards and, in theory, it ought to work very well, but somehow it never does and I go back rather reluctantly to the Rugosa understock.

As you move on and circle round the ruin there is a steep, high bank on the left completely hidden under a great mass of 'Nevada', a sight to dazzle the eyes in early summer with its snowy whiteness, as scarcely a leaf can be seen beneath its mantle of bloom. Further on

there is yet another special garden, hedged round, which is devoted to white-flowered shrubs, to which 'Mme Plantier', 'Blanc Double de Coubert', *R. × alba* 'Maxima', 'Mary Manners' and 'White Cécile Brunner' all contribute. Nearby a very long border, with the wall of the vegetable garden behind it, houses roses in various stages of health or senility. Once grown especially for cutting, they are now due for replacement, while in the vegetable garden itself, the walls of which are literally lined with 'New Dawn', are more Hybrid Teas and Floribundas for cutting.

There are two ways in which you can drive in to Arthingworth from the road, so make sure that you take the right one, either coming in or going out – or both. On one of them you drive past a Rugosa hedge that beats all others for sheer length. It is, though, of a single variety, 'Roseraie de l'Hay', and although I prefer, perhaps, the mixture of red and white roses in the hedges at Clapton and St Albans, this one is still magnificent, and a fitting exit from a magnificent garden.

'Complicata' is, surprisingly, a Gallica hybrid, but much more resembles a wild rose.

Doddington Hall

Lincoln

From Lincoln, 5 miles south on A46, turn west on
B1190 for Doddington.
Tel. 0522 694308
Mr Antony Jarvis
Open, house and garden, from May to end September on
Sundays, Wednesdays and Bank Holiday Mondays.

Doddington Hall is an example of an Elizabethan mansion which has remained virtually unchanged since the day it was completed in 1600. It is a vast, turreted building of brick and stone and the walled garden to the west, now given over largely to roses and irises, still has its original walls. This was replanted under the supervision of Kew Gardens in 1900, replacing the Victorian style with something more in keeping with its Tudor origins. The central area is now a four-part knot garden, the beds of the upper part nearer the house divided by low box hedges and those of the lower half set in lawns. All are planted with either roses or irises.

There is a drawing by Kip, dated 1705, proving that the overall layout of the garden has changed very little since his day. On this you can recognize clearly the long vista that you still see when standing on the terrace that overlooks the walled garden. On the far side and directly ahead, large eighteenth-century wrought-iron gates lead into a long avenue that stretches away into the distance, lined at first by Irish yews and then by Lombardy poplars (though the latter are due to be replaced in the future by broad-leaved limes). The plantings of old roses wherever you go, which Mr Jarvis is extending every year but particularly in the Wild Garden, were started by his parents. It was a relative of his, who took part in Kingdon Ward's last plant-hunting expedition in the 1930s, who introduced many of the rhododendrons you can find there too.

The terrace is a good place to start on a tour of the garden. Part paved and part grass, it runs almost the full width of the house. On the walls are some of the more usual old-time climbers such as 'Zéphirine Drouhin', 'Mme Caroline Testout' and 'Félicité et Perpétue', but the Bourbon 'Mme Isaac Pereire' and 'Gipsy Boy' are also trained most effectively against the walls instead of being grown as shrubs. 'Gipsy Boy', especially, covers a wall extremely well with its dark, purplish-red blooms, as it freely sends out new canes from the base which not all climbers will do.

There is a lavender hedge at the edge of the terrace and broad steps lead down to a gravel path with wide beds of herbaceous plants and old roses, edged with old-fashioned pinks between it and the terrace.

Turning to the left, some of the roses you will find are 'Chinatown', 'Rosa Mundi' and 'Empress Josephine', with day lilies, yellow loosestrife and campanulas keeping them company. On the right are the parterre beds with their plantings of iris and bedding roses, and as you reach the first corner of the path the roses continue, backed now by the mellow brick walls that give the garden such character. Among them are *R. californica* 'Plena', 'Golden Wings', 'Complicata', 'Mme Alfred Carrière' on the wall itself, 'Félicité Parmentier', with its soft-yellow buds and double blush-pink blooms, and *R. glauca*, with irises, hardy geraniums and other plants to set them off. By the time you reach the next corner the area with beds set in grass to your right has replaced the parterre. A terracotta urn forms a focal point on either side of this and among the roses to be found here are 'Dusky Maiden', 'Plentiful' and one of the best new deep-red Floribundas of recent years, 'The Times'.

Moving on across the bottom wall you see the striped Gallica 'Perle des Panachées', 'St Nicholas', 'Reine des Violettes' and, on the far side of the gate into the yew avenue, 'Complicata' runs riot against the wall. Nearby is a big bush of the Gallica 'Alain Blanchard' with its wide-open deep-maroon flowers with their central boss of golden-yellow stamens, while in the beds in the grass to the left are 'Penelope' and creamy-pink 'Grace Abounding'. The bed along the final wall that completes the circuit of the walled garden has a second 'Alain Blanchard' in it and some of the other roses are 'Officinalis', 'Thisbe', 'Maiden's Blush', 'De Meaux', 'Mme de la Roche-Lambert', 'Cardinal de Richelieu', 'Pink Prosperity' and *R. ×*
dupontii used as a climber. Below the terrace on this side are more roses and potentillas.

An opening in the wall at the north-west corner of the house leads out onto a wide gravelled area and a left turn down steps, flanked by the soft-pink blooms of huge bushes of 'Fritz Nobis', brings us to the side of a croquet lawn. Turn right on reaching the far side of this and a long avenue stretches ahead.

To one side of the avenue hornbeams have recently been planted. They are still only seedlings and you have to visualize what they will look like in six or seven years time. However, there are roses as well as hornbeams along the avenue and to the right the most grotesquely contorted ancient Spanish chestnut, seedlings from which apparently take on equally incredible forms. Nearby is a small bower over which the white rose 'Mme Alfred Carrière' climbs.

At the end of the avenue is a large urn, but before you reach it a left turn down some steps takes you into the long grass of the Wild Garden, where you can wander at will over its 2 hectares (5 acres). Apart from the rhododendrons mentioned earlier, many of the larger shrub roses are found in this part of the garden, especially species such as *R. californica* and *R. sericea pteracantha*, while climbers and ramblers like 'Paul's Himalayan Musk' and 'Sir Cedric Morris' form pink or creamy-white waterfalls of bloom cascading down from the tree-tops.

Bearing to the left through the Wild Garden you come eventually to a grass maze, one of the most ancient forms, and beyond that is the yew avenue first glimpsed while you were standing on the terrace, which leads back towards the house past an orchard on the left and the tennis court on the right. In spring the grass between the yews is bright with spring bulbs, lighting up the rather sombre green of the trees, and at rose time colour is provided by huge bushes of *R. moyesii* beside the wrought-iron gate that leads you back once more into the walled rose garden and so to the end of the tour.

Little Ponton Hall

Grantham

Three miles from Grantham. Turn off A1 for Great Ponton at south end of Grantham by-pass.
Tel. 047683 221
Mr and Mrs Alastair McCorquodale
Open under the National Gardens Scheme.

Little Ponton Hall is approached down a long curving drive and you see as you draw near to the Hall that there are roses on either side. I will discuss these in rather more detail later, but in the meantime the long frontage of the house itself comes into view with 'Paul's Lemon Pillar', 'Gloire de Dijon' and 'Mme Alfred Carrière' spreading over the walls on either side of the front door. Pulling up on the wide gravel forecourt, you look back over wide lawns, the more distant foreground (if that makes sense) dominated by a magnificent Cedar of Lebanon, with a small stream beyond.

The house was built in 1640, but added to at a later date. Mr McCorquodale says, like his father before him apparently, that to him everything in the garden is a poppy, but no one takes him too seriously for both he and his wife have a great love of plants of many kinds. It is his wife who is especially fond of roses.

The evidence of this is visible before you even move from the front of the house. Immediately to the left, against the wall, is a long bed with old shrub and modern roses in it. Some of the varieties here are 'Moonlight', 'Ballerina', 'Kathleen Ferrier', 'Hunter', 'Cardinal de Richelieu' and the Moss rose 'Monsieur Pelisson', while that lovely rambler 'Apple Blossom' lights up the wall behind with its soft-pink flowers. 'Mme Alfred Carrière' and *R. longicuspis* are its neighbours.

You now turn right over a small stream and retrace your steps for a short way down the drive. On the left, beyond the bridge, is a mixed planting of the two hybrid musks 'Penelope' and 'Felicia', making a hedge about 22.5 m (25 yds) long, under which bulbs are planted for the spring. There are several Rugosas on the other side of the drive, and box and yew trees clipped informally.

Soon a view opens up to the right down a small slope and back across the stream towards the house. If you turn down this slope and move along the water to the left there are clumps of 'Nevada', 'Complicata' and 'Cerise Bouquet' in island beds, with 'Canary Bird' beyond them. However, from this point you turn back along the stream past more island beds of Hybrid Musks, 'Cornelia', 'Buff Beauty' and then a *R. rugosa* 'Alba', which has suckered most attractively to form an enormous thicket overhanging the bank of the stream. Ahead a number of trees are being rapidly engulfed by climbers such as 'Wedding Day' and 'Bobbie James' and there are one or two more roses planted round about.

A small footbridge leads across to the other side of the stream and 'Raubritter' is gradually spreading right across its parapet of rustic poles. The house is now almost directly ahead over the wide lawn, but you turn to the left and stroll 90 m (100 yds) or more to where there are

'Fritz Nobis' is a comparatively modern hybrid that blends well with the old roses.

more beds with 'Agnes', *R. paulii*, *Philadelphus* 'Belle Etoile', *Rubus tridel* and the roses 'Hunter' and 'Fritz Nobis' planted in them. 'Wedding Day' climbs an elder in front of a group of other trees and the 'Ednaston Rose' climbs yet another tree. This spectacular and very vigorous climber has huge panicles of white flowers and will not be found in any of the reference books or nursery lists. It came originally from Holker Hall in Cumbria and was given by Mrs Cavendish to Mrs Stephen Player of Ednaston Hall in Derbyshire. Nobody knew its origin, so it was christened the 'Ednaston Rose' and in due coı rse a few friends acquired cuttings, so it is spreading gradually.

If you now work your way round the perimeter of this vast lawn along a bed with many grey-leaved plants, paeonies, irises and roses, you reach an arbour with an urn on either side planted with geraniums. Mrs McCorquodale rescued the arbour from a rubbish dump and it now forms one of the most pleasing features of the garden. The rose 'Minnehaha' and *Clematis henryii* climb the sides and the Gallica rose 'Charles de Mills' is planted to one side of it. You can sit there and admire the fine prospect across the grass to the stream and beyond.

Passing on, there is a long herbaceous bor-der backed by a beech hedge leading you nearer to the house. There are roses here, too, with 'Rosa Mundi' and *R. glauca* at one end and, in the centre by a seat, 'Paul's Himalayan Musk Rambler' climbing a walnut tree. Along the north side of the house is a small planting of 'Anthony Waterer' and then a stroll under chestnuts and willows takes you to a wall on which are many climbers, 'Parkdirektor Riggers', *R. longicuspis*, *Clematis montana* 'Rubra' and 'Grandiflora' among them.

A door in the wall leads through into the vegetable garden and, past a great range of greenhouses, is a corner where an ancient octagonal dovecote stands, in which the McCorquodales keep something like sixty fantail pigeons. Hybrid Teas and Floribunda roses are grown near this, largely for cutting for the house, and just beyond it a wrought-iron gate indicates the way to the swimming pool. Here roses such as 'Maigold', 'Albertine', *R. virginiana* 'Plena' and 'Scarlet Fire' are to be found either on the walls or planted as specimens in the grass.

This gracious garden has a great feeling of serenity; roses have been used with much skill, blended in with the other plantings so that you do not realize until you look back and take stock just how many there are.

The Manor House

Bitchfield

Take A52 from Grantham and turn left onto B1176 to Bitchfield. House on right in village just beyond a disused inn (frame for inn sign still in place as a landmark).
Tel. 047685 261
Mr John Richardson
Open under the National Gardens Scheme and by appointment.

The Manor House garden at Bitchfield – some 0.6 hectares (1½ acres) – is not especially large, but it is an enchanting, first-rate example of how roses, mostly old but in some cases quite modern, can be used imaginatively as part of a whole scheme, rather than as a feature on their own.

From the forecourt of the house (really a stable yard) a door leads out onto a paved terrace where the purplish-red flowers of 'Violette' grace one of the walls and geraniums grow in attractive, glazed Chinese pots. A low stone wall with a planting trough built into the top, bright with colour, surrounds the terrace. To the right the view takes in a wide stretch of countryside with the spire of Bitchfield church in the distance.

It is, however, the subtly blended colours of a long border, running down a gentle slope from the terrace and along the whole of one side of the garden that catches the eye. Backed for half its length by a long, low brick building, an annexe to the Manor, it is broken up at intervals by yew buttresses. At the near end immediately below the terrace, beside steps that lead down onto the lawn, is that lovely, but rarely seen, Pemberton rose 'Nur Mahal' and just beyond it *Alchemilla mollis* has been allowed to run riot. Backing these on the wall are the dark, dusky-red, almost black, blooms of the sweetly scented climber 'Guinée'.

Moving on down the border you find roses galore, obviously very carefully nurtured, for they have a robustness that is not by any means always seen elsewhere. Among them are 'Reine des Violettes', 'Paul's Lemon Pillar' on the wall, 'Pax', 'Aloha', 'Rosa Mundi', that strange, ghostly climber 'Ash Wednesday' (described on page 152), 'Gipsy Boy', *R.* × *alba* 'Maxima' (the Jacobite Rose), 'Chanelle', 'Constance Spry', 'Penelope' and *R.* × *harisonii*. Blended

with them are *Buddleia alternifolia*, poppies, foxgloves and many other plants.

As you reach the end of the border and, in fact, the bottom of the garden you discover that Mr Richardson has had the imagination to replace the fence with a ha-ha, which was invisible from the terrace so that the view to the church and beyond is quite uninterrupted. You go along it past an island bed with yellow 'Charles Austin' and two bushes of 'Cerise Bouquet', set off by the foliage of a purple rhus and other shrubs. A grey-leaved weeping pear and a yew hedge are to the right, with a golden, cut-leaved elder forming a striking feature.

Moving on, you come to an informal pool on the left, with a small cascade at its farther side. So well does it blend with its surroundings, that it is hard to believe that it is not a natural feature and was created by Mr Richardson. Moisture-loving plants surround it and where the ground rises on the side towards the house are roses predominantly in yellows and creamy-white, such as 'Graham Thomas' and 'Tynwald'.

Beyond the pool, at the point by the yew hedge where you begin to move up the gentle slope towards the top of the garden, is a specimen planting of 'Nevada' and a grey-painted seat, with more shrub roses in a long bed edged with *Viola cornuta* in both its white and blue forms. 'Wilhelm' and 'Celestial' are two of the roses and there is a massive planting of one of Mr Richardson's favourites, 'Raubritter'. Beyond, interplanted with tree paeonies, are 'Tuscany Superb', 'Mme Isaac Pereire' and her light pink sport, 'Mme Ernst Calvat' (both equally sweet-smelling), *R.* × *alba* 'Maxima', 'Tour de Malakoff', 'President de Sèze', 'Chianti', 'Fritz Nobis' and 'Paul Neyron' of the vast, mop-like, deep-pink flowers that outdo even those of 'Peace' for size.

Near the top of the slope you bear left past more 'Raubritter', 'Hunter', 'Golden Wings' and 'Felicia', while a little further on is another group including 'Fellemberg' and 'Thisbe', and beyond them *R. sancta* (the Holy Rose of Abyssinia) making a starry mound. 'Rambling Rector', 'Bobbie James' and 'François Juranville' are among the roses climbing into fruit trees to your left, together with a 'Wedding Day' so vast that it is difficult to believe that it was planted only seven years ago.

The house is now in front of you once more, with the creamy-white of 'Mme Alfred Carrière' and the pink of 'Parade' showing against its walls. Immediately in front of it at this side is a small topiary garden, the formality of the low box hedges contrasting with the informality of the planting in the rest of the garden. In the middle is a square bed with an armillary sphere on a pedestal, a nice period touch. It sums up the successful blending of new with old that is so much a feature of this garden.

Brewery House Cottage

Gamston

A638 Retford–Markham Moor road, 3 miles south of Retford. Turn into village, cross River Idle bridge; cottage on right.
Tel. 077783 585
Mr C. M. D. Polhill
Open under the National Gardens Scheme.

Brewery House Cottage, dating from about 1860, was built over the foundations of a candle wick factory, and the remains of the floor of this are only just below the surface of parts of the garden near the house. This has meant the use of a pickaxe whenever Mr Polhill wished to plant a shrub, a difficulty triumphantly overcome. The roses and other plants and shrubs, all most skilfully blended, revel in the conditions and each variety is seen at its very best.

Almost at once in this delightful garden you are faced with a mystery. Covering a large part of the cottage to one side of the porch and reaching right up to the pantiled roof is a climber, and neither Mr Polhill nor anyone else who has seen it knows what it is. To me, it is quite indistinguishable, except in its habit of growth, from the Hybrid Musk 'Penelope'. I have compared the two, flower to flower and leaf to leaf, and found them identical, but who has heard of a climbing sport of 'Penelope'? No one that I can discover. There are, however, some climbing genes somewhere in the Hybrid Musk family, as witness 'Francis E. Lester', a child of the Hybrid Musk 'Kathleen', and one parent of 'Penelope' might possibly be the Noisette climber 'William Allen Richardson'. So for my money Brewery House Cottage has the only 'Climbing Penelope' in the country, and perhaps in the world! An interesting start, as its creamy blooms look very good against the mellow brick of the cottage wall.

Standing in the doorway you can see enormous bushes of 'Iceberg', one to the left and one to the right at each corner of the cottage, and there are roses and other shrubs in whichever direction you look. They ring the small lawn and line the narrow, secret paths that lead away from it in various directions. Without moving from the spot, the most superficial glance round in a clockwise direction takes in a fine philadelphus, 'Cerise Bouquet', the biggest 'Empress Josephine' I have ever seen mingling with *R. californica* 'Plena', 'Constance Spry' flanked by a white and a yellow potentilla, a purple-leaved berberis and a weeping pear, 'Celeste', 'Felicia' with 'Pink Grootendorst' behind it, 'Rosa Mundi' and, up some steps to the right, the soft pink blooms of 'Paul's Himalayan Musk' tumbling from the branches of a tall lilac.

Which way should you go first after this quick and tempting survey? For this garden does not have a clearly defined route to follow. It is not large and the roses and shrubs are closely planted, merging exuberantly with one another and tending to disguise and hide the entry to a path until you are almost upon it. However, there is an opening to be seen across the lawn to the left, which leads into a short path and, taking it, you are at once surrounded by roses and the heady scent of many of them is in the air. They include 'Königin von Danemarck', *R. rugosa* 'Rubra', 'Complicata', 'Cornelia', 'Penelope' (handy for comparison with the one on the cottage wall), 'Mme Pierre Oger', 'Louise Odier' and 'Great Maiden's Blush'. In an island bed, where the path loops back on itself, are 'Mutabilis', 'Bloomfield Abundance', 'Old Blush', *Dianthus* 'Loveliness', purple sage, yellow foxgloves and many grey-leaved plants, while the lax shoots of 'Vanity', bearing their clusters of deep-pink, single flowers, partially bar the way into a small branch path with a view of open fields at its farther end.

And so back towards the lawn past 'Chinatown', 'Buff Beauty' grown as a standard and 'Maigold' as a shrub, 'Cantabrigiensis', *R. moyesii* and other shrubs, intertwined with species clematis and the hybrid 'Royal Velours'.

On the other side of the lawn the way to go is more clearly marked and you wander under trees towards the area round the drive. 'Scarlet Fire' is to the left and 'F. J. Grootendorst' to the right under a large hawthorn, its branches already weighed down by an all-conquering 'Kiftsgate'. By the drive itself are the Sweet

Brier (*R. rubiginosa*), *R. sericea pteracantha*, 'Heather Muir' and *R. soulieana* off to the left. All of which leads you to another area where, in the last five years, many more shrub roses have been planted. Such is Mr Polhill's enthusiasm for them, they are, in fact, invading (with permission) the orchard of a neighbouring farm which adjoins Brewery House Cottage. There is no defined boundary between the two, so there is no saying how far the roses will have advanced by the time anyone reads this account.

A fine selection exists already – 'Fantin Latour', 'Mme Legras de St Germaine', 'Empress Josephine', 'Mme Hardy' of the immaculate white blooms, 'Amy Robsart', 'The Portland Rose' (also known as 'The Duchess of Portland'), 'Hippolyte', 'Belle de Crécy', 'Baron Girod de l'Ain', 'Nymphenburg', 'Lykkefund', *R. × dupontii*, 'Shailer's White Moss', 'Tuscany Superb', 'Mousseline' and many, many more. In a small bed, as befits their size, are 'Little White Pet' and 'Carol', one of the Garnette group of roses (Floribundas really) which has been traditionally grown for the cut-flower trade and is not supposed to do too well in the open in the United Kingdom. I have grown them myself, however, and found, as Mr Polhill has, that they are perfectly satisfactory in the garden, provided you have genuine sports of the original deep-red 'Garnette' and not the fairly large number of roses on which the appellation of Garnette has been fastened.

I have probably not emphasized enough Mr Polhill's use of the mock orange for he has shown to perfection how the many forms of philadelphus blend with the old roses and mingle their fragrance. You leave this garden with memories of the heady scents of both, and of the sumptuous double blooms of old roses with their subtle pinks, mauves and purples, in perfect harmony with the more simple, but no less lovely, flowers of 'Belle Etoile', 'Virginal' and the rest.

A rose arching over one of Brewery House Cottage's many paths, with a glimpse of the open fields beyond.

Flintham Hall

Newark

On A46 six miles south-west of Newark. Turn off at
Flintham sign. Flintham Hall drive on right.
Tel. 0636 85214
Mr Myles Thoroton Hildyard
Open under the National Gardens Scheme and by
appointment.

The Thorotons were living in the vicinity of
Flintham in the Middle Ages and the Hall itself
goes back to 1300. In 1815 the families of
Thoroton and Hildyard were united by mar-
riage and Colonel Thomas Thoroton adopted
his wife's name, which has been the family
name ever since.

The house, rebuilt at the end of the eighteenth century, was drastically altered again in
the 1850s to the designs of the Nottingham
architect, T. C. Hine. He added the tower and,
most notably, the long library with its gallery
and tall windows, which leads in turn to the
conservatory. This, with its high, arched, glass
roof, its decorative ironwork and central fountain, is a true reminder of the Victorian age and
one of the most perfectly preserved examples
of such architectural extravagance surviving in
the country today. In itself it would make a
journey to Flintham Hall worthwhile, but there
is a notable garden too. The creators of the conservatory would have felt very much at home in
it, for much of it is more in tune with the last
century than this one. It has that indefinable air
of calm and permanence that comes only after
many years have passed.

On leaving the conservatory, ahead and
slightly to the right you see a great stretch of
grass leading to a distant lake, with trees and a
classical statue nearer the house. To the left,
beyond the shade cast by an enormous chestnut and a walnut tree, is the long outer wall of
an enclosed garden. In front of this is a wide
mixed border of herbaceous plants, small
shrubs and roses, and at the nearest corner
more shrubs and roses have been allowed to
run riot, mounding one upon the other, producing a spectacle of rare beauty in its blend of
colouring. 'Zéphirine Drouhin', 'Nevada', the
tall plumes of *Macleaya cordata*, the flat pink
heads of *Spiraea* 'Anthony Waterer', 'Rosa
Mundi' and 'The Fairy' are some of the plants
that spring first to mind in this corner and

behind them is a great thicket of *R. × paulii*, the
white flowers star-like against the green of its
leaves and the warm red of the brickwork. To
the left, in island beds, are more roses:
'Complicata', 'Constance Spry' and 'Rosa
Mundi' showing in many places the deep pink
blooms of 'Officinalis' to which it has reverted.

Leave the rest of the long border for the
moment, and pass through a wrought-iron gate
into the walled garden, taking in the beauty of
the apricot-pink single flowers of the climber
'Meg' beside the gate as you go and the fine
show of semi-double pink blooms of the rather
rare Bourbon rose 'Adam Messerich' nearby.
This walled part of the garden dates back to
1790 and some of the cordon fruit trees, with
their gnarled and twisted trunks, look as if they
could well have been planted when it was first
laid out. Several of the paths are lined with
them, though there are more recent plantings
of fruit trees too, and opposite, across the path
you take first, are broad borders under the
walls in which grow hollyhocks, delphiniums,
mulleins, sweetly scented tobacco plants and a
vast selection of roses, some old but some quite
modern. Many, early Hybrid Teas and the like,
are impossible to name, but 'Jacques Cartier',
the Centifolia 'Bullata', 'Charles de Mills' and
'Phyllis Bide' are there, just to mention a few of
the more obvious older ones.

You could ramble for hours in this walled
garden, such is its size and fascination, but the
route takes you along one of the cross paths
and through a great arch in the wall into the
rose garden proper, which Mr Hildyard created some twenty-five years ago, though he is
still adding to it.

Here again it is possible to wander off in
many directions, for there are roses everywhere among the trees, but a stroll along the
wall you have come through will give a flavour
of the rest. The wall itself is worth a pause and a
special mention for, vast though it is, it has
heating channels built into its entire length,
another reminder of the days when gardens of
this kind were run without any considerations
of expense.

In front of it, in a wide bed, roses are
massed: 'Marguerite Hilling', 'Duchesse de
Montebello', 'Gipsy Boy', 'Fantin Latour', 'Fritz
Nobis' and 'Mme Caroline Testout' among
many others on the wall. But branch off after a
while and take a path past a statue of a discus
thrower – one of a number of such classical
statues in the garden – with roses still beside

the way, including *R. pomifera* 'Duplex', the White Rose of York, 'Stanwell Perpetual', 'Complicata', 'Fritz Nobis', 'Celeste' and, in the trees, 'Rambling Rector', 'Kiftsgate' and their clan. However, for sheer mass of bloom one of the most outstanding roses in this part of the garden is 'The Ednaston Rose' (encountered in one or two of the other gardens in this book and described in the account of Little Ponton Hall on page 121) – it really is something very special.

Along another path now, mown like the rest through the long grass in which many of the roses grow, you come across another wall. A door in it leads down some steps into a pheasantry dating from Regency times with many of the brick buildings, though not the Georgian pheasants, still in a remarkable state of preservation.

Unsurprisingly, roses have invaded the pheasantry, including many of the Scotch roses and their hybrids, 'Conrad Ferdinand Meyer', 'Heather Muir', 'Honorine de Brabant', 'Boule de Neige', 'De Meaux', 'Sarah Van Fleet' and many more. Although scattered apparently at random, they were, in fact, planted by Mr Hildyard. They lead you eventually to the far end of the long high wall through which you passed into the walled garden at the beginning of your walk.

Along this are ramblers and climbers, some just beginning to revive from recent harsh winters, and, as already mentioned, there are roses and other plants in the long border in front of it. 'Mary Wallace' and 'Meg' are the two most notable climbers.

By now you have seen just about all the roses, but this garden is worth a visit at other times of the year too, for away on the far side of the house is the Spring Garden, noted for its snowdrops and for its unusual trees, among them four *Quercus* × *hispanica* 'Lucombeana' or 'Lucombe Oaks', a hybrid between the Cork Oak and the Turkey Oak, with dark-grey corky bark and deep fissures.

There is just one more group of roses of interest. To one side of the front door is a bed of Floribundas, almost certainly some of the very early Poulsen varieties, that have been there for many years, probably planted when they first came out under the classification not of Floribundas but of Hybrid Polyanthas. They more than likely date from the 1930s, the period when the Floribunda really started its rise to eminence.

Hodsock Priory

Blyth

Off the B6045 Worksop–Blyth road.
Tel. 090976 204
Sir Andrew and Lady Buchanan
Open under the National Gardens Scheme.

The house here, though largely Victorian, has a Tudor gatehouse and the whole vast building is on the site of a moated manor house, parts of the moat still visible in the garden. It seems likely, however, that man dwelt here even earlier than this, as eleventh- and twelfth-century earthworks have been discovered in the vicinity.

The massive gatehouse is no longer used and you enter from the other side of the house, from a yard at the far corner. From here you can start to explore the garden with the first planting of shrub roses – 'Canary Bird', *R. primula*, 'Complicata' and a number of others – on a grassy bank to the left as you leave the yard. Trees shade them to some extent, but they do not seem to mind, and other roses in the area are 'De Meaux', 'Scarlet Fire', 'Pax', 'Max Graf', *R.* × *paulii*, 'Boule de Neige', *R.* × *alba* 'Maxima' and 'Fritz Nobis'.

A winding gravel path now leads ahead past a small glasshouse and then alongside a small stream, all that remains of the moat at this point. On the far bank are beech trees, and wooden footbridges give access to that part of the garden, but for the moment continue along the path, which rises gently, until you are some way above the stream, and the terraced beds on your left now lead down to it.

The rose plantings begin again here with a great show of 'Iceberg' on your right and a pink Floribunda (anonymous) on your left, together with the bush form of 'Cécile Brunner'. 'Frühlingsgold' marks the spot where the path forks, but keep to the top level, past an enormous bush of 'The Alchymist' on a pillar, more 'Iceberg', 'Officinalis', *R. glauca*, 'Felicia' and 'Alfred de Dalmas', a pink Moss rose.

A line of the Floribunda 'Allgold' follows to the right, giving a great splash of yellow but looking a little incongruous among the predominant pinks and whites of the old roses. Lady Buchanan intends to replace it when she can get around to it and agrees that there are roses that blend more happily with the old ones than this particular variety. Looking across the stream, on the farther bank, great clusters of white flowers show among the branches of an enormous but very dead pear tree; 'Bobbie James' in this case.

On along the path now with many shrub roses on the right where the ground rises slightly – 'Maiden's Blush', 'Mme Hardy' and others – until you reach a point where the gravel path turns to grass and you swing left up the slope and along the back of the border. At the turning point 'Snow Carpet', a miniature ground-cover rose, has been planted, one that really does hug the ground though its use is restricted because of its size. It will eventually cover an area about 1 m (3 ft) across, which is useful in the right place, and it looks most attractive with its double, snowy white flowers.

There are many Sweet Williams planted here among the roses, together with Love-in-the-Mist, blending beautifully with the pink and white striped blooms of the Gallica 'Perle des Panachées', the pinks of Rugosas, the soft mauve petals of 'Belle de Crécy' and the blush tints of 'Félicité Parmentier' and 'Fantin Latour'.

You emerge from the shade of trees onto a wide lawn with the front of the house to your right and, some way to the left, the sun (when it is there) glints on the waters of a small lake, formed by damming part of the stream. There is a formal garden of bedding roses on a wide terrace between you and the house and you are now directly below the terrace's 1.5 m (5 ft) retaining wall, along which a number of roses have been trained, with other shrubs, such as *Carpentaria californica*, mingled among them. In the middle of the wall, steps lead up to the formal garden above you, but for the moment you carry on.

At the far side of the lawn, a gravel path leads towards a short pergola, but before you reach it you pass fruit and vegetable cages and a long border in which those two fine, if slightly temperamental, Floribundas 'Rosemary Rose' and 'Elizabeth of Glamis' mingle happily. On the pergola old blends in with new, 'Karlsruhe' and 'Danse de Feu' with 'Goldfinch' and another white rambler that neither the Buchanans nor I can put a name to. A few shrub roses, such as 'Fantin Latour', grow between the pillars.

Across another wide lawn, this time with the gatehouse and the original front door of the house on your right, you come across plantings of rhododendrons and roses amongst the trees.

They are in groups of three or more, 'Nevada', 'Rosa Mundi', 'Complicata', 'William Lobb' and a number of others, allowed to grow as they will and all the better for it.

With these behind you, you move back towards the south-west corner of the house, where steps lead up to the formal rose garden. There is another mystery rambler (looking very much like a China rose of some kind) by the entrance and on the left a low fence behind which *R. sericea pteracantha* and 'Fritz Nobis' have been planted. 'Aimée Vibert' and other climbers and ramblers grow on the parapet that surrounds the terrace and in the beds cut in the grass are Hybrid Teas and Floribundas, though the selection includes two that have come to be regarded more as shrubs because of their size. These are the yellow and sweetly scented 'Mountbatten', raised by Jack Harkness, and the Kordes rose 'Robusta', which was introduced in 1979 and is probably the most modern rose in the garden. It carries clusters of large, single, scarlet flowers and is reputed to be a Rugosa hybrid, though it is difficult to detect any sign of a Rugosa in its makeup.

Although there are (at present at any rate) no roses in the bog garden which is still being developed at one end of the lake, you should not leave Hodsock Priory without seeing it. A stroll under the willows at the waterside there makes a fitting conclusion to a very pleasant visit.

David Austin Roses

Albrighton

Take exit 3 off M54. For Albrighton turn left off A41, going towards Wolverhampton. Nursery in Bowling Green Lane which leads off High Street, some way out of village.
Tel. 090 722 3931
Show garden and nursery open every day.

This is not, of course, a garden in the same sense as most of the others in this book. A show garden, it is designed primarily to show off what the nursery sells, but it is nevertheless well worth a visit by anyone with any interest in roses at all. In it you will see an incredible range of roses – species or wild roses, all the old rose groups and modern shrub roses, quite a few of the more modern bedding roses and, of course, the varieties that David Austin has bred himself, his English Roses. With most of these, old roses have been crossed with moderns to combine in many cases the best attributes of both – the lovely flower forms and scents of bygone days with the recurrence and more compact growth of modern times.

There are too many roses in the Austin show garden to attempt any kind of listing and the multitude of interesting and, in some instances, unusual varieties would make it rather meaningless to pick out just a few for special mention. If there is a particular rose from any period of history that you wish to buy or study, you are likely to find it here: the nursery has a plan of the garden with details of what is planted where.

The roses in the main part of the display garden, behind the office building, are planted in three straight borders with pillars and other forms of support down the centre of each. The varieties are labelled, but their growth is so exuberant that as the season progresses and the bushes mingle one with another, the supports vanish beneath a tangle of shoots so the labels take a bit of finding. You can walk down each side of all three borders and at the height of summer they are a stunning sight with the scent of roses filling the air.

Towards the far end of the left-hand border a side path leads you into a circular garden with rose beds in three concentric rings. These are used primarily as a show place for the Austin English Roses, though there are some other varieties there as well.

The route from this round garden back to the offices takes you past (but not into) the hybridizing house where, through the glass door in the second half of the summer, you can see the pot-grown roses that have been used in that year's breeding programme, each one decorated with the white tie-on labels that record the details of each cross. Through the door of the next greenhouse new seedling roses from the previous year's hybridizing can be seen beginning to show their paces.

One exception to my policy of not mentioning varieties must be made for David Austin's own 'Dapple Dawn', a huge bed of which runs along the front of the offices. It is a rose that will grow up to 1.5 m (5 ft), and the very large, single, delicate pink flowers have great charm. It is a sport of another Austin rose, 'Red Coat', and both are unrivalled in their profusion of bloom and for continuity.

Shugborough

Milford, Nr Stafford

On A513, 5½ miles east of Stafford. Entrance in Milford.
Tel. 0889 881388
The National Trust, but administered by the Staffordshire County Council.
Open Tuesdays to Fridays and Sunday afternoons.

The River Sow winds through the park here, with a wealth of neo-Grecian buildings and monuments forming focal points among the trees. Among them is the Temple of the Winds designed by James Stewart (known as the 'Athenian Stewart' for reasons that become obvious as one moves about), though the Chinese Pavilion near the ironwork bridge over the river is the work of Sir Piercy Brett. The house dates from 1693, though the impressive portico with its wooden pillars is a late eighteenth-century addition. The present magnificence of Shugborough is due to George Anson and his brother Thomas, later Admiral Lord Anson, who returned from a four-year voyage round the world with booty worth a fortune, and lavished it on the house and grounds.

The rose garden is, in fact, relatively modern. In terms of the overall scale of Shugborough it is also quite small – about 27 by 27 m (30 by 30 yds). It was laid out in 1966 in the Victorian manner: completely symmetrically, with roses in beds cut into the grass, a sundial in the middle and with arches and pillars for the climbing and rambling roses. The climbers, and indeed all the roses, have been chosen for their colourings, which fit in with the Victorian period, although comparatively few of the varieties would actually have been grown in gardens of the time. In fact the only three that might have been are the climber 'Zéphirine Drouhin', 'Little White Pet' and the much older Portland rose 'Jacques Cartier', which has been planted to form the centrepiece of long beds at each end.

Each variety has been used several times, either in the beds or on the pillars or arches, so that the total number is smaller than it might seem at first glance. Although there are twelve pillars and ten arches, only six climbing roses are used, but to great effect. Apart from 'Zéphirine Drouhin', there is 'New Dawn', 'Violette', 'Kathleen Harrop' (which is, of

The climbers 'New Dawn', 'Mary Wallace' and 'Kathleen Harrop' are among those on the arches and pillars in the Victorian-style rose garden at Shugborough.

course, a lighter pink sport of 'Zéphirine Drouhin'), 'Mary Wallace' (which is a Van Fleet climber from 1924 with semi-double rose-pink flowers of considerable size) and 'Climbing Iceberg', the most modern of them all and bidding fair to outflower the lot.

In the beds are 'Yesterday', 'Clarissa', 'Little White Pet', 'Natalie Nypels', 'The Fairy', 'Pink Posy' (like a pink 'Little White Pet'), all of them of the Polyantha type, plus the new, low-growing, deep-red shrub 'Cardinal Hume' and 'Innoxa Femille'. 'Fru Dagmar Hastrup' flanks 'Jacques Cartier' and 'Roseraie de l'Hay' bulks large, and fragrant, at each corner. 'Ballerina' is used in standard form in many of the beds and each pillar has at least one clematis on it as well

as a rose. Here again the varieties and species are restricted with no loss of effect. They are *macropetala*, deep-purple 'Gipsy Queen', *Clematis alpina* 'Columbine', and 'Perle d'Azur'.

Apart from the rose garden, there are not many other roses at Shugborough, though you will find small groups of such varieties as 'Golden Wings' and thickets of Burnet or Scotch roses here and there. Otherwise, there is only a mass – and I do mean mass – planting of 'Allgold' in two huge beds between the house and a lawn of immense proportions dominated by eighteen golden yews planted at intervals across its entire width. You can see both the yews and the 'Allgold' planting from the rose garden; in fact, you cannot miss them.

Arley Hall

Knutsford

*Leave M6 at junction 19 or 20 and join the A50
Knutsford to Warrington road. Turn south at High Legh
for Arley Green. Signposted.*
Tel. 056 585 284
The Hon. M. L. W. Flower
*Open every day, except Mondays, from March to early
October.*

The earliest records of the Arley Hall garden are in the form of a map dating from 1744. The first walled gardens were built in 1746 by Sir Peter and Lady Elizabeth Warburton, who also laid out the shrubberies and pleasure walks on the east side of the house. To see the beginnings of the garden as it is today, you must, however, go to a plan of 1846, displayed in the Tudor Barn. Created between 1840 and 1860 by Rowland and Mary Egerton-Warburton, the garden remains substantially as it was all those years ago, though subsequent generations have made some changes. The present owner's mother, Viscountess Ashbrook, was largely responsible for the extensive plantings of old roses near a small building known as the Tea Cottage, but there are many other roses in this beautiful 3.2-hectare (eight-acre) garden.

If you follow the long drive that opens out into the yard (with the ticket office, shop and Tudor Barn on the left), you glimpse the house through an archway surmounted by a remarkable wooden clock tower. Turn right through the arch and through a small gate into the Flag Garden. Its paved paths divide up the triangular beds which house a mixture of Floribundas and Hybrid Teas, including 'United Nations', a good salmon-pink Floribunda that has long since disappeared from sale, 'Aloha' grown as a shrub (instead of as a climber) in one corner and 'Mme Alfred Carrière' on a wall nearby. This little garden serves as an appetizer to the rose walk – a long straight path with an extensive glasshouse known as The Vinery (but which could equally well be called The Figgery as there are more fig trees than vines in it) on

one side and the kitchen garden on the other, glimpsed through a double line of Rugosa roses on each side of the path. Most of these are a mixture of 'Blanc Double de Coubert' and, I think, 'Belle Poitevine'.

At the far end of the rose walk is an arch in a high brick wall that leads into the walled garden, but the climbers on either side of the entrance are worth a second look. One is the Centifolia shrub 'Fantin Latour', which has climbed to about 3 m (10 ft), and the other the Portland rose, 'Comte de Chambord', which has reached about 1.8 m (6 ft). Both were grown from cuttings by the head gardener, Tom Acton.

The walled garden in its present form dates only from 1960. For many years it was the kitchen garden, with fruit trees trained on the walls, but from 1946 to 1960 it was managed as a commercial market garden. Now it is purely ornamental with a large central pond and surrounding lawns, the beds round the walls filled with plants noted for their attractive foliage and some with striking flowers too, such as *Cranber cordifolia*, like a giant gypsophila, and carpenteria, as well as roses like 'Nymphenburg', the Hybrid Musks 'Felicia', 'Moonlight', 'Buff Beauty' and 'Penelope', and the single-flowered Hybrid Tea 'White Wings'. On one wall is a fine specimen of another rose that can no longer be bought, 'Chaplin's Pink Companion', a much more pleasing pink than 'Chaplin's Pink' itself, which is still quite widely stocked.

At one end of the walled garden there is a paved area with a stone urn on either side and a seat in the middle that gives a view down the whole length of the garden. Around this is a planting of 'Rosemary Rose', that cherry-pink Floribunda with the old-rose look, surrounded in turn by the soft blue of nepeta. Behind the seat is a line of dark-leaved, bright pink 'Buisman's Triumph' and behind that again the shrub roses 'Autumn Fire' and 'Mrs Anthony Waterer'. It always seems odd that a rose breeder would call a rose his 'Triumph', let alone 'Supreme', as in 'Poulsen's Supreme'. What do you follow it with? But the reason for naming many other roses is equally baffling.

Opposite: The Flag Garden at Arley Hall has a mixed planting of Floribundas and Hybrid Teas.

Statuary and roses in the huge walled garden at Arley Hall, with 'Iceberg' in the foreground.

Another view of the walled garden, this time featuring the Hybrid Musk 'Cornelia'.

Hybrid Musk roses frame most of the gates into the walled garden. This one is 'Felicia'.

Nepeta admirably sets off the red roses surrounding the urn at the end of the walled garden.

Through the gate at the far end of the walled garden you can see the end of Arley Hall's famed *Ilex* avenue and can glimpse the park beyond. The trees in the avenue have been clipped in the form of very tall cylinders, though an early painting shows that they were originally pyramidal. It is thought that during the First World War the tops filled out so much, as a result of lack of proper care, that it was decided to change their shape permanently.

Eye-catching as these trees are, as you come out of the walled garden through a handsome pair of wrought-iron gates there is an even more impressive sight immediately to your left. Stretching away into what seems to be the infinite distance – 83 m (90 yds) in reality – is a pair of the most beautiful, and possibly the oldest, herbaceous borders in the country. Flanking either side of a broad grass walk, they are backed by brick walls with yew buttresses at intervals. At midsummer the borders look breathtaking, their colours bright but carefully blended. Beyond them, the shrub rose planting can just be glimpsed but you should first, perhaps, carry on along the *Ilex* avenue.

At the far end, wide steps lead down to the Sundial Circle. The sundial is surrounded by grass and two half-circle beds of the Kordes Hybrid Musk 'Erfurt', a rose so lovely that I am surprised it is not planted in every garden in the country. The large, fragrant, semi-double flowers are lemon-yellow edged and shaded carmine, carried in clusters on long, strong stems. Eventually it will reach about 1.5 m (5 ft) and it is, of course, a recurrent flowerer. Silver-foliaged plants in the Sundial Garden set the roses off to perfection and mock orange bushes form the background, while up a tree nearby is a climber with globular, soft-pink, many-petalled flowers that the experts have, so far, failed to identify.

To reach the shrub roses from the Sundial Circle you can either retrace your steps along the *Ilex* avenue or else follow the Furlong Walk, a grass terrace that separates the garden from the park. Here you will find the principal planting of roses near a small wooden building known as the Tea Cottage, which stands near the edge of the walk in the shadow of a weeping willow. There is a magnificent old cedar nearby and grass paths undulate gently in all directions between the rose beds, which also include a few other shrubs, such as *Cotinus coggyria* (the Smoke Bush), planted here and there to provide attractive contrast.

One of the first roses to catch your eye as you start from the Tea Cottage is the curious little *R. horrida* (*R. biebersteinii*), which has such small white flowers and leaves and such a prostrate habit that it reminds me of nothing so much as a *Cotoneaster horizontalis*. It never grows much higher than 60 cm (2 ft) and spreads out to about the same distance. It does not really justify its name, but as it is the one rose that Lady Ashbrook says she might dispense with, it is clearly not widely loved.

For the rest, the roses are a mixture of species and old garden varieties. Among the former are *R. californica* 'Plena', *R. virginiana* 'Plena', the 'Double Yellow' Scotch rose, *R. fedtschenkoana*, the white flowers of which appear all summer, *R. multiflora carnea* with light pink double flowers, *R. stellata mirifica*, *R. moyesii* 'Geranium', *R. californica* and *R. × dupontii*. Of the old roses, among many others, you will find *R. × centifolia*, 'Tour de Malakoff', 'Mme Isaac Pereire' and its light pink sport 'Mme Ernst Calvat', 'William Lobb', 'Kathleen Harrop', 'Rosa Mundi', 'Fantin Latour', 'Sarah Van Fleet', 'Cardinal de Richelieu', 'Max Graf', 'Henri Martin', 'Félicité Parmentier' and one of the healthiest of all Gallicas, 'Gloire de France'.

There is an atmosphere of peace about the whole rose garden, and in fact tranquillity is a word that comes to mind when thinking of the gardens at Arley Hall. This is not something that happens by accident. It is only achieved by the most careful thought and a feel for the plants that will blend, not only together, but with old brick and stone walls and paved paths that date back many hundreds of years and so have a built-in tranquillity of their own. At Arley Hall this has been achieved to perfection.

Cholmondley Castle

Malpas

Off the A41 Chester to Whitchurch road; signposted.
Tel. 082 922 202
The Marquess and Marchioness of Cholmondley
Open Sundays and Bank Holidays from Easter to September.

'Romantic' is a description that can easily be over-used when writing about great houses and their gardens, but it is certainly appropriate for this 'Gothic' hilltop castle with its glorious garden and the surrounding park. The pre-

*The climbers 'Pink Perpetue' in the foreground and 'New Dawn' on one of the
arches in the rose garden at Cholmondley Castle.*

sent house, with its crenellated towers at each corner, dates only from the turn of the century, although there have been Cholmondleys at Cholmondley Castle since the twelfth century. The present Lord and Lady Cholmondley have lived here since 1950 and have carried out many imaginative schemes to create a garden of great beauty, with roses everywhere.

The Rose Garden itself is not particularly big but it has great charm. It runs along one side of the tennis court, the side netting of which is used to support climbers and ramblers such as 'Dr Van Fleet', 'Kathleen Harrop', 'Zéphirine Drouhin' and the almost obligatory 'New Dawn', through all of which honeysuckle twines itself. Lavender is planted under the roses and features again, in the variety 'Hidcote Blue', as an edging to the raised beds of the central part of the garden. As Lady Cholmondley points out in her guide to the gardens, the rose varieties are changed from time to time so that naming them in a book like this would be rather misleading. The ones I saw there may well not be there now, but the bed on the side of

the garden farthest from the tennis court is more permanently planted and includes such varieties as the two Hybrid Musks 'Buff Beauty' and 'Cornelia', 'Maigold' and the little-known Floribunda-shrub 'Lafter' ('Laughter') which puts on a fine twice-yearly display of cupped, semi-double, salmon-flame coloured flowers.

Steps at the far end of the Rose Garden lead down between herbaceous borders and more roses; 'Mutabilis' from China, 'Auguste Roussel' from France (a salmon-pink hybrid between *R. macrophylla* and the Tea rose 'Papa Gontier', raised by Barbier in 1913) 'Constance Spry' and 'Cerise Bouquet'. Roses trained on metal arches include (once again) 'New Dawn', 'Albertine', 'Leverkusen', 'The Garland', 'Félicité et Perpétue' and 'Evangeline', the latter one of the many ramblers raised from *R. wichuraiana* crosses by M. H. Walsh of Massachusetts early in this century (see also page 78).

The other roses in this vast garden are scattered throughout its length and breadth and the best plan is to follow the route described in

The small shrub rose 'Ballerina' makes an effective standard, as seen at Cholmondley Castle.

the guide book which takes you to all parts of the garden, and to enjoy the beauty of other plants as you walk around. So, on coming through the small gate from the car park, mount the steps as far as the path that runs across the slope ahead of you and turn to the right. Almost straight away you will be rewarded by a massed planting of 'Nevada' and 'Scarlet Fire' down the slope to your right, while on the left are Rugosa roses, tree heaths, a Mount Etna broom and various other genistas.

Carry on and then turn left when you reach the Cherry Walk to stroll under the overhanging branches of *Prunus* 'Shimidsu Sakura' towards the castle. Near the top of the walk, *R. brunonii* 'La Mortola' and *Clematis montana* 'Elizabeth' compete for dominance of a metal arch on their way up into a large yew tree. The white flowers of one and the pink of the other are only seen together if the clematis is late into bloom and the rose exceptionally early, for they do not normally overlap.

Along a grass track below a terrace wall are more cherries and a number of shrubs, and here the climber 'Pompon de Paris' scrambles into the branches of a *Prunus* 'Kanzan' making a nonsense, except perhaps in terms of its flower-size, of its classification as a miniature.

At the end of the terrace a path leads down to The Glade, a sheltered site for the more tender plants though the rose to note especially here is 'Maigold', which is as tough as old boots. 'Maigold' in full bloom is a marvellous sight especially when, as here, it is underplanted with *Primula denticulata* and *Trillium grandiflorum* and with the American *Cornus florida* 'Rubra' with its red bracts and autumn colouring foliage nearby. Grown in a group as shrubs rather than climbers, 'Maigold' roses make a wonderful display quite early in the year, though, sadly, there is little repeat-flowering. Many of the other modern, less rampant, climbers could be used in just the same way and a number of them have a full second flowering.

You now approach the Rose Garden, but before that you pass a tall laurel supporting, so far, a plant of *R. filipes*, of which, of course, 'Kiftsgate' is an extra special form. Does the laurel know what it is in for? I wonder.

Beyond the Rose Garden I have already mentioned some of the roses to be found, mostly integrated into a harmonious whole with other plants. In addition to those mentioned earlier there is 'Fritz Nobis', 'Golden Wings', 'Golden Showers' (another climber that will make a good free-standing shrub), some more Hybrid Musks, 'Lavender Lassie' and the two Floribundas 'Scented Air' and 'Ivory Fashion', the last of which has long been a great favourite in America but is seldom seen in the United Kingdom.

Apart from the main areas with roses, the Temple Garden down near the lake provides a home for 'Kiftsgate' and its offspring 'Diany Binny' which are scaling two ancient oaks, but as they were only planted in 1978 they have not yet taken command. 'Scarlet Fire', *R.* × *cantabrigiensis* and *R.* × *paulii* can also be found in this area and 'Cerise Bouquet' can be seen on the main drive.

The final ascent to the castle leads between beds of 'Queen Elizabeth' and there is a circular bed of the fine, scented, yellow shrub rose 'Chinatown' in the terrace area, where 'Albéric Barbier' and 'Max Graf' tumble over a wall on which climbing roses, abutilon, solanum and the clematis varieties 'Mrs Cholmondley', 'Ville de Lyon', 'Perle d'Azur', as well as the species *montana*, make a fine show early and late.

Chatsworth

Bakewell

Near Bakewell, 2 miles south of Baslow on B6012. Well signposted.
Tel. 024 688 2204
The Duke of Devonshire, but administered by Chatsworth House Trust Limited, Bakewell
Open daily from late March to end October.

The subject of roses does not usually come up when anyone speaks of Chatsworth. In the mind is a picture of a vast, magnificently and intricately landscaped garden, a great deal of it the work of Joseph Paxton who worked for the sixth Duke of Devonshire. There is the seventeenth-century Orangery, Flora's Temple, the Canal Pool with its spectacular Emperor Fountain built to impress an Emperor of Russia whose visit never materialized, and above all the Great Cascade of 1694, with water flowing down the hillside towards the house over a series of terraces from the Cascade House at the top.

Paxton was only twenty-three when he first came to Chatsworth, which makes the scale and the imagination of his achievements there all the more remarkable. The Emperor Fountain, conceived by him, is capable of shooting a jet of water 87 m (290 ft) into the air, the pressure coming solely from the largest of the ponds on the hilltop above, but his most ambitious achievement, the great conservatory, is no longer there. It had to be demolished shortly after the First World War, and its site is now occupied by the Maze.

But what of the roses? There is a formal rose garden quite near the entrance but I do not think that it could be claimed to be exceptional, despite the presence of some good Hybrid Musks. There is also some skilful blending of the lovely white 'Iceberg' with lavender and delphiniums in beds along the east face of the house and near the entrance to the Orangery, which is now the shop. And what else?

On a large area of the hillside north of the site of the Conservatory, Paxton created an incredible landscape of huge rocks, piled one upon another among the trees, with narrow paths leading between them, twisting and turning, up and down, into quiet dells and beside secret pools where the water is black as night. It is the sort of place where the only sounds to break the stillness are the hum of insects or the racketing alarm call of a blackbird.

Over the years many shrubs as well as the trees have grown up, and so have the roses. All through this area climbing and rambling roses cover the shrubs with masses of white or pink bloom or fall in cascades from tree after tree. 'Seagull', *R. longicuspis, R. helenae, R. moschata floribunda*, 'Kiftsgate', 'Francis E. Lester', 'Paul's Himalayan Musk Rambler' are just some of the ones that I think I recognized, and I feel that 'Silver Moon', 'Wedding Day', *R. filipes, R. brunonii* 'La Mortola', 'Bobbie James' and all the rest must be in there somewhere, not just in ones but in twos and threes or more, a great congress of beauty. It is quite breathtaking and a revelation as I have never seen them mentioned anywhere, even in the official guide to the gardens.

A different kind of rose garden indeed, and there is an epilogue for, as you return towards the entrance, ahead and not far from the Rose Garden itself, three or four more of 'Paul's Himalayan Musk' have invaded a small clump of trees and now completely envelop them in their soft pink blooms.

So go to Chatsworth for the roses, neither too early nor too late in the season, for their hour of glory is fairly brief.

Dam Farm House

Brailsford

Five miles south-east of Ashbourne take the Bradley road from A52 opposite the Ednaston Village turning. House 450 m (500 yds) on right.
Tel. 0335 60291
Mrs S. D. Player
Open under the National Gardens Scheme.

The stable yard is as good a place to start as any for a walk round the garden at Dam Farm House. A large, wrought-iron gate in the wall leads out onto a broad grass walk, alive with the colour of herbaceous plants and roses on either side. There is a fascinating, white-painted metalwork bower at the far end and arches leading off into side paths about half-way down. But before going further, a glance back at the wall shows yellow-flowered *R. ecae* and others trained on it, a new way of growing this particular rose which tends as a rule to make a rather ungainly shrub. In fact, most of the old roses will make very successful climbers on a wall, at times reaching undreamed of heights, though mainly staying within manageable size. *R. × paulii*, for instance, is an impressive climber on a wall at Charlecote Park (a National Trust house without much else of interest in the way of roses) and I have seen many other instances elsewhere, like the 'Gipsy Boy' described at Doddington Hall.

There is also much of interest in the mixed borders ahead of you that have been so carefully planned and visualized by Mrs Player. Among the roses you first see are 'Tuscany', 'Mrs Oakley Fisher', 'Little White Pet', 'Ballerina', 'Golden Wings', lanky 'William Lobb' supported by a tall stake, and 'Chapeau de Napoléon'. Then the Jacobite Rose, *R. × alba* 'Maxima', is used to cover the arch on the left, another instance of the imaginative planting to be found everywhere in this garden. Through it you can see the small vegetable garden, and an enormous bush of the Rugosa 'Hunter' is nearby. Mrs Player is one of a growing army of admirers of this deep pink Rugosa, which seems only to be stocked by the nursery of John Mattock, who introduced it in 1961.

Beyond the arch can be found 'La Noblesse', 'Henri Martin', 'Duc de Guiche', 'Königin von Danemarck', 'Celestial' and 'Mme Hardy', with potentillas and other plants and low-growing shrubs. Roses near the bower at the end of the path, picked for their short stature, include the seldom-seen but dainty white Floribunda 'Irene of Denmark', 'Natalie Nypels', deep-pink 'Rose de Rescht' and 'Gruss an Aachen', which some people hold to be the first Floribunda. This argument is hard to follow as one of its parents was the Hybrid Perpetual 'Frau Karl Druschki' and the other a soft-yellow Hybrid Tea 'Franz Deegen'. Not a whisper of the necessary Polyantha strain is anywhere to be heard and the flowers, creamy-white and very double, are twice the size of those of the average Floribunda. It is certainly low-growing and floriferous, and a marvellous bedding rose, but there, to me, the resemblance ends.

The second arch, when you walk back to it, is draped with everlasting sweet peas and honeysuckle and leads out onto a lawn, where a left turn takes you along the other side of one of the borders, past a massive 'Heather Muir' and several bushes of the dwarf-growing Centifolia 'Petite d'Hollande', forming a showy pink mound. An opening in a hedge then leads into a long, fairly narrow part of the garden, bordered on one side by a fence and beyond it a field with the drive running across the middle of it. This gravel-covered area has been planned to be the first part of the garden visitors see so it was important to choose something fairly showy for it. Buddleias, mixed Rugosa roses, including 'Hunter', *R. glauca* and, at the far end, *R. setipoda*, 'Highdownensis' and 'Bobbie James' up a tree, were among the plants decided on.

Leaving this part of the garden, your way takes you back across the lawn. A stable block ahead has 'Chianti' on one corner and 'Climbing Ophelia', 'The Alchymist', 'Mutabilis' and *Cytisus battandieri*, the Pineapple Broom, covering its walls, but before reaching this you turn through openings in the low yew hedge and across the drive. Immediately on the right now, leading almost to the house, is a scree garden and beyond it on the house walls 'Golden Showers' is interlaced with the loveliest of light-blue clematis, 'Perle d'Azur', to give colour in August, 'The Alchymist' and 'Phyllis Bide', which provides colour pretty well nonstop the entire summer. Nearby are 'Cupid' and the American climber 'Inspiration' (dating from 1946), which has fragrant, semi-double, pink flowers and large, glossy leaves.

A turn to the left as you reach the house takes you into a paved area below a retaining wall, needed because the lawn beyond it is at a con-

Looking from Dorothy Vernon's door at the roses on the upper terrace.

siderably higher level. Along the top of this many roses have been planted, a mixture of pinks and whites, *R. sancta*, 'Raubritter' and 'Max Graf' trailing down, 'Scabrosa', 'Blanc Double de Coubert', 'Sarah Van Fleet' and 'Mary Manners', a white Rugosa with double flowers named after Mary Manners of Haddon Hall in Derbyshire.

The paved area runs round two sides of the house, but when the retaining wall ends you can turn left up a grassy slope to the lawn above. Here among trees, *Prunus* and others, roses are planted as specimens: *R. × paulii, R. californica* 'Plena' and 'Cerise Bouquet'. More trees lie ahead, including a collection of *Sorbus*, and a tapestry hedge, only just recovering from gaps left in it by hard winters but looking remarkably mature for a seven-year-old planting, borders the garden to the right. At its far end is a large corner bed of mixed shrubs and roses, with 'Hunter' again perhaps outstanding among the latter.

From here you can move back onto the drive and from there return to your starting point in the stable yard, reflecting perhaps more than anything on the skill with which the various components of this lovely garden have been blended, one with another.

Haddon Hall

Bakewell

On A6, 2½ miles south-east of Bakewell. Car park across the road from the entrance.
Tel. 0692 81 2855
The Duke of Rutland
Open, house and garden, from April to end September, Tuesday to Saturday, and on Bank Holiday Sundays and Mondays.

With a little imagination Haddon Hall could well be mistaken for a twelfth-century castle, perched as it is in an ideal defensive position high above the River Wye. Parts of the house do, in fact, date from that period, though there is an Elizabethan wing; and the terracing and steps which form such a feature of this garden date from the seventeenth century. When the roses are at their glorious best, Haddon Hall has a fairy-tale atmosphere about it.

The approach to the Hall lies over the river and then up a steep slope to the entrance to the first courtyard. You have to go through this, and through the house itself, to reach the rose garden, but pause at the tall archway that leads

from the courtyard into the Banqueting Hall, the oldest room in Haddon, built in 1370 by Sir Richard Vernon. For framing it are two spectacular climbers, scarlet 'Allen Chandler' to the right and sweetly scented 'Albertine' to the left.

After moving through numerous state rooms and the Long Gallery you reach Dorothy Vernon's door and, leading down from it into the top terrace of the rose garden, her steps. Her story is certainly the stuff of which fairy tales are made. She eloped with John Manners, son of the Earl of Rutland, through whom Haddon in due course passed to the Manners family. From the terraced gardens, you can still see the tiny packhorse bridge, spanning the river Wye, on which Dorothy is said to have waited for her lover.

Above this terrace, at the top of a wall, which must be all of 3 m (10 ft) high, is another terrace which is private and used only by the family. From Dorothy's steps you can get the best view of what is planted along the top of it – great masses of a large-flowered creamy-white Floribunda that I think may be 'Moonraker' and further along the old favourite 'Frensham' and the Hybrid Musk 'Cornelia'. Others less recognizable from a distance are banked up behind them, making an impressive sight.

This wall forms the backdrop for the whole of the wide terrace which you are about to explore. At the end nearest to you there are roses, both old and new, in beds cut in the grass, but by far the largest part of the terrace is lawn, with conical yews planted at the corners to give a pleasing change of height and shape. A gravel path surrounds the lawn and beyond it, against the walls, are beds with roses and other plants. Among the climbers on the walls, emblazoning them with a patchwork of colour, are 'Variegata di Bologna' (really a Bourbon, of course, but here going up to about 3.6 m [12 ft]), 'Lawrence Johnston', 'Shot Silk', 'Altissimo', 'Albertine', 'American Pillar', 'The Alchymist', 'Dortmund', 'Dance du Feu', 'Bantry Bay', 'Meg' and 'Leverkusen', many of them duplicated, which gives some idea of the expanse of wall to be covered. In front of a low wall at the farther end, a number of Floribundas has been planted, but they suffer from the shade of trees.

Not so those in the beds nearest to Dorothy Vernon's door. Here the species R. hugonis is the centre-piece, presumably to give the earliest possible colour with its creamy-yellow

blooms early in June, and round it are grouped a number of the best Hybrid Teas, 'Alec's Red', 'Wendy Cussons', 'Ernest H. Morse', the sweetly scented and strangely neglected Gold Medal rose 'My Choice', 'Mischief', 'Amatsu Otome' from Japan, 'King's Ransom', and a real veteran in 'Mme Louis Laperrière'. Two bushes of 'Celeste' frame the path nearest to the lawn and there are pillar roses at each corner.

There is a drop of something like 3 m (10 ft) from this terrace to the one below. You look down over the stone balustrade onto a further sea of roses, not just in the beds all round the lawn, with its central square pool and fountain, but on the walls of the house that tower over the garden on the right-hand side. Climbing roses look particularly well against the grey stone of the walls, which are such a feature of the garden of Haddon Hall, and indeed of all the houses of Derbyshire, and some of those to be seen are 'Bleu Magenta', 'Paul's Scarlet', 'Raymond Chenault', 'Guinée', 'Parkdirektor Riggers' (a good rose which might be better known if it were not for its name), 'Parade', 'Mme Grégoire Staechelin' and pink 'Christine Wright', which used to be in Miss Murrell's list and has 'Mme Caroline Testout' as one parent. 'Albertine' lines each side of the broad steps that lead from one terrace to the other.

A low wall borders the second terrace instead of the open stonework of the top one and runs round two sides, for there is now a long drop beyond it both ahead and to the left. More climbers almost hide the wall in the exuberance of their blooming, each seemingly wishing to outdo the other. Among them are 'Climbing Gruss an Teplitz', 'Climbing Aurora', which is a mixture of orange and pink, and another that looks remarkably like 'The Alchymist' but which the head gardener assures me is 'Colonel Poole'.

Because of the roses growing along the top, it is easier to look down from this terrace from a small side terrace by the house wall. There you will find, a long way below you, yet another terrace garden with roses, at present not accessible to the public. Smaller than the two already explored, its planting is simpler. The predominant features are shrubs and the great mass of bloom of 'Complicata' at its best, together with 'American Pillar' on the walls. Beyond it, lower still, the river winds its way between trees and through lush meadows and under the fateful bridge.

Opposite: *The Floribunda 'Dearest' surviving surprisingly well in the shade on the lower terrace at Haddon Hall.*

At Winale Hall, a garden of predominantly modern roses, a few older ones are used for special features.
Here white flowered 'Seagull' makes a spectacular hedge.

Windle Hall

St Helens

Pass north of St Helens on A580. Bridge with blue-painted handrail arches high over road; half a mile beyond this, turn left at traffic lights towards St Helens. Keep turning left until you reach Abbey Road on left. This leads to south end of bridge, passing cemetery. Go over bridge (the only access); Windle Hall on right.
Tel. 0744 23534
The Lady Pilkington
Open, garden only, under the National Gardens Scheme.

Windle Hall dates from 1750 but it has been much changed over the years. So too has the surrounding property, notably by the East Lancs Road cutting through the hillside on which the house stands. Now the only access is over the blue-painted bridge. However, a 200-year-old walled garden remains surrounded by 2 hectares (5 acres) of lawns and woodland which are lit up early in the year by the fresh yellows and blues of spring flowers.

The roses are in the walled garden and if ever flowers expressed the personality of the owner of a garden, the roses of Windle Hall, vibrant and full of life, do just that. They are mostly modern varieties, though the first one to be seen, rambling over an arch that leads to a small courtyard on the west side of the house, is 'Zéphirine Drouhin', which goes back to 1868 and is probably the oldest rose in the garden except for a species or two.

Passing 'Zéphirine Drouhin' you reach a wicket gate. Once through it you are on a paved path with 'American Pillar' first of all and then 'Seagull' on a low fence on the left. To the right is a forsythia hedge (which, sadly, never has a chance to flower because of the drastic cutting back that is necessary) and at the end of the path are two fine standards of the rather neglected McGredy Floribunda 'Kerryman' in whose flowers different shades of pink are blended most attractively.

A general view of Windle Hall garden, St Helens. The foreground roses are
'Lancashire Life', 'Happy Anniversary' and 'Alexander'.

Turn right along another path and such Hybrid Teas as 'Polar Star', 'Gold Crown', 'Silver Jubilee', 'National Trust' and 'Percy Thrower' are planted in the bed on your right. Also there are orange 'Fyvie Castle' and bright-red 'Sir Harry Pilkington'. The latter, a vigorous grower from Tantau of Germany, was named after Lady Pilkington's husband. Both the Pilkingtons were leading exhibitors of roses and you can still find the evidence of this in the many varieties in the garden that are winners on the show bench, and in the vigour of the bushes and the size of the blooms, as well as by the care obviously lavished on them. 'National Trust', for instance, is generally considered to have small (though immaculately shaped) flowers. In this garden they are a match for any in size.

Half-way along the path you can turn right up some steps to a round formal pool with a fountain in the centre and a seat behind. It makes a good place to sit and look out across the garden, with a massive old brick wall cov-

ered in ramblers at your back. 'Albertine' and 'Dr Van Fleet' are there and another, probably much older, climber with many-petalled flowers in deep pink, which might, I suppose, be even older than 'Zéphirine Drouhin'. On either side of the pool is a small lawn with a standard 'Ballerina' in each corner.

After this pleasant diversion the path leads on towards a large greenhouse filled to the brim with pot plants for the house. Turn left when you reach it, past small beds planted with dwarf conifers, potentillas, *Spiraea* × *bumalda* 'Goldflame' and other low-growing shrubs. Another wall of the garden is then on your right with a long herbaceous border in front of it. In it the roses 'Iceberg' and 'Queen Elizabeth' blend very happily with other plants, while across the way beds are cut in a wide lawn for bedding varieties like 'Sarabande', the brilliant scarlet 'Lancashire Life', 'Sunblest', salmon-pink 'Happy Anniversary' and 'Alexander', shown off to best advantage. So, too, is the Kordes climber 'Leverkusen' growing on a rus-

*Another older rose at Windle Hall: 'Kiftsgate' grows up an
old apple tree and arches over the path.*

tic wooden frame alongside a path that bisects
the lawn. All too often a prey to mildew, this
very beautiful soft-yellow climber excels at
Windle Hall and seems to be perfectly healthy.

All round you as you make your way towards
the farther side of the garden are beds of roses
with some new varieties and some not so new
ones. Among them are 'Cheshire Life', pink
'Lakeland', 'Red Lion', 'Circus', 'Allgold', 'Paul
Shirville' (one of the best new Hybrid Teas for
some time), 'Mischief', 'Pink Favourite' (one of
the healthiest Hybrid Teas of all time), 'Gail
Borden', 'Champion', 'Opera', 'Lady Belper',
'Admiral Rodney', yellow 'Ethel Sanday' and
pink 'Tiffany'. The presence of 'Red Lion',
'Champion' and 'Admiral Rodney' indicates
Lady Pilkington's interest in showing but who,
on the evidence here, would believe the oft-
repeated assertion that 'Admiral Rodney' is not
a rose for the garden? It looks magnificent, as
they all do, and since the oldest of them ('Lady
Belper') goes back to 1948 you are really looking at the progress of the Hybrid Tea over the
last forty years. It has not changed very much.

In the south-east corner of the walled garden
is a long pergola with laburnum trees trained
in espalier fashion along its sides to form a
tunnel of yellow bloom in early summer. The
few roses on the pergola, including another
'Zéphirine Drouhin' and 'Etoile de Hollande',
seem to have something of a struggle to reach
the light, but at the far end, right in the corner,
is a white-painted iron gate in the wall with
'Goldfinch' clambering over it with greater
freedom. More herbaceous borders follow the
west wall, and again there are roses in them,
sweetly scented 'Alpine Sunset', 'Yesterday',
'Dearest', and 'Matangi', the species *R. glauca*
and two standards of the fairylike 'Nozomi' at
the end.

Back-tracking through the laburnum tunnel
and turning to the right, you pass under an arch
formed by *R. filipes* 'Kiftsgate' growing up, and
hanging down from, an old apple tree and
arrive almost at the point from which you
started. However, by no means all of the garden, or all of the roses, have been seen yet. A
turn to the right along a paved path, past a

planting of azaleas and, further on, geraniums on the left and begonias and standard fuchsias on the right, and you reach steps that lead down to a large formal paved rose garden in front of the house. There is a standard of 'Ophelia' on each side of the steps and in the beds are 'Sir Harry Pilkington', 'Just Joey', light peach-orange 'Royal Romance', 'Margaret Merril', 'Glenfiddich', 'Champs Elysées', 'Sally Holmes', 'Silver Jubilee', 'Pernille Poulsen', 'Pink Parfait', 'Prima Ballerina' (another rose that seems to escape its customary mildew in this garden) and, last but not least, 'Shot Silk', which dates from 1924 and which, in my own garden, gives more flushes of bloom each summer than any other variety.

That is just about the end of the roses, but if you wander down across the gently sloping lawn at the end of the rose garden you come to a pool with Cinnamon Teal and Mandarin and other ducks. Beyond it is woodland, and a stroll through the trees and then back up the lawn to the stone grotto brings a visit to Windle Hall to a pleasant conclusion.

Aislaby Hall

Pickering

On A170 Kirkbymoorside–Pickering road on right in
centre of village of Aislaby.
Tel. 0751 72830
Mrs Patricia Cooper
Open under the National Gardens Scheme.

The front door of Aislaby Hall (which dates from the reign of Queen Anne, but with a wing added in 1900) is in the village street, but you can enter the garden from the yard at one side. There you will find a foretaste of the roses to come, for 'Meg', 'Albertine', 'Mme Grégoire Staechelin', 'Paul's Lemon Pillar' and 'Mrs Sam McGredy' are to be found on the house walls in the yard and on those of the stables opposite.

A door in the wall leads through into the garden, to a shaded area of ferns and hostas, with steps leading upwards from there towards the house, and out into the sunlight once more. Across a gravel forecourt is a stone porch with the climber 'Meg' on the wall to the left of it and 'Royal Gold' to the right. Stone troughs filled with pansies edge the gravel area, and beyond these a long lawn slopes gently down to where

a wooden fence separates the garden from the fields beyond. To the left a huge copper beech throws its shade and, as you move down the lawn, you pass the massed white flowers of 'Bobbie James' climbing through the branches of an oak on the western boundary. Roses nearby are 'Anna Wheatcroft', 'Celestial', 'Gipsy Boy', 'Nevada', 'Roseraie de l'Hay' and 'Maigold'.

A left turn at the bottom of the garden takes you across the lawn and under a mulberry tree, then between ancient yews with shrub roses such as 'Fritz Nobis', 'St Nicholas', 'William Lobb' and 'Ferdinand Pichard' making a brave show in quite shady conditions.

You now come across one of the most intriguing features of this fascinating garden – a building which I suppose should be called a pavilion, its roof supported by a fourteenth-century carved Woodwose or Wise Man on the left-hand side and another carved, painted figure on the right. Their origin is uncertain, despite considerable research by Mrs Cooper, but it would appear that a Woodwose forms some kind of link between the pagan deities of olden times and those of the later Christians, and the figures may at one time have formed the side pieces of a fireplace in an old house. Both of them are carved in oak and each clutches a very large wooden bone.

Interestingly enough, the rose itself formed a similar link between the old and the new religions. For thousands of years it was a pagan symbol and as such reviled by the Church, but people would not be denied their roses and the Church had to adapt. Gradually the white rose became the symbol of Christian purity and the red rose was said to have gained its colour from being stained by the blood of Christ rather than the blood of Adonis. But back to Aislaby Hall.

After the pavilion, turn right and immediately left again by a greenhouse, where the path leads past a small, semi-circular trough garden and then along the side of another long greenhouse and a herb garden. Open fields can now be glimpsed to your right on the far side of a wall, and then the path ends in another small garden, the beds this time set in bricks laid most ingeniously by Mrs Cooper in interlocking fan shapes. Here you are back among the roses once more, a large planting of 'Penelope', 'Rosemary Rose' (showing no sign of its usual mildew), 'Margaret Merril', 'Ice White', 'Moonlight' and 'Mme Legras de Saint Germaine', with dianthus and other grey-leaved plants.

From this garden an arch in a high wall and then a left and a right turn leads into what is specifically known as the Old Rose Garden, though there is no lack of roses elsewhere. If you can resist the temptation to sit and doze on the seat on the far side of a circular pool, with the gentle hum of insects and the scent of a white rambler seedling that frames the seat drifting over you, you might, perhaps, take note of some of the roses: 'Baron Girod de l'Ain' with its sumptuous crimson, white-edged blooms, striped 'Commandant Beau-repaire', 'Henri Martin', 'F. J. Grootendorst', 'President de Sèze', 'Mme Legras de St Germaine', the rarely seen 'Petite Lisette' (a China rose with small, rich pink, pompon style flowers which will grow to about 1 to 1.2 m [3 to 4 ft]) 'Camaieux', 'Belle de Crécy', 'Général Kléber', 'Empress Josephine', 'Shailer's White Moss', a huge 'Fritz Nobis' and David Austin's

'The Squire'. 'Ballerina' is to be found on each side as you enter the garden, and you leave it to pass through into the Gold Garden next door.

Here, as might be expected, there are yellow flowers and golden foliage. Yellow foxgloves, yellow and orange lilies, alchemilla and golden conifers and, among the roses, 'Arthur Bell', 'Chinatown', 'Lawrence Johnston' and 'Buff Beauty'. As a contrast the deep purple-magenta blooms of 'Chianti' fill one corner.

You now retrace your steps, back through the Old Rose Garden, until a high brick wall can be seen ahead on the eastern boundary of the garden. You turn left along it past a varied selection of fruit trees, but you have by no means done with the roses. On the wall are 'Mme Grégoire Staechelin', 'Mme Alfred Carrière', 'Bantry Bay' and others, 'Kiftsgate' and 'Bobbie James' disporting themselves among the trees, and below them are, to men-

The Old Rose Garden at Aislaby Hall where roses surround a circular pool.

tion only three among a multitude, Moyesii seedlings, 'Wilhelm' and the Alba 'Amelia' with its large, double, fragrant, bright-pink flowers with deep-yellow anthers.

In the corner ahead where the wall changes direction is a large brick-built gazebo, a listed building of great interest. Under this is what used to be a fruit and vegetable store until animals started to show an interest in its contents, but to get into the gazebo proper you must climb steps to a door in the side. There are frescos on the walls, and on the ceiling, in a round, painted frame, is the figure of Queen Anne holding hands with her husband, George of Denmark. The heating system, though it is no longer used, is particularly ingenious, with pipes from the fireplace running behind the brickwork.

After the gazebo the path along the top wall leads back in the general direction of the house, though a diversion can be made down side paths to the left if you feel inclined. On the wall the long, arching branches of an exochorda show off their racemes of small white flowers in May, and there are delphiniums, hardy geraniums and *Astrantia major* with its star-shaped, parchment-pink flowers among many others along the way. 'Danse de Feu', 'Hamburger Phoenix' and 'Zéphirine Drouhin' are some of the roses on the wall, and on the left as you near the end of the path and the corner of the house comes into sight, is a fine 'Cornelia', the yellow Rugosa 'Agnes' and 'Shropshire Lass', a David Austin rose with Alba parentage and pale pink, almost single, flowers.

Two bushes of 'Buff Beauty' and the climbers 'Maigold' and 'Leverkusen' make a fitting climax to your visit to Aislaby as you turn the final corner and come out onto the gravel forecourt of the house once more.

Roses on the top wall of the garden at Aislaby Hall include 'Danse du Feu' and 'Hamburger Phoenix'.

Castle Howard

York

Off A64 York–Scarborough road, take left (signposted)
turning at Barton Hill. Follow signs thereafter.
Tel. 065 384 333
Castle Howard Estate Limited
House and garden open daily from late March to end
October.

The inspiration for the building of Castle Howard came from Charles Howard, Third Earl of Carlisle, back in the early 1700s. He it was who first recognized the potential genius of the soldier-playwright, Sir John Vanbrugh, as an architect and designer in the grand manner and gave him a free hand. The result was this vast mansion that dominates an east–west ridge in the Howardian Hills with its magnificent prospect over the Vale of York. The gardens were originally laid out by the nursery firm of London and Wise in about 1705 and certainly match the imaginative originality of the buildings. Many of the design features appeared at Castle Howard for the first time and were subsequently much copied in other gardens.

The approach from the main road, along a beech and lime avenue several miles long, is stunning though you turn off before the end. Entry is through Vanbrugh's Carrmire gate with its pedimented arch and from the car park the rose garden is well signposted. The work of the late George Howard and James Russell, who set out to create one of the finest collections of old roses in the country, it is very recent compared with the rest of the garden, and is remarkably successful. Like Mottisfont Abbey, it does not lend itself easily to description, as it is basically the same square walled garden with roses planted in beds within it.

The Castle Howard garden, however, is big enough to accommodate tall hedges that divide it up in a number of different ways, but primarily into four separate units. In addition, a long hedge runs down each side inside the walls, forming two wide avenues planted with roses, with an urn at the end of each.

A list of the varieties that can be seen there contains more than 500 different kinds, so it is impossible to single out even a few of them for description: how would one choose them? And how could one even attempt a representative selection from so many? It can be said, though, (give or take a few after the recent hard winters) that there are no fewer than 77 different species, 54 different Teas, 5 different Albas, 22 Bourbons, 17 Centifolias, 20 Damasks, 30 Gallicas, 12 Hybrid Musks, 95 Hybrid Perpetuals, 29 Moss roses, 13 Noisettes, 18 modern shrub roses and, rather surprisingly, only 9 different Rugosas. And, of course, there are all the rambler groups, such as the Wichuraianas, Sempervirens ramblers, Multifloras, the Ayrshires and the rest, while 'Amblyotis', 'Baronne Henriette de Snoy', 'Bernard Verlot', 'Chastleton', 'Comte de Bobrinsky', 'Comtesse de Lacepede', 'Gustave Piganeau', 'Hortense Vernet', 'Mme Driout' or 'Nubienne' are none of them varieties you would commonly see from a train flashing past suburban gardens. But they are here in the garden of Castle Howard, together with countless other interesting rarities.

Even though I cannot give descriptions, or even brief comments on so many, the way they are grown and trained is of some interest. There are individual wooden frames for many of the taller roses like the Bourbon, 'Mme Lauriol de Barny'. For those that are also very tall but can support themselves to some extent like the three Albas, 'Maxima', 'Semi-plena' and 'Celeste' and the Moss rose 'William Lobb', long and strong bamboo canes have been pushed into the ground in among the shoots, providing sufficient support, apparently, without the shoots being tied. In other places there are wooden lattice-work pyramids to which ramblers are tied in, and of course more climbers and ramblers are trained on the walls. Grey-leaved weeping pears and fastigiate conifers are planted at strategic points to give height or colour contrast and paeonies, lavender and other plants in many of the beds enhance and complement the roses. Here and there are bowers with honeysuckle and ramblers twining themselves about them, and one of the four main gardens, the Venus Garden (named after the statue in the centre) has a long pergola round two sides, again for climbers and ramblers.

Next to the Venus Garden is what is known as the Sundial Garden, planted almost exclusively with modern Hybrid Tea and Floribunda bedding roses, so that Castle Howard caters for all tastes and all periods in the history of the

Opposite: A general view of the garden at Castle Howard, with 'Empress Josephine' in the foreground.

rose. In the wall is Vanbrugh's Satyr Gate (now permanently closed) with the grotesque stone carvings that give it its name on pillars on either side.

Near the centre of the garden, in a wide grass circle edged round with box, is a fountain. Behind it is a solid bank of the deep purple-maroon rose 'Chianti', which, in full bloom, is one of the most striking sights imaginable. Beyond it is Lady Celia's Garden (where the lattice-work tripods are) and then a broad area of grass overlooked by the head gardener's house. From his windows he can look out over one of the greatest and most beautiful rose collections in the country or, indeed, in the world.

Newby Hall

Ripon

Two miles south east of Ripon, taking B6265. Turn right at Bridge Hewick; signposted.
Tel. 09012 2583
Mr R. E. J. Compton
Open from April to end September, Tuesday to Sunday, and on Bank Holiday Mondays.

Newby Hall was built in the late seventeenth century, but the garden as you see it today is relatively modern. Originally, as early prints of it show, it was formal, with a series of symmetrical terraces and parterres, but little of this now remains. In 1923 the late Major Edward Compton created, in this wonderful setting on the banks of the River Ure, a completely new garden, which is one of the finest and most varied in concept in the north of England. It is also a garden for all seasons and a visit at any time of year brings rich rewards. By no means only a rose garden, it features roses prominently throughout and they are clearly one of the first loves of Major Compton's son, the present owner, a knowledgeable and dedicated gardener.

You approach the house through extensive parklands, passing Newby church, inside the boundary of the park, on the way. A path from the entrance kiosk leads towards the house but before you reach it broad steps lead down to the left into the Statue Walk, flanked by Venetian statues and Irish yews, planned by the Victorian architect, William Burges. At one end of the walk the south front of the house comes

fully into view, while in the opposite direction a broad grass walk leads down between Newby's famed herbaceous borders to the river Ure which flows serenely along the southern border of the garden. This fine double view is from a point in the walk where it is bounded on one side by a curved balustrade, from the centre of which steps lead down to the grass walk. *R. × paulii* decorates the balustrade on both sides with its large, star-like white flowers and *R. primula* and 'Scarlet Fire' can be seen at the end of the borders below.

If you now move a little way in the other direction towards the house and turn left where a sign points to Sylvia's Garden, the path takes you through an opening in a high hedge into a long, fairly narrow plot that Mr Compton has nicknamed 'The Wars of the Roses'. On each side of the path he has planted first a row of lavender and then a line of the brilliant deep-pink *R. gallica* 'Officinalis', the Red Rose of Lancaster. Behind it and much taller is another double line, this time of the White Rose of York (*R. × alba* 'Semi-plena'), and acting as a kind 'peacemaker' between the two, is the pink- and white-striped 'Rosa Mundi'.

Although some might suggest that a more logical choice would have been 'York and Lancaster' (*R. damascena* 'Versicolor'), I think that Mr Compton was right to opt for 'Rosa Mundi'. It is a much better garden rose and makes a far better show. Towards the end of the path, amongst some trees, is an enormous *R. holodonta* (*R. moyesii rosea*), a pink-flowered form of this species.

Steps flanked by a further massed planting of 'Rosa Mundi' lead down at the end of the path into Sylvia's Garden, named after Mr Compton's mother and completely replanted by his wife. Here there are few roses, though 'Ballerina' is used as a centrepiece in four of the semi-triangular beds that surround an old Byzantine corn-grinder, which forms the focal point of the whole. Otherwise the beds, surrounded by paved paths, have plants that give their main show of colour in the spring and early summer, with a large number of foliage plants for later effect. Delphiniums are there, as well as paeonies, irises, artemisias, campanulas, rock roses, salvias and potentillas and, a great favourite of Mrs Compton, *Tanacetum densum*.

If you then take the steps immediately opposite you will come to an area heavy with the scent of philadelphus and then on, through a

The steps leading from 'The Wars of the Roses' garden to Sylvia's Garden at Newby Hall.
The Gallica 'Rosa Mundi' grows on the left, backed by philadelphus.

grove of trees, to the far end of the Statue Walk which you left earlier. Its end is marked by a huge curved stone seat which Burges obtained from Caen in Normandy.

A left turn here takes you into the rose pergola, its square stone pillars sporting recently restored metal hoops over the top to support the roses, and underplanted with *Alchemilla mollis*. Behind the pillars on either side shrub roses are planted, including 'Complicata', 'Anthony Waterer' and 'Fritz Nobis' among others, and on the arches, forming a canopy of beauty at midsummer, are 'Mme Alfred Carrière', 'Goldfinch', 'Bobbie James', 'Albertine', 'Lady Hillingdon', and 'Lady Waterlow'.

At the end of the pergola where the path drops steeply you can, if you wish, explore the rock garden beyond, designed by Ellen Willmott at the turn of the century. A fascinating place, the term rock garden hardly does it justice – it is a shady land of rocks and boulders rising to shoulder height and more, with the sound of water trickling over them, and ferns

and mosses growing from every cranny. *R.* X *paulii* can be seen there in a small clearing between the trees, but to reach the main rose garden you must retrace your steps and turn right half-way along the pergola at a point where pink geraniums surround a sundial. The way leads on beneath the shade of an enormous copper beech and then past fine specimens of the Korean dogwood, *Cornus kousa*, which has rather smaller bracts than its Chinese relative but is still attractively showy. A gravel path runs across at right angles at this point but you cross it and move on between a magnificent double hedge of sweetly scented *Philadelphus erectus* through to the rose garden. A grey-leaved weeping pear on either side forms the portals to a virtual Ali Baba's cave of treasures.

A copper beech hedge forms a screen all round the rose garden, which was designed by Mr Compton's father just before the last war and which replaces a former tennis court. Steps lead down into it between two large urns. Laid

A general view of the paved old rose garden at Newby Hall.

out in neat beds with paved paths between them, the rose garden soon loses its formality in the exuberant growth of the roses, which mingle one with another and, in places, tumble onto the path. They are divided, in a general way, bed by bed, into their respective families, the Bourbons together, the Albas, the Centifolias and so on, while self-heal, *Prunella* × *webbiana* 'Loveliness', campanulas, pinks and *Viola cornuta*, in both its mauve and white forms, are used for underplanting and edging. A central urn is surrounded by the soft grey-green and blue of lavender.

Some of the roses you will find in the garden are, in no particular order, 'Celestial', 'Rosa Mundi', 'St Nicholas', 'Königin von Dane-marck', 'Hebe's Lip', 'Trigintipetala', *R.* × *alba* 'Maxima', 'Perle des Panachées', 'Stanwell Perpetual', 'Reine des Violettes', 'Fantin Latour', 'Ferdinand Pichard', 'William Lobb', 'Constance Spry', 'Nevada', 'William III', 'Blush Damask', *R. pomifera* 'Duplex' and 'Mme Plantier'. There is a weeping pear in each corner, which always looks most effective with the roses.

There are roses, in fact, throughout the whole garden in ones or twos and, in places, in groups of four or more. For instance 'Cerise Bouquet' is allowed its head so that its long thorny canes range far afield and you can see its bright pink blooms from a long way off as you walk among the trees and other shrubs. And then there are *R. webbiana*, 'Headleyensis', *R. setipoda*, *R. macrophylla doncasteri* and 'Mme Plantier', used properly as a climber. On the walls near the restaurant are numerous other climbers, including 'Ramona', 'Wedding Day', 'Lawrence Johnston', 'New Dawn', 'The Alchymist', 'Claire Jacquier' and the strange-looking 'Ash Wednesday'. Its blooms are a haunting pale bluish-mauve, an impossible colour to describe, but if you remember McGredy's 'Grey Pearl' of 1945, used so extensively in the breeding of the so-called 'blue' roses, you will know what I mean. Nearby is the White Garden, where the Rugosa 'Blanc Double de Coubert', philadelphus, deutzia and *R.* × *paulii* mingle, but go where you will at Newby in search of roses and you will not be disappointed.

Pennyholme

Fadmoor

From A170 Kirkbymoorside–Nawton road turn north and then left half a mile before Fadmoor. Signposted Sleightholmdale only, the road leads, over three cattle grids, to Pennyholme garden.
Tel. 0751 32313
Mr C. J. Wills
Open under the National Gardens Scheme.

You could justifiably question whether this should be classed as a rose garden, although there are many roses in it. But it is such a lovely spot, and such a spectacular garden, not least because of its setting, that if you are visiting Sleightholmdale Lodge down the valley, you should not miss Pennyholme, provided, of course, that they are both open at the same time, for Pennyholme generally opens rather earlier, when the Wild Garden of azaleas, rhododendrons and heathers is at its best.

To reach Pennyholme you must take the long, winding (and in places single-track) road up the Bransdale valley, continuing on and on until you think it will never end. It is hard to imagine a more remote place but it was here, at the turn of the century, that Lord Feversham decided to create a garden near the old farmhouse at the end of the road. You can go no farther, nor would you want to, for the scene is breath-taking. As you stand on the wide sweep of gravel that fronts the house and look down over the low wall to the south, the whole valley is spread out below you, the garden sloping steeply down to Hodge Beck, a small stream that meanders its way along the valley floor. On the other side of the stream, where the land rises up once more, is the Wild Garden where the rhododendrons grow.

And the roses? 'Golden Showers' grows on the house, 'Zéphirine Drouhin' on the stable block, and 'Paul's Himalayan Musk' tumbles over the low wall over which you have been looking. Near it a gate leads down some steps to where the long grass slope begins its descent, but at the top, immediately under the wall, are roses and shrubs. Some way along to the right the retaining wall of a terrace juts out from the side of the house, for you are now well below it, perched as it is on the steep hillside. On this wall is 'New Dawn' and above it on the house itself is 'Mme Grégoire Staechelin'. You

can climb up steps to the terrace and from there look down on one of the most striking features of the garden, a cascade with the water actually tumbling out from under the house and down in a series of steps to the stream below. It is thickly planted on either side with a fine selection of shrubby potentillas.

Elsewhere in the garden you can find climbing roses on walls and shrub roses planted as specimens in the grass. 'Bobbie James' envelops an old apple tree and *R. longicuspis* weaves its long canes in and out of the parapet of one of the two footbridges that span the stream. Philadelphus, weigela, kolkwitzia, geraniums, 'Belle Poitevine', *R.* × *alba* 'Semi-plena', 'Roseraie de l'Hay' and 'Sarah Van Fleet' can be found on the far bank, with honeysuckle and *R.* × *dupontii* on the low wall behind them. Beyond this you climb up to the Wild Garden, but by then most of the roses will be behind you.

Sleightholme Dale Lodge

Kirkbymoorside

From A170 Kirkbymoorside–Nawton Road turn north and then left half a mile before Fadmoor. Signposteld Sleightholmedale only.
Tel. 0751 31233
Mrs Gordon Foster and Dr and Mrs O. James
Open, garden only, under the National Gardens Scheme.

Hidden away in Bransdale, this house faces south with a grand view across the valley to forests that stretch into the distance on the far side of Hodge Beck. Brick walls, many of them built by the present owner's father, do much to shelter this northern garden from the icy winds of winter. He also laid out the original garden in 1910, but from 1935 onwards Mrs Foster took over and much of what you see today is her creation, though now she works in it with her daughter, Mrs James, who is playing an ever-increasing part in its running and development.

In all, the estate consists of 60.8 hectares (152 acres), for there is a farm as well as the garden, and the whole is an ornithological survey area with a special interest in the migrant Pied Flycatcher and with some 300 numbered nesting boxes. The Lodge was built in 1898 by Lord Feversham (who also created the garden at Pennyholme, discussed on page 153) for his youngest daughter and it is still the family home. In 1910 the rose plantings were largely Hybrid Teas which would flower at the time when Mrs Foster's father returned for his summer holidays, but sadly few, if any, of these early varieties now remain. Sad in one way, true, but they have been replaced by the most glorious collection of other roses which have spread far beyond the confines of any formal rose garden.

On your arrival you go down a steep drive from the road into the forecourt of the house. At the top of a high, grassy bank to the right you can glimpse the first roses, reached by climbing up a path at the end of the bank and bearing to the right. The main rose garden now stretches away up the slope ahead behind a low stone wall, with 'The Alchymist' among the first roses you see and with 'Easlea's Golden Rambler' in tremendous form nearby. At Sleightholme Dale this is grown as a bush rather than in the way Walter Easlea intended when he introduced and named it in 1932, but, in fact, it is now classed as a large-flowered climber rather than a rambler, for its gold-yellow blooms are fully 10 cm (4 in) across. It was the winner of a Rose Society Gold Medal in its year of introduction.

Through a wrought-iron gate, you find a flagged path that leads ahead up the slope, with a magnificent display of herbaceous plants (including the dazzling blue spikes of giant delphiniums) and many roses along both sides. The rose garden, of considerable size, is roughly square, and cross paths at intervals divide it into smaller areas. The path ahead runs up one side, but, instead of taking this, turn to the right along the bottom of the garden. Plantings of 'Felicia' and 'Perle d'Or' are on the corner as you make the turn and a wooden arch supporting 'Climbing Lady Waterlow' is overhead, one of countless rose arches you pass through as you go. Past the Easlea rambler there are 'Mme Isaac Pereire', 'Fantin Latour', and the Floribundas 'Margaret Merril' and 'Alain' beside the path. 'Penelope' grows in profusion as you turn the corner and begin to climb upwards under an arch with 'American Pillar' rampant. Beside it are 'Empress Josephine', 'Gipsy Boy' on a frame, 'Fantin Latour', 'Josephine Bruce' and many more.

A left turn at the half-way point on the slope takes you along a path with fences on which

roses flourish on either side – 'Aloha', 'Dr Van Fleet', 'Souvenir de la Malmaison' among them – and more are on arches overhead. At the farther end you turn right up the hill once more, onto the path where the delphiniums grow, moving between the rambler 'Minnehaha' on one side and the Bourbon 'Mme Pierre Oger' on the other.

On a wall ahead where you turn right yet again is the climbing sport of the 1907 Hybrid Tea 'Mrs Aaron Ward', its large double flowers a warm orange-buff with an occasional hint of salmon. A rose of variable colour, it is nevertheless attractive at all times and is set off well here by the brilliant white of a nearby clematis and the handsome shiny green foliage of *Choisya ternata*.

At the top of the rose garden you find, once again, a mixture of roses and other plants. On a rustic wooden frame to one side grows 'Crimson Conquest' but it is likely to be replaced because it has not flourished as it should and is a martyr to black spot. 'American Pillar' is on the openwork fence further along and *R. polyantha* 'Grandiflora' (*R. gentiliana*) covers the wall opposite with its racemes of white flowers. As well as the roses, paeonies, lavender, Sweet Williams, mullein and poppies are planted along the way until you reach a summerhouse from where you can look down past the house to the valley beyond. A more entrancing prospect is hard to imagine.

You could take a path straight down the slope from the summerhouse, though you would miss many roses in doing so; 'Paul's Lemon Pillar' on the second half of the top wall, together with 'Bobbie James' and 'Zéphirine Drouhin'; 'Complicata' and a multitude of others on the path downwards at the far end. One particular rarity, the carmine-pink Floribunda from 1930, 'Frau Astrid Späth', grows there. I doubt if there is another garden in the country where it can be seen today, and the same might well be said of another rose at Sleightholme Dale – the pale orange-yellow Wichuraiana rambler 'Aviateur Blériot'.

Though the estate is vast, the garden itself is confined to 1.6 hectares (4 acres). To see more of it you move out of the rose garden and stroll, under the shade of lime trees, down a grassy slope towards the tennis court. Here there are extensive plantings of species roses and a few others, including 'Roseraie de l'Hay'. Among the species are *R. roxburghii*, with its grey, peeling bark and prickly chestnut-like hips, *R.*

*forrestiana, R. soulieana, R. × paulii rosea, R. ×
andersonii* (a chance hybrid of *R. canina* with
deep-pink flowers that occurred in 1912 and
was introduced by Hilliers), and a great mass
of the early-flowering, pale yellow *R.
pimpinellifolia altaica* right down one side of the
tennis court. There are a number of others and
a good many native wild roses as well, probably
self-sown rather than the understocks of roses
from the past that you see in so many old gardens. Since wild roses abound in the hedges all
along the road to Sleightholme Dale, there is
plenty of source material and birds will do the
rest.

It is only on beginning to move back towards
your starting point that you can see for the first
time, on this side of the house, the terracing of
the garden right down to the valley floor below,
where a pool has been made. Since the drop
must be all of 15 to 18 m (50 to 60 ft), creating
the terracing must have been a massive task.
But the result is superb. Each terrace is wide,
with a broad grass sweep at the top running
right across the back of the house. Along its
edge, above the drop down to the next terrace,
a line of small shrubs and roses has been
planted: Moyesiis, Rugosas, 'Cantabrigiensis',
R. glauca, 'Andrewsii' (with its deep-pink semi-
double flowers), 'Buff Beauty', a great bank of
'Raubritter' tumbling down the slope, rivalled
by 'Max Graf', 'Grouse' and 'Partridge', the last
two among the latest additions to the growing
list of ground-cover roses. There, too, is
'Autumn Delight', one of Bentall's Hybrid
Musks, which has enchanting, semi-double
white flowers with red stamens. In fact, the first
terrace down is largely planted with Hybrid
Musks, and when you see the breathtaking display, you realize what an enormous debt all
gardeners owe to the raiser, the Reverend
Joseph Pemberton, and to Mrs Bentall who
came after him.

The door that opens from the house onto the
top terrace is garlanded by the magical blooms
of 'Complicata' while the more retiring 'Clair
Jacquier' with its creamy-yellow Noisette flowers is to be found on a wall at the far end. Others
in the beds under the windows include 'Rosa
Mundi', 'Königin von Danemarck' and 'Old
Blush'.

A check through Mrs James' rose list would
seem to confirm that none of the Hybrid Teas
planted by Mrs Foster's father in 1910 remain.
But 'Mrs Wemyss Quin' of 1914 is included in
the tally and may have been one of the very
early plantings as it was the first reasonably
hardy and healthy yellow bedding rose. 'Mrs
John Laing' and 'Hugh Dickson' are also in the
garden and, though both are Hybrid Perpetuals, they were introduced in the period when
the two classes overlapped and may well have
been in some early nursery lists as Hybrid Teas.
But that is all pure guesswork; however, the
planting of the early roses at Sleightholme Dale
was entirely done by members of the same
family, adding immeasurably to the charm of
a beautiful garden, loved and cared for by
succeeding generations.

The soft pink blooms of 'Fantin Latour', one of the best of all Centifolia roses.

Other Gardens with Roses Worth Visiting

All, except where specific details are given, are open under the National Gardens Scheme.

SOUTH

Hampshire
Laverstoke House, Whitchurch. Mr and Mrs Julian Sheffield. Tel. 0256 770245

Marycourt, Odiham. Mr and Mrs M. N. Conville. Tel. 025671 2100

Pyramids, South Harting, Nr. Petersfield. Miss G. Jacomb-Hood. Tel. 073 985 396

The Wakes, Selborne (The Gilbert White Museum). Tel. 042 050 275. Open, house and garden, March to October, daily except Mondays

Kent
Goodnestone Park, Nr. Wingham, Canterbury. The Lord and Lady FitzWalter. Tel. 0304 840 218

Sussex
Cooke's House, West Burton, Nr. Pulborough. Miss J. B. Courtauld. Tel. 079 881 353

SOUTH-WEST

Devon
The Glebe House, Whitestone. Mr and Mrs John West. Tel. 039 281 200

Dorset
Chilcombe House, Chilcombe, Bridport. Mr and Mrs John Hubbard. Tel. 0308 3234

Somerset
Tintinhull House, Yeovil. The National Trust. Tel. 0935 822509. Open April to end September, Wed, Thur, Sat and Bank Holiday Mondays

CENTRAL ENGLAND

Bedfordshire
Stagsden Bird Gardens, Stagsden. Mr P. Kaninski. Tel. 023 02 2745. Open every day

Berkshire
Cliveden, Taplow. The National Trust. Tel. 06286 5069. Grounds open March to end December daily

Gloucestershire
The Chestnuts, Minchinhampton. Mr and Mrs E. H. Gwynn. Tel. 045 383 2863

Hunts Court, North Dibley, Dursley. Mr and Mrs T. K. Marshall. Tel. 0453 47440

Oxfordshire
Brook Cottage, Alkerton, Nr. Banbury. Mr and Mrs David Hodges. Tel. 029 587 303

Manor Farm, Old Minster Lovell, Nr. Witney. Sir Peter and Lady Parker. Tel. 0993 75728

The Old Rectory, Farnborough, Nr. Wantage. Mrs Michael Todhunter. Tel. 048 82 298

EAST ANGLIA AND HERTS

Cambridgeshire
Abbots Ripton Hall, Huntingdon. The Lord de Ramsey. Tel. 048 73 234

Hertfordshire
Furneaux Pelham Hall, Buntingford. Mrs Peter Hughes. Tel. 027 978 224

Hatfield House, Hatfield. The Marquess of Salisbury. Tel. 070 72 62823. Open end March to early October, daily except Mondays

MIDLANDS

Lincolnshire
Gunby Hall, Nr. Spilsbury. The National Trust. Open April to end September Weds and Thurs. Other days by written appointment

Nottinghamshire
Green Mile, Babworth, Nr. Retford. Mr and Mrs A. C. M. B. Scott. Tel. 0777 702422

Staffordshire
Little Onn Hall, Church Eaton. Mr and Mrs I. H. Kidson. Tel. 0785 840 154

NORTH

Cheshire
Chester Zoo, Chester. Tel. 0244 380 280. Open every day

Cumbria
Dalemain, Nr. Penrith. Mr and Mrs Bryce McCosh. Tel. 08536 223

Northumberland
Wallington Manor, Cambo, Nr. Morpeth. The National Trust. Open every day

Yorkshire
St. Nicholas, Richmond. Lady Serena James. Tel. 0748 2328

Bibliography

American Rose Society *Annuals* from 1916 on. Informative articles on all aspects of roses.

Bagatelle et ses Jardins (Librairie Horticole, Paris 1910). Describes the French Château and its gardens.

Peter Beales *Classic Roses* (Collins Harvill 1985) Encyclopedic cover of old roses and climbers. Colour throughout.

W. J. Bean *Trees and Shrubs Hardy in the British Isles* (Murray 1914–1933. 8th edition edited by Sir George Taylor, 1973–1980). 4th volume has comprehensive survey of the genus *Rosa*.

Robert Buist *The Rose Manual* (Lippincott, Grambo, Philadelphia 1844; re-issued as *The Culture of the Rose*, 1854. Facs ed, Heyden 1978). Roses in the eastern states of America.

E. A. Bunyard *Old Garden Roses* (Country Life 1936, Scribner NY 1936. Facs ed Heyden 1978). Bunyard was a nurseryman and pioneer of the old rose movement. A standard work.

P. Coats *Flowers in History* (Weidenfeld and Nicolson 1970).

P. H. M. Cochet & S. J. Mottet *Les Rosiers* (Paris 1896). The transition from the Hybrid Perpetuals to the Hybrid Teas.

H. R. Darlington *Roses* (J. C. & A. C. Jack 1911, Stokes NY 1911). One of the best guides of the period.

Rev. H. H. D'Ombrain *Roses for Amateurs* (The Bazaar 1887). A practical handbook by a founder of the RNRS.

Dawn and Barry Eagle *Miniature Roses* (Collins 1988).

H. B. Ellwanger *The Rose* (Dodd-Mead NY 1882) 965 roses of the period discussed by a very knowledgeable grower.

Rev. A. Foster-Melliar *The Book of the Rose* (Macmillan 1894) Very interesting on the Hybrid Perpetuals.

S. M. Gault and P. M. Synge *The Dictionary of Roses in Colour* (Ebury Press and Michael Joseph 1971, Grosset and Dunlap NY 1971). Colour photographs and descriptions of over 500 roses by leading authorities.

Michael Gibson *Shrub Roses, Climbers and Ramblers* (Collins 1981), *The Book of the Rose* (Macdonald 1980), *Growing Roses* (Croom Helm 1984, Timber Press, Portland 1984).

C. F. Gore *The Book of Roses or The Rose Fancier's Manual* (Colburn 1838, Facs ed Heyden 1978). Descriptions of over 1400 roses available in France in the 1830s, plus hybridization and rose culture.

Jules Gravereaux *Les Roses* (Edition d'Art et de Literature, Paris 1912). By the Director of Roseraie de l'Hay.

Trevor Griffiths *The Book of Old Roses* (Michael Joseph 1984), *The Book of Classic Old Roses* (Michael Joseph 1987). Between them describing about 1200 old roses, some great rarities, marred by uneven picture quality.

Jack Harkness *Roses* (Dent 1978). A fascinating *tour de force* on roses and rose history by one of our leading nurserymen and rose breeders.

N. P. Harvey *The Rose in Britain* (Souvenir Press 1951, Van Nostrand NY 1950). An authoritative work on rose history with a wider scope than its title suggests.

F. S. Harvey-Cant *Rose Selection and Cultivation* (MacGibbon & Kee 1950). Particularly good on rose exhibiting.

Roy Hennessey *On Roses* (West Coast Printing, Portland, Oregon 1942). Irreverently robust and highly informative.

Shirley Hibberd *The Rose Book* (Groombridge 1864, retitled *The Amateurs' Rose Book* 1874). Growing roses on the grand scale in the 1890s.

Hillier & Sons *Manual of Trees and Shrubs* (David and Charles 1972). Hardcover edition of this encyclopedic catalogue of the Hillier nursery.

Dean S. R. Hole *A Book About Roses* (Blackwood, Edinburgh 1874). An opinionated but entertaining classic of rose literature by a founder of the RNRS.

L. Hollis *Roses* (Collingridge 1969, re-issued in new format 1974). Still considered a standard work on rose growing.

Gertrude Jekyll & Edward Mawley *Roses for English Gardens* (Newnes 1902). Garden design using roses, especially the ramblers and climbers then coming into fashion. Many photographs.

F. L. Keays *Old Roses* (Macmillan NY 1935. Facs ed Heyden 1978). An indispensable book on the 19th century roses, including early Tea roses.

Wilhelm Kordes *Roses* (Studio Vista 1964). Rose history, cultivation and hybridizing by the leading German authority.

Gerd Krüssmann *Roses* (B. T. Batsford 1982, Timber Press, Oregon 1981). The translation of a classic German rose book, an encyclopedia of roses and rose law with much information unobtainable elsewhere.

Mary Lawrance *A Collection of Roses From Nature* (1799). 90 plates from hand-coloured etchings which, despite some inaccuracies, are a wonderful contemporary record.

Edward Le Grice *Rose Growing Complete* (Faber 1965, revised paperback 1976). Just what the title says, by a noted Norfolk nurseryman.

John Lindley *Rosarium Monographia* (Ridgeway 1820). An early descriptive work by the distinguished botanist.

J. H. McFarland *Modern Roses 1* to *Modern Roses 7* (McFarland, Harrisburg, 1930–1969). *Modern Roses 8*, 1980 taken over by the International Rose Registration Authority and the American Rose Society. *Modern Roses 9*, 1987, much less comprehensive. The international check list of every rose in cultivation throughout the world.

T. C. Mansfield *Roses in Colour and Cultivation* (Collins 1943, Dutton NY 1943). Comprehensive coverage of the roses of the time with many colour plates of varying quality.

Bertram Park *Collins Guide to Roses* (Collins 1956). A replacement for the previous book with much the same coverage and better colour.

John Parkinson *Paradisi in Sole Paradisus Terrestris* (1629). 24 roses described by this plantsman, apothecary and herbalist.

Francis Parkman *The Book of Roses* (Tilton, Boston 1866). Parkman became the first professor of horticulture at Harvard University.

William Paul *The Rose Garden* (Kent 1848. Last ed. 1903. Facs ed Heyden, 1978). The most comprehensive coverage of rose varieties and cultivation in the second half of the 19th century. Colour plates of first edition omitted later because of cost. A classic, even if Paul's rose history is a little shaky according to modern research. Fascinating nevertheless.

Rev. J. H. Pemberton *Roses, Their History, Development and Cultivation* (Longmans, Green 1908; rev ed 1920). An authoritative account of its time, but information on the early Hybrid Musks only comes in the last edition.

W. Prince *Manual of Roses* (Clark, NY 1846). Written by an American nurseryman.

P. J. Redouté *Les Roses* (Paris 1817–1824. Facs ed in 4 vols, Schutter, Belgium 1978). 170 of the roses from the Empress Josephine's garden at Malmaison depicted in colour with a text by the botanist Thory.

Thomas Rivers *The Rose Amateur's Guide* (Longmans, Green 1837). An entertaining treatise by a Hertfordshire nurseryman.

William Robinson *The English Flower Garden* (Murray 1883). An exhaustive (but not exhausting) coverage of the subject that was written by the man who helped to change our ideas on gardening. A section on roses and rose growing.

Royal National Rose Society Annuals from 1907 on. Informative articles on all aspects of roses.

Roy E. Shepherd *History of the Rose* (Macmillan, NY, 1954, Facs ed Heyden 1978). The standard American reference work on the genus *Rosa*, particularly good on the species.

Sacheverell Sitwell and James Russell *Old Garden Roses Part 1* (Rainbird/Collins 1955; *Part 2* by Wilfrid Blunt and Russell, Rainbird/Hutchinson 1957). The first covers history and the main rose families, the second rose literature and the Gallicas in detail. The remaining four volumes of what was planned as a six-volume folio work were never published.

Nancy Steen *The Charm of Old Roses* (Jenkins 1967). By the noted authority on old roses from New Zealand, lavishly illustrated in colour. Tells of the rediscovery of many old roses originally planted by the early settlers.

Graham Stuart Thomas *The Old Shrub Roses* (Phoenix House 1955), *Manual of Shrub Roses* (Sunningdale Nurseries 1957), *Shrub Roses of Today* (Phoenix House 1963), *Climbing Roses Old and New* (Phoenix House 1965), which comprise the 'Bible' of the old rose lover. Also by Graham Thomas are *The Gardens of the National Trust* (Weidenfeld and Nicolson 1979) and *A Garden of Roses* (Pavilion/Michael Joseph 1987), a commentary on a selection of the watercolours originally painted for Ellen Willmott's *The Genus Rosa*.

R. Thompson *Old Roses for Modern Gardens* (Van Nostrand, NY, 1959). Especially good on the early Hybrid Teas.

Ellen Willmott *The Genus Rosa* (Murray, in parts, 1910–1914). Fine plates by Alfred Parsons poorly printed and a flawed text by Miss Willmott. (See entry for Graham Thomas above.)

Norman Young *The Complete Rosarian* (Hodder and Stoughton 1971). Incomplete as there is nothing on cultivation, but a treasure house of information, even if the author's views are sometimes controversial.

Index